STUDENTS BY DAY

McGill-Queen's Indigenous and Northern Studies
(In memory of Bruce G. Trigger)
John Borrows and Arthur J. Ray, Editors

The McGill-Queen's Indigenous and Northern Studies series publishes books about Indigenous peoples in all parts of the northern world. It includes original scholarship on their histories, archaeology, laws, cultures, governance, and traditions. Works in the series also explore the history and geography of the North, where travel, the natural environment, and the relationship to land continue to shape life in particular and important ways. Its mandate is to advance understanding of the political, legal, and social relations between Indigenous and non-Indigenous peoples, of the contemporary issues that Indigenous peoples face as a result of environmental and economic change, and of social justice, including the work of reconciliation in Canada. To provide a global perspective, the series welcomes books on regions and communities from across the Arctic and Subarctic circumpolar zones.

98 Forty Narratives in the Wyandot Language
John L. Steckley

99 Uumajursiutik unaatuinnamut / Hunter with Harpoon / Chasseur au harpon
Markoosie Patsauq
Edited and translated by Valerie Henitiuk and Marc-Antoine Mahieu

100 Language, Citizenship, and Sámi Education in the Nordic North, 1900–1940
Otso Kortekangas

101 Daughters of Aataentsic
Life Stories from Seven Generations
Kathryn Magee Labelle in collaboration with the Wendat/Wandat Women's Advisory Council

102 Aki-wayn-zih
A Person as Worthy as the Earth
Eli Baxter

103 Atiqput
Inuit Oral History and Project Naming
Edited by Carol Payne, Beth Greenhorn, Deborah Kigjugalik Webster, and Christina Williamson

104 Ǫ da gaho dę:s
Reflecting on Our Journeys
Gae Ho Hwako (Norma Jacobs) and the Circles of Ǫ da gaho dę:s
Edited by Timothy B. Leduc

105 Called Upstairs
Moravian Inuit Music in Labrador
Tom Gordon

106 Otter Skins, Boston Ships, and China Goods
Voices of the Maritime Fur Trade of the Northwest Coast, 1785–1841, Revised Edition
James R. Gibson

107 Cultural Change among the Algonquin in the Nineteenth Century
Leila Inksetter

108 Métis Music
Stories of Recognition and Resurgence
Monique Giroux

109 Students by Day
Colonialism and Resistance at the Curve Lake Indian Day School
Jackson Pind

STUDENTS BY DAY

Colonialism and Resistance at the Curve Lake Indian Day School

JACKSON PIND

McGill-Queen's University Press
Montreal & Kingston • London • Chicago

ISBN 978-0-2280-2604-4 (cloth)
ISBN 978-0-2280-2605-1 (ePDF)
ISBN 978-0-2280-2606-8 (ePUB)

Legal deposit fourth quarter 2025
Bibliothèque et Archives nationales du Québec

Printed in Canada on acid-free paper that is 100% ancient-forest-free, containing 100% sustainable, recycled fibre, and processed chlorine-free.

This book has been published with the help of a grant from the Federation for the Humanities and Social Sciences, through the Awards to Scholarly Publications Program, using funds provided by the Social Sciences and Humanities Research Council of Canada.

Funded by the Government of Canada | Financé par le gouvernement du Canada | Canada | Canada Council for the Arts | Conseil des arts du Canada

We acknowledge the support of the Canada Council for the Arts.
Nous remercions le Conseil des arts du Canada de son soutien.

McGill-Queen's University Press in Montreal is on land which long served as a site of meeting and exchange amongst Indigenous Peoples, including the Haudenosaunee and Anishinabeg nations. In Kingston it is situated on the territory of the Haudenosaunee and Anishinaabek. We acknowledge and thank the diverse Indigenous Peoples whose footsteps have marked these territories on which peoples of the world now gather.

Library and Archives Canada Cataloguing in Publication

Title: Students by day : colonialism and resistance at the Curve Lake Indian Day School / Jackson Pind.
Names: Pind, Jackson, 1993- author
Description: Series statement: McGill-Queen's Indigenous and northern studies ; 109 | Includes bibliographical references and index.
Identifiers: Canadiana (print) 20250194902 | Canadiana (ebook) 20250194937 | ISBN 9780228026044 (cloth) | ISBN 9780228026051 (ePDF) | ISBN 9780228026068 (ePUB)
Subjects: LCSH: Curve Lake Indian Day School. | LCSH: Ojibwa Indians—Education—Curve Lake First Nation. | LCSH: Curve Lake First Nation. | CSH: First Nations students—Curve Lake First Nation. | CSH: First Nations—Ontario—Residential schools.
Classification: LCC E96.6.C87 P56 2025 | DDC 371.829/973330713—dc23

This book was designed and typeset by studio oneonone in Minion 11/14.
Copyediting by Kaitlin Littlechild.

McGill-Queen's University Press
Suite 1720, 1010 Sherbrooke St West, Montreal, QC, H3A 2R7

Authorized safety representative in the EU: Mare Nostrum Group BV, Mauritskade 21D, 1091 GC Amsterdam, the Netherlands, gpsr@mare-nostrum.co.uk

CONTENTS

FIGURES

FOREWORD

Day Schools

One of the questions I am often asked as I travel the country and lecture is, "Did you go to residential school?" The answer is no, I went to a day school. Specifically, the Mud Lake Indian Day School located on my reserve (Curve Lake First Nation). I don't remember much about my experiences there, as it was grades 1 and 2, and there's been a lot of other memories filed into my mind since then. For subsequent grades, my fellow students and I were bused twenty minutes away to various schools in nearby Lakefield. But my first experience understanding the outside world came from that little two-room building by the lake.

I know my mother went to that same school, as did most of my relatives and community members. In some First Nations, day schools have the same horrid reputation as residential schools. Places where White people were paid and encouraged to help facilitate the genocide of Indigenous languages and cultures. Often brutally. Who knew colonization could be a make-work industry? All in the name of education. You'll notice the irony there. My mother told me, among other things, that she wasn't allowed to speak her language, which was primarily all she knew. For one reason or another, I was somewhat more familiar with that tongue and its complicated "th" sounds. So, the transition for me wasn't as harsh.

Education – now that's a funny thing. It's supposed to improve us, make us more worldly, and help us navigate this complex rule. Under normal circumstances, it's supposed to be a wonderful thing. Those who say that obviously have never been Indigenous in Canada.

The misadventures and tragedies of the residential school system across Canada have been well documented, thanks to the efforts of the Truth and Reconciliation Committee and their final report. If you want to learn something about Canadian history, give it a read. But lesser known are the day schools, the little sister of that colonizing presence.

It's estimated that over the decades they existed, over 200,000 Indigenous youth attended these day schools. It's difficult to imagine how our community of Curve Lake was shaped and influenced by the ninety years the school stood and operated on the shores of Buckhorn Lake. We all speak English very well, unfortunately far better than our Anishnaabemowin. But the language continues to live and breathe as the next generation, free from the effects of governmental/church influence, struggles to embrace the words that sprang from the land underneath our feet, not some faraway land with Kings and crumpets.

These schools, way more often than naught, were staffed by those we refer to as *Chuganash*, or euphemistically the colour challenged or the pigment denied (Caucasian for the more literal), who had little understanding of the people they were teaching or frequently, came with limited teaching experience or knowledge. Part of the mandate was to make us good little Canadians. Their success rate is somewhat dubious.

Today, most Indigenous communities run and staff their own schools. Education is now a community activity. One cousin of mine is working on her PhD in Indigenous education. Another cousin is the principal of our on-reserve school, no longer referred to as a "day school." Graduation and success have increased exponentially. There is no light at the end of the tunnel. We have, in fact, exited the tunnel and are driving our own train.

Jackson Pind's groundbreaking research into the world of day schools is the next brick in the platform of reconciliation and decolonization. Murray Sinclair, the chairman of the Truth and Reconciliation Committee, once said, "Education got us into this mess, and education will get us out of this mess." Start reading.

Welcome to my community.

Welcome to my … our … childhood.

DREW HAYDEN TAYLOR
Curve Lake First Nation
September 2022

ACKNOWLEDGMENTS

This book would not have been possible without the support of Curve Lake First Nation. I am deeply grateful to both the former Chief and Council, led by Emily Whetung, and the current Chief and Council (2024), led by Keith Knott, for their unwavering support in facilitating this research. I also extend my heartfelt gratitude to the community members who generously shared their knowledge about the Curve Lake Indian Day School, allowing me to share these stories with others interested in learning more about this understudied period in Canada's history.

In particular, I want to thank Shelly Knott Fife, Stanford Taylor, and Val Whetung, who welcomed me into their homes and engaged in dialogues that shaped the direction of this book and deepened my understanding of the impacts of the Indian day school system in Canada. Chief Keith Knott kindly welcomed me into the former Indian day school building, which now serves as his office, and shared not only stories about the school but also profound wisdom about what it means to be Anishinaabeg today. Lorenzo Whetung, a cultural advisor at my university, took me to the petroglyphs and offered invaluable insights into the true meaning of education, alongside sharing painful memories of how the Indian day school system worked to sever his Anishinaabeg identity and language.

I would also like to thank Drew Hayden Taylor for contributing the foreword to this book. His often humorous yet deeply poignant writing has paved the way for future Indigenous authors and illuminated what it means to be Indigenous in "Canada" today. My colleague and friend, Jack Hoggarth, also deserves special acknowledgment for helping to set up interviews, introducing me to relatives, and contributing a hopeful afterword that sheds light on the path forward for Anishinaabeg. He has helped track down sources, provided helpful context to enrich the historical narrative, and offered invaluable insights into the community's ongoing efforts toward cultural revitalization. His dedication and expertise have been instrumental in ensuring this book authentically reflects the lived experiences and histories of Curve Lake First Nation. He continues to offer ceremony and guidance to all those who want to learn more about being Anishinaabeg.

This research began in 2017, a process that was profoundly affected by the COVID-19 pandemic. I owe a deep debt of gratitude to Theodore Christou for supporting this project, as well as to the following academics for strengthening my methodological approach and historical research: Heather McGregor, Lindsay Morcom, Nicholas Ng-A-Fook, Helen Raptis, Thomas Peace, and Sam McKegney. Their guidance is woven throughout this book, and I am a stronger scholar because of them. Along the way, I was fortunate to receive the help of Teri-Ann McDonald and Kaitlin Littlechild, who played a crucial role in meticulously editing my work, as well as Alexandra Peace, who created an excellent index. I am also deeply appreciative of the entire team at McGill-Queen's University Press, specifically Joanne Pisano and my editor, Emily Andrew, who believed in this project and provided helpful and encouraging advice every step of the way.

Finally, I would like to acknowledge the support of my family, who stood by me throughout the years of research and writing that often intruded on family obligations. Chi-miigwetch to my parents, David and Angela Pind; my brother, Jordan; my sister, Caroline; and my partner, Danielle Marsh. I also want to thank my grandfather, James (Jim) Marsden, for sharing his experiences growing up in Lakefield, Ontario, and attending school as a mixed-Indigenous person alongside fellow Curve Lakers, including Doug Williams-ban. Your stories provided invaluable insights into the resilience and complexities of our shared history. This connection between past and present is even more meaningful as I look to the future with my son, Rain Ziibi Marsh, who was born during the final stages of this project. Rain, your presence gave me the strength and motivation to complete this book, and I hope one day it will serve as a testament to the importance of knowing where we come from and honoring those who came before us.

STUDENTS BY DAY

CHAPTER 1

Introduction to Place: Growing Up in Michi Saagiig Anishinaabeg Territory

Aaniin, Boozhoo. Jackson, nindizhinikaaz. Ma'iingan nindoodem. Nogojiwanong nindoonjibaa. Sydenham zaaga'igan, nindaa. Hello, welcome. My name is Jackson. I am from the Wolf Clan. I am originally from Peterborough (place at the end of rapids) and currently live on Sydenham Lake. I wanted to begin by introducing myself in Anishinaabemowin, the language of the place where I am writing and living. Before we begin, we must establish the identity of the storyteller and the setting in which this narrative will unfold. The field of historical research has, after all, moved away from the illusion of absolute objectivity to acknowledge the subject position of the researcher.[1] This aligns with existing practices within Indigenous research and offers a bridge between methodologies. In his book *Research Is Ceremony*, Shawn Wilson explains the importance of assuming the subjective role of the storyteller rather than an "objective" researcher. He argues: "When listeners know where the storyteller is coming from and how the story fits into the storyteller's life, it makes the absorption of the knowledge that much easier."[2] Thus, I will begin by introducing myself and my cultural location as a historian. During the nineteenth century – when thousands of Europeans fled instability – most of my ancestors left Denmark and settled in what would later become Ontario. With the expert knowledge of dairy production they brought from Denmark, my ancestors quickly established a farm outside of Toronto and later expanded to Lakefield, Ontario.

I was born in Nogojiwanong – Anishinaabemowin for "place at the end of rapids" – but until the age of twenty-five, I had only heard it referred to by its English name: Peterborough, Ontario. The public education system in which I was brought up told the story of Peter Robinson, who founded the city in 1825 along the banks of the Trent River with a group of Irish pioneers. Given its geographical location at the end of a twenty-metre waterfall, the city began harvesting hydroelectric power, becoming known as the "electric city" and attracting multinational corporations, including General Electric, Quaker Oats, and Outboard Marine.[3] It became, or so I was told, famous for constructing the largest concrete hydraulic lift dam in the world, which allowed for the passage of boats over the rapids. The engineer, Richard Birdsall Rogers, relied on techniques developed for the canals in European nations, including France, Great Britain, and the Netherlands.[4] The lift locks were completed in 1904, but the Trent-Severn Waterway would not be completed until 1920 – eighty-seven years after construction began.[5] The creation of this system of forty-five interlocking dams, which spans 386 kilometres across central Ontario, provided easy access for industry and recreation, enabling settlers to flood into these regions and establish a new relationship with the waterway.

As I entered Laurentian University to study Canadian history, I began investigating my family history in Alderville First Nation, as it appeared frequently in the books I read. In 2015, the Final Report of the Truth and Reconciliation Committee (TRC) was published. Alderville was mentioned multiple times as the site of one of the first residential schools in Canada.[6] I became interested in whether these schools impacted my family.

This chapter will reveal how the creation of the Trent-Severn Waterway, much like the education under Indian day schools, separated the minds, bodies, spirits, and emotions of Anishinaabe peoples from their traditional interactions with the waterway and the land. It will incorporate Anishinaabe pedagogy developed by Rebecca Chartand, which utilizes the four directions as a teaching philosophy: "The east represented our physical self, the south our emotions, the west our mind/cognitive self, and the north our spirit self."[7] Sheila Cote-Meek also uses the four dimensions in her conceptualization of colonization: "It concerns the land, it requires a specific structure of ideology to proceed, it is violent, and it is ongoing."[8] In this section, each direction will be understood through the perspective of this waterway and the changes that occurred due to the canal system, similar to the changes brought about by education under Indian day schools. Much like colonial education, canal architecture was introduced by European colonists as they sought to bring their own cultures, traditions, and methods of transportation to Canada. I will tie these significant changes to my own life and perceptions as an Anishinaabe and to the broader Anishinaabe community impacted by the development of the Trent-Severn Waterway.

By the end of my third year at Laurentian, I was connected to Maurice Switzer, an Indigenous writer and activist who was also one of my grandfather's first cousins. He shared stories he had written about the life of my great-great-grandfather Moses Marsden. He discussed my grandfather's experience at residential schools, which framed his decision to remove the "Indigenous" designation from his thirteen children so that they could attend a regular provincial school. In 2018, Switzer shared in *Anishinabek News* that Moses Marsden was "a master log cabin builder who had to teach himself how to read and write after running away at the age of eight from Alnwick Manual Labour School, part of Canada's network of Indian Residential Schools."[9] I realized that my lack of knowledge on the topic was directly related to racist and colonial decisions related to enfranchisement in the first half of the twentieth century. These new understandings of the past have allowed me to reconnect with my Indigenous culture and are valuable for other Survivors and their families to decolonize.

As a mixed-settler and Anishinaabe historian from central Ontario, I have developed several connections and relationships with Curve Lake First Nation as I have grown up in the Canadian context of truth and reconciliation. My relationship with Curve Lake First Nation was through the land adjacent to the reserve my family moved to in the early 2000s, where we spent every summer at a growing trailer park. I grew up biking to the reserve to rent movies at Garfield's convenience store and picking strawberries in the nearby fields for my first summer job. I also stood on the shores watching countless sunsets over lower Buckhorn and Chemong Lakes, which surround the peninsula-shaped community. Reflecting on this relationship with the land, I am acutely aware of the different experiences I had growing up compared with those of my ancestors and the Curve Lake community members.

Physical – East – Waabanong. Indigenous groups still occupy and live traditionally on parts of the Trent-Severn Waterway, including the Mississauga communities of Hiawatha, Curve Lake, Alderville, and the Chippewas of Rama First Nations. Yet, during the twentieth century, these communities were forbidden from accessing the traditional diet they had perfected through their relationship with the waterways. They were not allowed to plant their manoomin (wild rice), a sacred food found in the Great Lakes region and used for thousands of years to sustain their lives. Curve Lake member Drew Hayden Taylor's recent play and documentary *Cottagers and Indians* contextualizes the relationship between settlers' leisure experiences of the water with Indigenous food sovereignty and sustainability.[10] It shows that the flooding caused by the creation of the Trent-Severn Waterway submerged wide swaths of traditional rice beds, creating ideal territory for cottages but not for sustainable food systems. In an internal memo held within the federal archives, the Department of Indian Affairs noted that Chief Marsden and his councillors from Alderville had visited government officials in 1905 to explain how 6,000 acres of privately owned rice beds denied his community access to the wetlands. A twenty-one-year lease had been sold to an individual living in Toronto at $160 per year, preventing the Anishinaabe from "trapping, shooting and gathering wild rice in those parts of the lake."[11] Marsden's request for access was ultimately denied.

Another example of settlers physically removing the Indigenous Peoples of this area from their waterways occurred in 1984. George Howard, an angler from Hiawatha First Nation, was charged under the *Ontario Fishery Regulations* for illegally harvesting walleye from Rice Lake outside the prescribed season. He had been fishing to provide food for his family, who lived on the reserve. Howard appealed his case to the Supreme Court, but it was dismissed in a 1994 ruling that indicated that Hiawatha had "given up its traditional hunting and fishing rights" (*R. v. Howard*). In other cases relating to Curve Lake First Nation and its relationship with the land, the courts made similar final decisions on traditional activities such as the harvesting of frogs.[12]

South – Emotions – Zhaawananong. As human emotions regarding this waterway are based on our experiences interacting with the canals, this direction will focus on my perspective of the water. My family has benefitted tremendously from this new relationship to the water. My grandfather was employed for forty-two years at General Electric, which enabled my mother to pursue her postsecondary education at Trent University. They lived on the canal for over twenty-five years, enjoying tourist activities such as boating, camping, and water skiing. Their experience of the waterway was completely different from those of the previous generations and was based on the canal system and the ideas that it brought. This is the reality now for many Anishinaabe descendants in this region: they are born without their language, connection to water, or reliance on traditional foods.[13] We must grapple with the benefits of this new system that almost destroyed the old knowledge system. Reminders of the past are everywhere along the waterway, but my family's connection to the Indigenous language and cultural sites was completely divorced, as we rarely talked about that history. How could we speak about this past without the language, places, and memories of the environment? My grandfather has mentioned that the sites' "desecrations" remind us of how we are treating the waterway and how it has changed into something that would be unrecognizable to our ancestors. He remembers where various "Indian islands" used to be located, where his family and relatives would gather, but these have since been destroyed by flooding and replaced by cottages.

Colonialism is a process that favours new ideas on resource management while divorcing the minds, bodies, spirits, and emotions of Indigenous Peoples from the land and water. Historians and educators have shown how human activity has changed waterways worldwide. Curve Lake First Nation member Madeline Whetung calls the canal a monument of "colonial violence," as "the disruptions and dispossession across our individual and collective lives as Mississaugas are real and are felt; the dams stand still. The specific claims for flooded lands are ongoing and being settled through the Canadian court system. The eels and salmon no longer travel to our inland lakes. The beavers and muskrats are fewer. Our shoreline access is obstructed by private property to the water's edge. As a result of this, our governance has shifted as well."[14]

Across Canada, and particularly in the numbered treaties signed between the British Crown and First Nations, the phrase "as long as the sun shines, the grass grows, and the rivers flow" is a foundational element in many agreements. However, what do these treaties signify when the rivers no longer flow freely along their natural rapids but are instead controlled, maintained, and diverted?[15] Acting as a metaphor for the control institutions place on Indigenous Peoples, such as education, healthcare, and the criminal justice system, the treatment of water demonstrates a systemic issue throughout the community of Curve Lake First Nation.

My grandfather's grandfather remembered a time when the canals were used differently to what they are now. In an experimental oral history interview conducted at Trent University in 1965, my great-great grandfather shared his knowledge of lumber extraction through river drives in this region. The historian conducting the interview, George Cobb, never asked my great-great grandfather – who was both a residential school Survivor and Chief of Alderville First Nation – about his Indigenous heritage. He focused on building a log church and river drives along a set of rapids that no longer exist. Cobb, who was interested in how lumbering operations used the waterway, asked, "Well those canals were built for the logging then, not for the boats, particularly?" My great-great-grandfather's reply, "Well, no, I think the boats were running then. That was, that was the main traffic then,"[16] indicated that at the turn of the century, boats filled with cottagers and tourists were the main traffic on the canal system, not logging operations. The interview, which is less than an hour long, ends with a final question by Cobb: "Well that was all rapids down from here down to Peterborough, wasn't it?" My great-great-grandfather responded: "Yeah ..."[17] If given the opportunity, what could he have explained about the waterway before the lift locks? Those memories and the environment he experienced are lost due to the locking of water in this area.

Mind – West – Ningaabii'anong. During her childhood, my mother's family lived near Lakefield, Ontario, on Katchewanooka Lake, three locks north of the lift locks along the Trent-Severn Waterway. Although I heard the original Anishinaabemowin word for the water body, I never realized it meant "lake of the many rapids," as rapids were no longer visible due to the lock system. My mother's family was the first Indigenous family to move to Lakefield after being enfranchised – the process of giving up your Indigenous rights in return for citizenship – shortly before the First World War. Their experience of the waterway was much different from that of previous generations of Anishinaabe descendants, as their section of the water was defined by the nearby town of Lakefield and the stories that were created by early settlers. These included writers Susanna Moodie and Catherine Parr Traill, who, respectively, wrote the popular books *Roughing It in the Bush* (1852) and *The Backwoods of Canada* (1836) and thus defined the new quintessential pioneer experience on the land. These books used derogatory terms such as *squaw* to describe Indigenous Peoples, even after the Anishinaabe saved settlers during brutal winters.[18] While they didn't attend the Indian residential school system and segregated Indian day schools, my grandparents and parents were sent to a public school that taught them that Indigenous ways of connecting to the land and water were wrong, savage, and unfit for the modern world of postwar Canada.[19]

Spirit – North – Giiwedinong. As a result of the canal and, more generally, settler colonialism, some Indigenous individuals were mentally and spiritually disconnected from their traditions. For example, no one spoke Anishinaabe, and the water flow to sacred sites had been diverted into concrete dams.[20] The waterway that the Trent-Severn Waterway is built on shows evidence of Indigenous life from over 3,000 years ago. This route, which stretches across central Ontario from Georgian Bay to the Bay of Quinte in Lake Ontario, was an essential transportation network for the Anishinabek.[21] Cultural sites along this waterway are connected with ancient ceremonies and funeral practices. These sites, which were created, visited, and maintained for thousands of years, connected Indigenous Peoples to the water, their traditions, and the spiritual world of their ancestors. However, these traditional connections were severed, and the sites were turned into tourist attractions after the canal was built.

For example, the creation of the petroglyphs building in Petroglyphs Provincial Park has prevented the trickling of water under the rocks, which was traditionally used to listen for messages from the Spirit World. Dagmara Zawadzka argues, "The construction of the building severs the complex relationship between the images, the sacred rock which is considered a living entity and the landscape" including the ability to see shadows and the cosmos, hear echoes, or even feel the wind as you interpret the site.[22] As a result, "the building fails to reflect Indigenous ideas regarding spirituality and sacred locales where connection with the natural setting is important."[23] In Anishinaabemowin, the petroglyphs are called Kinoomaagewaabkong or the "rocks that teach." These lessons do not have the same resonance when delivered under a constructed dome. The site is now operating as a provincial park under the control of the Government of Ontario and, like education, is ultimately managed by the province in this region. Along with the largest collection of Indigenous petroglyph carvings in the country, the largest funerary Serpent Mound structure in Canada can also be found along these waterways. Both these sites have been studied, and bodies and artifacts have been removed from the Serpent Mounds in the name of anthropology and archaeology.[24] All directions of potential connection between the descendants of the Anishinabek have been disrupted by the impacts of colonialism.

In the heart of central Ontario is a bioregion known as the "the land between" – a place where the Great Lakes Basin and the Canadian Shield meet. This area was connected through a network of ancient waterways that began in Lake Huron's Georgian Bay, snaked through significant rapids and falls, and emptied into the Bay of Quinte in Lake Ontario. During the Ice Age some 10,000 years ago, retreating glaciers created this network of finger-like rivers and an estimated 250,000 lakes.[25] This complex ecosystem of falls, wetlands, and forests relied on a constant stream of water from Georgian Bay into Lake Ontario. In Anishinaabemowin, the terms used to describe key areas on this waterway include Katchewanooka (lake of many rapids) and Nogojiwanong (place at the end of the rapids); indeed, the name of the people Mississauga came from the word Misizaagiing, (those at the Great River-mouth). These waterways had been used for thousands of years as a means of trading and traversing the central parts of the province.

Several local historians have provided necessary background to the life of the Anishinaabe in this area. The late Elder Doug Williams-ban

(Gidigaa Migizi) of Curve Lake First Nation is one prominent example. Williams was the director of the PhD program in Indigenous Studies at Trent University and a respected historian of the Anishinabek.[26] After turning seventy, and with the help of Leanne Simpson, he wrote a history of the Michi Saagiig in central Ontario.

According to Elder Doug Williams-ban, the main Indigenous group in this region called themselves the Michi Saagiig Nishnaabeg (people who live at the mouth of the river).[27] Williams said that the group occupied the land "west of Gananoque … along the north shore of Lake Ontario and all its tributaries and rivers that drain into it, is the territory of the Michi Saagiig Nishnaabeg."[28] These Indigenous groups rarely settled for more than a few months; they regularly followed the seasons but visited the same places yearly.

Since the beginning of colonization, this area had been under attack by waves of settlers, the flooding of land, and new forms of education that began dominating central Ontario's society.[29] The canal system had thoroughly altered the physical environment, and the settlers' new ideas for education would similarly impact the remaining Indigenous Peoples. When the federal government first opened the Indian day school in Curve Lake in the mid-nineteenth century, cottages for urbanites moving into the area due to settlement from the emerging canal system were already becoming prominent.[30] The new settlers' education system promoted farming as it taught students during the winter but allowed them to "turn off" education over the summer months to help with the harvest. This seasonal control of time would continue to cause disruptions to the traditional way of life for the Indigenous community as the Indian day school grew in power over its almost one hundred years in operation.

Due to their prominence in the country's largest province, the Michi Saagiig Nishnaabeg were participants in and firsthand witnesses to the earliest attempts at settlement and disputes in the "new world." During the War of 1812, Doug Williams's great-great-grandfather George Taylor, a member of the future Mud Lake reserve, fought for the British and defended Fort York from the invasion of the Americans.[31] In fact, many Michi Saagiig Nishnaabeg fought for the British and pioneered the use of guerrilla warfare, helping defend British territory. After the war, the government signed a treaty with some of these Indigenous Peoples in Cobourg, Ontario that further increased the settlement of Europeans and reduced the amount of viable land. Despite being veterans of the previous wars, the Chief at the time, Buk-kwa-kwu, "felt that if he did not sign this treaty his women and children would starve because his hunting area was taken."[32] According to the agreement, each person was permitted $10 worth of goods per year, and the treaty was to last until each member of the Band passed away.[33] From the beginning, the treaty's terms were not followed and its renegotiation in 1822 created the reserve system in Ontario. Over the next two decades, three reserves would be created in central Ontario specifically for the descendants of the Michi Saagiig Nishnaabeg: Alderville, Hiawatha, and Mud Lake. These communities continued to help the early settlers – including well-known Europeans such as Peter Robinson (who founded Peterborough), Susanna Moodie, and Catherine Parr Traill – survive in the harsh winters of Upper Canada.[34]

The Mud Lake reserve was primarily funded by the New England Company, a missionary society tasked with Christianizing the Indigenous Peoples who lived along the north shore of Lake Ontario. Doug Williams explained, "Many of our people were living around Rice Lake and Lake Ontario and slowly ended up showing up in Curve Lake because it was more of a distance from settlers."[35] By 1829, the missionaries had received permission from the federal government to establish full-fledged reserves and force Indigenous Peoples to live on them. Influenced by the Wesleyan Methodist and Baptist movements, the New England Company was provided with a sixteen-hundred-acre land grant for the Curve Lake Reserve and hired Rev. Richard Scott and a translator to operate the mission; in 1837, the company added a schoolteacher.[36]

The Curve Lake Reserve had access to land north of the European settlement, giving them access to hunting and fishing grounds to sustain their traditional lifestyles. Their method of education provided the Michi Saagiig Ninshaabeg with sacred teachings that were constantly reimagined to fit changing contexts and passed down for at least ten thousand years. Therefore, the communities in this region had very little use for Eurocentric schooling before the arrival of settlers and the New England Company.

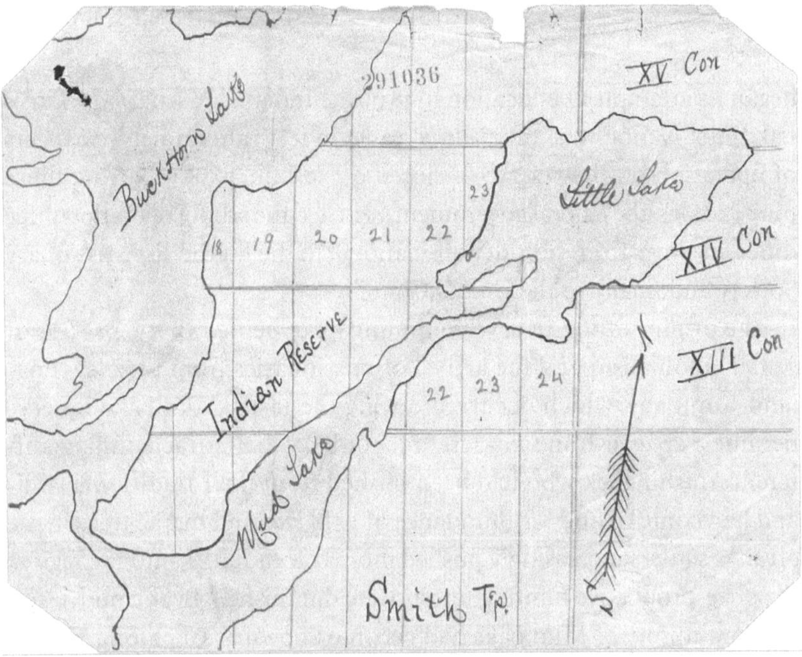

Figure 1.1
A hand-drawn map of the Mud Lake Indian Reserve, showing the surrounding area, including Buckhorn, Mud Lake, and Little Lakes. This map highlights the geographical boundaries and locations significant to Curve Lake First Nation at the turn of the century.

Doug Williams noted in 2018 that traditional education is based on a connection to the land and that teachings are passed through oral history. He shares one such oral history about his older friend Madden, who would later become a respected Elder in Mud Lake. He said: "Madden hated school. There was a truant officer in Curve Lake, but Madden was really good at hiding from him … Every morning he would leave the house and hide in the bush with the other kids who hated school. They lived off the land, hiding all day long."[37] Williams's friend was able to learn "traditional Nishnaabeg education" from his grandparents and to speak Anishinaabemowin as his primary language until he passed away at the age of ninety-five. We learn from Williams's work that his stories "document Michi Saagiig Ninshaabeg as provocateurs, strategists, connectors, agitators, and intellectuals. They show that resistance and resurgence have always been part of us."[38] While the New England Company began its attempts at education in 1837, the Indian day school on Curve Lake First Nation was "officially" created in 1886; after ninety-two years of operation on the reserve, it closed on 30 June 1978.[39] During those nine decades, the federal government switched the school operation three different times from non-denominational to the Methodist Missionary Society and finally to the United Church.

The origins of the reserve community can be tied to the process of settler colonialism and the arrival of missionaries from the New England Company, which occurred during the 1830s. Mud Lake Reserve became a sixteen-hundred-acre tract of land that attracted many different Anishinabek who had been pushed from their traditional lands and had come to find an abundance of wild rice and maple trees in the area. As settlers increasingly pushed more communities into the region, the once-productive hunting forests were diminished. By the mid-1850s, the community of Mud Lake had become known as Chemong Village, based on the Anishinaabemowin word Oshkigmong, meaning "curve in the lake."[40] Due to its proximity to settlers moving into Upper Canada, the community regularly appeared in government documents of the time.

CHAPTER 2

Researching Indian Day Schools in Canada

The research for this book took place during the *Mclean et al. v. Canada* case, a decade-long class action lawsuit filed by Indian day school Survivors. Initiated in 2006, the suit was a response to their exclusion from the $5 billion Indian Residential School Settlement Agreement. As part of the *Mclean et al. v. Canada* announcement, the federal government admitted that the same crimes of cultural genocide also occurred in Indian day schools. Minister of Crown-Indigenous Relations Carolyn Bennett spoke on behalf of Canada:

> Close to 200,000 Indigenous children attended federally operated Indian Day Schools. Institutions where children went to school during the day and returned home at night. As a result of the harmful and discriminatory government policies at the time, students who attended these schools were subject to sexual, physical, and psychological abuse and forced to abandon their language and culture. Survivors across this country continue to suffer from the abuse and horrible experiences they were subjected to, which was perpetuated by the very people charged with educating them as children.[1]

Minister Bennett's statement acknowledged that the federal government of Canada had caused significant harms to Indigenous Peoples because of its Indian day school policies.[2]

The *Mclean et al. v. Canada* suit was filed after several Survivors came forward to advocate for justice, compensation, and an official apology from the federal government. Raymond Mason, one of the class action's founders, shared part of his horrific experience in an Indian day school on the reserve at Peguis First Nation in Manitoba: "Every time I tried to speak, I couldn't speak English, so I got strapped and I got my hair pulled, my tongue pinched, and I was ostracized, and I had to stand on a corner and balance a book on my head for a long, long time, it seemed like hours. And then, after that, I had to write on the chalkboard: 'I will never speak Indian again' about 100 times."[3]

Garry McLean, another of the class action's founders, described a similar experience at Dog Lake Indian Day School in Manitoba. Just five minutes into the school day, McLean was strapped because he couldn't say "good morning" in English.[4] Both Raymond and Garry were in attendance in December 2018 when the federal government announced they had reached a deal for the approximately 200,000 other Survivors. Speaking after Minister Bennett, Garry stated, "I know you may not know some of the damages that have happened. And for me, I forgive you for that, for me, without forgiveness, things stay the same. And my family, my aunts and uncles, my relatives, I assure you, we forgive you Canadians for some of the damages that may have happened. And we know we can correct that, and I truly believe, one hundred per cent, that we can correct that."[5] Garry passed away less than six weeks after the announcement. These words constitute his final public statement on the lawsuit he helped bring to fruition.

About 2,000 Survivors of the Indian day schools are passing away every year.[6] This history has not always been a priority of research aimed at understanding the history of Indian day schools. The study of Indian day schools in Canada has been overlooked as a result of the powerful legacy of Indian residential schools, which have garnered national attention because of the intergenerational trauma they inflicted on Indigenous Peoples. As the public learned from the 2015 Truth and Reconciliation Commission Reports, residential schools were intended to remove Indigenous children from their communities to assimilate them into the Canadian worldview.[7] The devastating effects of abuse, cultural genocide, and trauma inflicted by these institutions are still affecting Indigenous communities throughout the country.[8] The high prevalence of substance abuse, suicide, and low educational attainment is a direct result of this colonial education system.[9] The public's increasing awareness of the history of these schools has blurred its focus on Indian day schools.

Indian day schools were located on nearly every reserve in Ontario. Historians report that in British Columbia, Manitoba, and the Maritimes, Indian day schools tended to be one-room schoolhouses resembling rural public schools.[10] A partnership was formed between the federal government, which had a fiduciary duty to create and oversee the schools, and church organizations, which saw to the day-to-day operations. Christian education would become a key component as Methodist, United, Anglican, Roman Catholic, and Presbyterian organizations operated the schools. With limited resources, the education followed a traditional Eurocentric curriculum. The ideal result was to create "cookie-cutter" Canadian citizens who would be engaged in the workforce and assimilated from their Indigenous culture.[11] In addition, since the instructors specifically taught in English, Indigenous languages were forced out of the curriculum and, subsequently, the students. One teacher – usually someone with little or no qualifications – taught a variety of grades, from elementary to middle school.[12] By 1920, attendance became mandatory for any Indigenous child under the age of sixteen, thus increasing the number of pupils attending this type of school.[13] Some Survivors speak of the enduring impacts of the mental, emotional, physical, and sexual abuse that occurred at some of these schools.[14] The lasting repercussions of these schools in Ontario in the twentieth century have not been studied.

In reality, there is very little research on the Indian day schools in Ontario between the 1800s and 1900s, despite the thousands of Survivors who attended during this period. Only one source appears around this time that discusses the impact of Indian day schools: "'The New Generation': Cooperative Education at the Day School on Dalles 38C Indian Reserve, 1890–1910," by Brittany Luby and Kathryn Labelle. The research uses the oral history of Brittany Luby's grandmother, Matilda (Ogimaamaashiik), which was recorded in 1972 and explains the educational models used in Dalles 38C Indian Reserve. Located 225 kilometres from Winnipeg, the reserve was considered a remote northern Ontario community in Treaty 3 between 1890 and 1910. The authors found that "children educated at day school on Dalles 38C Indian Reserve retained control over their religious affiliation and do not appear to have been forcibly baptized like pupils of the nearby Cecilia Jeffrey Residential School."[15] The impact of the Indian day school varied based on the complex interplay between Indigenous Peoples, the government, and church organizations in each community. In the community, "the curriculum and pedagogical approach to learning at the day school followed a cooperative model due in large part to the program set out by the schoolmaster."[16] The missionary, in this case, was John Kipling, a mixed Indigenous and settler teacher who adopted Anishinabek teaching practices and Anishinaabemowin language lessons within his classes at the Indian day school.[17] Kipling also worked the school schedule around Indigenous parents' seasonal migratory changes and educated the students on methods for dealing with other colonial administrators. These efforts were curtailed in 1906 when Kipling suddenly died, forcing the Indian day school students to transfer to Cecelia Jeffery Residential School. At first, this occurred slowly, but by 1920, "Duncan Campbell Scott, Deputy Superintendent of Indian Affairs, required that Indigenous children from seven to fifteen years old attend residential school. Should parents withhold their children from federal agents, penalties like jail-time could be enforced by the state."[18]

Research on Indian day schools has focused mainly on British Columbia, with scholars such as Helen Raptis and Sean Carleton publishing important texts in the field. Raptis has published extensively on this topic. In particular, she examines the relationships between teachers in specific schools and the ongoing impacts of this education across two different generations.

Since 2007, Helen Raptis and colleagues have produced a number of historical articles and a book on the topic of day schooling in British Columbia. The first article is co-written by Thomas Fleming and Lisa Smith and focuses on the interwar period of 1929–42, when forty-nine day schools were in operation in British Columbia. The looming presence of the residential school is highlighted in the abstract: "Little historical attention, however, has been directed toward the operations of Indian day schools, although a large literature has otherwise documented the devastating effects of the Residential Schools."[19] Raptis and colleagues concluded that "evaluations of the federal government's historical role in the education of Indigenous Peoples in multiple broad historical settings have been hampered by historians' almost singular focus on residential schooling."[20] These remarks highlight the need for a broader focus on the Indian day school system that emerged in Ontario during the same period.

Raptis and colleagues also changed the perspective of this history to focus on "average individuals" or people employed in the Indian day school in British Columbia. Their research examined how an Irish immigrant, later a teacher, used different educational methods that valued Indigenous Knowledge and promoted their artwork in British Columbia. The authors framed the day schools as a hybrid between a residential school and rural school: "Physically, day schools were similar to the more than 700 one room schools that dotted rural and remote parts of the province, that is to say they were usually dilapidated wooden structures with sparse furniture and even less in the way of instructional supplies."[21]

Drawing on an extensive review of Library and Archives Canada's Record Group 10 (RG10) files for two schools, as well as the memoirs of war veteran Anthony Walsh, Raptis and colleagues show how Walsh used his position as a teacher to resist the assimilating nature of day schools. This perspective is highlighted by Walsh's comments that the Department of Indian Affairs' "concern was the three R's, and he [the Indian agent] did not recognize the creative work that was going on."[22] Walsh rebelled against that notion of education and changed the classroom into a studio where students learned a variety of creative arts, including drawing, sculpting, and musical lessons. This strategy worked as his class's Indigenous-themed works won numerous art awards.[23] The authors concluded that "the history of Aboriginal [*sic*] education in British Columbia is more than a simple morality play featuring oppressors and the oppressed."[24] Rather, different experiences were created based on the contextual and individualized classrooms that teachers managed as they negotiated between the demands of the community and government policies.

Raptis's study of Indian day schools in British Columbia culminated in the publication of a book with the fitting name *What We Learned: Two Generations Reflect on Tsimshian Education and the Day Schools.* For the first time in any of these studies, Raptis decided to write the book with twelve members of Tsimshian First Nation who share oral histories. This approach displays a shift towards acknowledging the Survivors as key data contributors to historical writing. Raptis concluded: "Yet both the day schools prior to the Second World War and the public schools afterward, also played important roles in eroding traditional Tsimshian learning and livelihood. Whether they were attending Residential Schools, day schools, or integrated public schools, Tsimshian students experienced the negative effects of ill-conceived government policies pertaining not only to schooling but also to the fabric of their individual and communal lives."[25]

Interviews with the children who attended day schools and their parents show that "the educational journeys of Tshimian students varied greatly across time and place. Their narratives remind us that 'each person has a unique and personal journey that will yield to their learning.'"[26] The book covers many different periods of Indian day schools, both before the 1951 changes to the Indian Act and during the period of integration. Interestingly, Raptis also found that members of the older generation were able to retain more of their traditional culture and language in Indian day schools; in comparison, the younger generation was forced into integrated schools that eroded their localized culture.[27]

In 2022, Sean Carleton published *Lessons in Legitimacy: Colonialism, Capitalism, and the Rise of State Schooling British Columbia*, a book on the history of public schooling and Indian day schools. The same federal policies of Indigenous education were enacted on various Indigenous communities throughout British Columbia. Drawing on the fields of political economy and settler-colonial studies, Carleton determines "how different kinds of state schooling supported this change by teaching Indigenous and non-Indigenous students, in overt and covert ways, to accept and adapt to British Columbia's emerging capitalist settler society."[28] By focusing on a variety of colonial schooling models, including Indian day schools, his book "offers a 'long view' of the development of state-supported schooling as a struggle and negotiated compromise, not a consensus."[29] Indigenous Peoples throughout the province continually resisted these efforts to control education and provided "reminders that schooling is continually contested, even though the terms of engagement are deeply unequal, which was especially the case for Indigenous parents and children."[30] Carleton agrees with Raptis and notes that "Canadians need to grapple with a more comprehensive history of education to implicate many kinds of schooling, not just residential schooling, in the colonial project."[31] Indian day schools are an important aspect of that history and more research is needed into the 699 schools that operated in Canada. While this book focuses on one Indian day school in Canada, there is still much research to be done in this area, as well as on other educational experiences endured by Indigenous Peoples, including the Indian boarding home program, the Sixties Scoop, and public schooling.

RESEARCH WITH CURVE LAKE FIRST NATION

In September 2020, after spending over a decade of my life growing up around the community, I approached Curve Lake First Nation with the intention of working collaboratively to better understand the history of the Indian day school in their community. This was a conscious decision as I had developed a relationship with them through my previous experiences. I contacted Chief Emily Whetung, who arranged for me to provide a research presentation to Council. This process allowed me to hear the community's concerns and highlight my research experience and methodology. The community was particularly interested in who I was and how this information could help their Survivors access more historical documents. They ultimately gave me permission and allowed me to access the potentially sensitive documents in the archives. In their letter of support, the Curve Lake community was clear about the active role they wished to play in the research relationship. They wrote: "We plan to work on the research advisory team. Specifically, we will be serving as research liaisons between the researcher and the community making sure the research is shared with Curve Lake First Nation members and forwarding interested oral history participants."[32] I am extremely grateful for the research relationship that was established with Chief and Council. The rest of this chapter reflects the research process that was undertaken with Curve Lake.

As this research intends to follow Indigenous concepts of relational accountability, the community I work with (Curve Lake First Nation) has personal and professional relationships with me. In addition, I have worked in this community in various roles, including as an Aboriginal Heritage Liaison and instructor of the Matariki Indigenous Student Mobility Program, which was offered in partnership with the Whetung Cultural Centre in Curve Lake. This relationship is ongoing and has continued through the election of a new Chief and Council, which Chief Keith Knott currently leads.

I draw on several local and place-based histories to help inform the overall picture of the Indian day schools within the context of the history of colonialism in Ontario. For example, the names of the places I mentioned previously can only be understood to mean the same thing once you learn that Curve Lake used to be called "Mud Lake." The individual nature of place-based knowledge makes it difficult for researchers combing through decades of archival research with changing names to keep track of places or provide a comprehensive overview of their studies.[33] Building upon the important research that these scholars have conducted, this book offers three significant contributions to the study of Indian day schools in Canada. The first is an exhaustive review of the federal archive relating to the Curve Lake Indian Day School between 1899 and 1978. The federal government's treatment of Curve Lake is traced over seven decades, and this information is used to draw conclusions regarding the management, operation, and legacy of the school on reserve. Second, this book provides a window into the control of Anishinaabe resources and the use of assimilating education to remove treaty rights. The third and most transferable for other contexts is a new method of organizing the RG10 files. New digital history techniques, such as optical character recognition (OCR), make these files more accessible to Survivors and educators.

This book has two major and complementary purposes. First, it brings to light information stored in the federal archive of Curve Lake First Nation regarding the Indian day school that operated on the reserve. Second, this information and understanding are offered back to the community to be preserved in a digital archive (a more easily accessible version) to help educate other people about the institutions' impacts on Indigenous Peoples. This book also examines the involvement and oral history of community members, including Chief and Council, in making decisions related to the operation of their school within their reserve.

This book documents and preserves Survivors' stories differently than what is available through the class action lawsuit. Claimant forms required Survivors to write their histories into a legal document. However, written history is not how most Indigenous communities pass on knowledge, so the forms represent foreign documents created by lawyers. As one Survivor stated: "This is a lawyer's game … Lawyers need to do this, because ordinary people are not going to do it … It's a legal document. I feel that a lot of us are going to fail, because we don't know how to do that."[34] Murray Sinclair, the late chair of the Truth and Reconciliation Commission, echoed these sentiments, stating that former students have to do all the work themselves to seek compensation. He argues that Survivors "have to find the documents; they have to prove they went to the school; they have to match the records that the department provides to the law firm, I assume to justify that they in fact are the same person whose name might be spelled four or five different ways according to school records, and who may not have had an English name … And we're talking about a population of people whose literacy rates are the lowest in Canada."[35] By providing easier access to these files, this book can help foster a better understanding of the Indian day school system and its influence on Indigenous communities. By applying the techniques of OCR and historical data management, I have been able to provide searchable, accessible, and improved documents that will enhance understanding of this history not just for this book, but all interested community members. Using OCR, I converted old, often difficult-to-read documents into searchable and editable text, making them more accessible to researchers and community members alike. Additionally, through historical data management, I organized, cross-referenced, and contextualized these records, ensuring that important details are preserved and easily navigable. These techniques not only improve the readability of historical materials but also allow a wider audience to engage with and interpret this history more effectively.

The settlement with Indian day school Survivors includes a compensation agreement between the Canadian government and Survivors, using a scaled compensation model that categorizes payouts based on the severity of harms experienced. To receive the highest compensation levels, Survivors must submit a written narrative and any additional records related to their claims. Some suggestions on the claim form include "report cards, enrolment forms, class photographs, letters from teacher or principal, other records, like yearbook or school articles, family narratives, written narratives, diaries, photographs, or other."[36] Any written document that can be traced to a particular school can, therefore, provide valuable information for claimants' forms. Curve Lake First Nation was aware of this value, as they stated, "Your exploration of this topic is particularly timely given the Indian Day School Settlement Agreement that was ongoing until 2022. In particular, Curve Lake First Nation, consents to the search of the federal and provincial archives for information regarding the Indian Day Schools and the sharing of information in the form of a final report on this subject" (see Appendix 1 for the full letter).

This book employs oral Indigenous history and archival analysis to understand the history of an Indian day school within the province of Ontario. In using these methods, I have framed the structure of the book around the methodology of Two-Eyed Seeing.[37] First adopted as an Indigenous storytelling method by Jo-Ann Archibald, the original two-eyed story was about a coyote; it was told by Terry Tafoya in 1982.[38] Archibald used the story as a metaphor to describe how to "bring together, in harmony and balance, a First Nations knowledge and way of knowing and research methodology."[39] Albert Marshall, a Mi'kmaq Elder, and other colleagues, including Cheryl Barlett and Murdena Marshall, helped popularize the term within Indigenous-scientific studies, stating that both sets of ontologies "need each other and must engage in a co-learning journey."[40] I argue that combining archival and oral history research can help First Nations communities reclaim and interpret their own histories on their own terms. This approach is particularly important for ensuring that historical records – many of which were created and held by external institutions – are not only returned to the community but also understood within Indigenous knowledge frameworks. This process supports data sovereignty as it enables communities to manage, govern, and interpret their historical records rather than relying solely on external institutions. By using these methods, I collaborated with Curve Lake First Nation to facilitate more equitable and culturally relevant access to documents currently held in federal archives. While historical records may be accessible without Indigenous research, their interpretation often lacks the lived experiences and knowledge systems that oral history provides. Integrating these perspectives ensures that the documentation crucial to understanding the impacts of colonial education practices is accessible.[41] Providing something tangible in return for the knowledge I have gained through this research ensures reciprocity. I also hope this book will serve as a useful reference that will enable the community to more easily search for information related to the Curve Lake Indian day school on reserve. I want to clarify that I did not "discover" anything included in this book. The documents I examined had all been collected, maintained, and shared by archivists who have made this information publicly accessible. Under the terms of the United Nations Declaration on the Rights of Indigenous Peoples (UNDRIP), all Indigenous Peoples "have inherent and inalienable rights relating to the collection, ownership and application of data about them."[42] I argue that this includes information gathered as part of the Indian day school system.

Initially, this research was part of my dissertation, and the intention was to record the community's archival and oral history. However, due to the second wave of COVID-19 and the challenges of interviewing Survivors online about this sensitive topic, the project was divided into two stages. The pandemic required a shift in focus to ensure the research remained relevant and safe for the community. The first stage, which comprises the next two chapters of this book, was focused on archival research and improving access to historical documents on Indian day schools. Once it was safe to do so (nearly three years later), I returned in 2024 to complete the oral history interviews, allowing for a comprehensive collection of archival and personal accounts.

During the pandemic, it was impossible to travel to the community to meet with individuals. The possibility of conducting interviews virtually was considered but dismissed, as I felt this could harm community members interested in participating. There was no way to ensure that the proper supports could be implemented online, so there was too big a risk that Survivors would be revictimized. Between 2020 and 2023, I decided to focus on data sovereignty and the repatriation of historical material for Curve Lake First Nation. This commitment was taken seriously, as all files that were examined were compiled into a folder to be provided back to the community. This required the downloading of approximately 9,965 pages of information from the RG10 school files series; these pages were then organized by record grouping and compiled into four PDFs that correspond with the relevant record groups: C-8207, C-8208, C-8798, and C-8141. These four PDFs, which represent all publicly available records of the Curve Lake Indian Day School, were combined into a single file rather than the 9,965 separate links on the federal online database. After this process was complete, I also applied OCR to the new single file; this allows for an extensive keyword search of those files that were typed (as handwriting is not picked up with OCR). This process converted isolated and unsearchable records into a more easily accessible format, providing a tangible benefit for the community. Survivors can now access historical evidence of their experiences as they can search for a particular period, teacher, school inspector, or Indian agent. In addition, the archival files relating to the community's history can now be stored in a different and more accessible form within the community itself, allowing the community to choose how to manage the records in the future. Other digital images and newspaper articles that were found during my research were also returned to the community. This book was submitted in the form of a final report that will serve as a resource for Survivors or family members. Finally, I compiled all the relevant information from the Indian Affairs Annual Reports into an Excel document, which lists grade distribution, attendance, and funding for the school over the three-decade period from 1899 to 1939. It is essential that historians in Canada return any knowledge or information that was not held in community archives to its rightful owners.

COVID-19 also limited this project to sources that could be obtained digitally or through the postal service, as the federal and provincial archives were closed during the provincial lockdown. Therefore, most sources have been obtained through the RG10 School Files series, 1879–1953 online database, and other institutional holdings, including the *Globe & Mail: Canada's Heritage from 1844* – an archive of the complete works of the *Globe & Mail* that is housed by the University of Prince Edward Island. After 1953, the history is supplemented by secondary sources relevant to the Indian day school and oral history interviews with Indian day school Survivors from Curve Lake, which have been digitized and stored in the Trent University archives. Finally, a general search of Library and Archives Canada's (LAC) integral holdings also produced helpful images, figures, and additional documents. These sources provide a window into the federal government's operation of the Indian day school in Curve Lake and represent over 9,000 primary source documents.

In pursuing the important work of sharing documents, a group of researchers at Queen's University worked with me over the past several years to help expedite this process so documents could be made available to the Survivors who are still alive. Together, we created www.indiandayschools.org in partnership with LAC, which re-digitized over 800,000 files in the RG10 School Files Series. These files contain all the publicly available information on LAC's website regarding most Indian day schools and residential schools in Canada. We used new digital history techniques such as OCR, which allows for some of the documents to be searched in a PDF form and greatly reduces the amount of time needed to search for a name, date, or place. In addition, we tied each of these files to the publicly accessible Indian day school locations so that Survivors and other community members could easily find the files relevant to them. Since launching in 2022, our website (www.indiandayschools.org) has garnered over 20,000 views. Several Indigenous communities are currently using it to search for archival documents regarding the Indian day schools on their reserves. We continue to build new features, such as overlaying treaty maps, a search function to find the closest Indian day school to any location in Canada, translations into Indigenous languages, and educational programming to support teaching this material in high schools. With partners such as the National Centre for Truth and Reconciliation, we hope this material will help other Survivors and historians tell their stories of Indian day schools in Canada.

To provide a more comprehensive and accurate understanding of the Indian day school experience, it was essential to incorporate oral histories alongside existing archival records. By including the voices of former students, this research expands the historical record, filling in gaps and offering perspectives that may have been overlooked or omitted in official documentation. The oral history research had to be re-approved and presented to a new Chief and Council of Curve Lake First Nation, now led by Chief Keith Knott. In the spring of 2024, five former students who attended the Curve Lake Indian Day School between 1951 and 1972 were invited to share their stories. These interviews were conducted at various locations, including people's homes in Curve Lake, one of the former Indian day school buildings (now a council room), and during a walk at the Kinoomaagewaabkong (Teaching Rocks), also known as Peterborough Petroglyphs Provincial Park. The interviews were largely informal and paced according to each participant. They were loosely structured around two primary questions: "What did you experience at an Indian day school?" and "How did these experiences impact you later in life?" At the end of each interview, participants were also asked, "What would you like to be remembered about the Indian day school?" The answers to this final question are shared in the conclusion. The oldest interviewee was Chief Keith Knott, born in 1937, who began school in the early 1940s. The oral histories in this book begin chronologically, starting in Chapter 6, and continue through the rest of the book. Unfortunately, no older students were available or alive to share their experiences. Therefore, the next two chapters contain exclusively archival history, transitioning to personal stories from individuals who attended the school post-1941. This framework effectively bridges the gap in the archival record, which is unavailable past 1951, making the oral histories crucial for understanding the school's transformation and its eventual integration into the Ontario education system.

As a result of its relevance to the community, the history that follows has been created within a completely different context than that of most works on the topic. By pursuing historical topics that have present-day meaning for the community, Indigenous-led historical research can contribute to a significant engagement with the past. More importantly, it can provide valuable access to information that may have been taken, misused, or misinterpreted because of previous colonial actions. Therefore, this research was based on federal archives that comprise most of the data that is inaccessible in its current form to the community.[43]

I also acknowledge that each Indigenous person's identity and understanding of the Indian day schools was created in the context of their personal social experiences, and so may be completely different from other Survivors. Therefore, this book will not generalize the experiences of Indian day schools in Ontario; rather, it will seek to highlight the relationships between the institution and individual Indigenous people within that system. Indigenous Peoples believe their "worldview is such that it is regarded as a network of relationships."[44] Within this web of relations are connections between the institution of Indian day schools in nearly every reserve in the province and the experiences that individuals had at these schools. Understanding Indigenous Peoples' multiple, varied connections with the history of Indian day schools is the goal of both this research and its methodological approach.

This book will explore the history and operation of a specific Indian day school within Anishinaabe territory. By weaving together oral histories and archival research, we can answer key questions such as: Who was responsible for these schools? What were their intended purposes? And what should be remembered about their legacy in the context of Canada's ongoing journey toward Truth and Reconciliation? This narrative begins with the mission that established Curve Lake First Nation and its first Indian day school, managed by the New England Company. As we progress through the chapters, we'll explore both the education provided at the school and the broader societal constructs imposed by colonial governments to marginalize Indigenous Peoples. This book aims to provide a window into the lived historical experiences of the Curve Lake Indian Day School, offering a deeper appreciation of the resilience and perseverance of the Anishinaabeg.

CHAPTER 3

The New England Company and the Creation of the Indian Day School

The New England Company was responsible for creating the reserve in Curve Lake and establishing the first formalized school for the community. These early classes would become the foundation of the Indian day school system that would spread quickly across the rest of the country in the late nineteenth century. This chapter will highlight the important roles that the New England Company and the Methodist Missionary Church played in establishing an education system with forced daytime attendance for Indigenous students. From the very beginnings of this new system, European ways of education were imposed on Indigenous communities to facilitate the assimilation of Indigenous students into the emerging Canadian state. Classes became a method to teach English religious practice and divide the Indigenous populations into smaller parcels of land.

In the *History of the County of Peterborough*, first published in 1884, author Dr C. Pelham Mulvany, an Anglican clergyman, explained the educational philosophy at the time. The New England Company focused on the spiritual enlightenment of the Indigenous Peoples, usually appointing a clergyman from a Protestant denomination as their agent. Most of the Indigenous Peoples around Peterborough adopted the Methodist Church, as its straightforward worship and emotionally charged preaching resonated more with them than the more elaborate rituals of the Church of England. It was noted that the emotional nature of both the Methodist and Roman Catholic religions seemed particularly well-suited to the Indigenous perspectives. Typically, at this time, the missionaries would preach through an interpreter provided by the government.[1]

This type of mission was seen as a form of charity that could increase the number of religious members in a particular organization and help the "poor" reach salvation. When the community of Curve Lake was established, each of the first thirty families who joined the reserve were provided with a log home and four acres of land to farm.[2] In 1837, this missionary work led to the creation of a school, which subsequently expanded into a required part of the community's life. The New England Company argued that the new school system was making a significant difference in the community's life.[3]

In 1868, the mission reported a growing need for a better school building. The school required more space – more people were being forced onto the reserve, and families already living there were expanding. The New England Company regularly remarked on the excellent work of the teacher and the local resident missionary who were responsible for "watching over them carefully and striv[ing] to keep them from the whisky."[4] In the same year, Mr Henry John Lister reported that "Chemong day-school wanted great improvements and that the boarding school ought to be abandoned as the children all lived within two miles."[5] The school also operated "for a short time as a residential school, with a few students from Hiawatha."[6] The New England Company tested different approaches to educational delivery, such as day or boarding schools, to find the method best suited to their goals of Christianizing the population.

Regulating the moral behaviour of the community was a constant goal in deploying this type of schooling. In 1873, a superintendent for the New England Company mentioned that "the moral status of the Band is generally good and improving and the progress in civilization very fair, and better than most Indian Bands in the Superintendency. They have an excellent teacher and missionary, who keep a strict supervision over them, both socially and morally."[7] As a result, the mission approved the renovation of both the day school and church to be "sustainably repaired."[8]

The 1878 Annual Report to the New England Company reported that a teacher named Alfred McCue earned $400 a year teaching a roster of twenty Indigenous students, fourteen of whom were in regular attendance. Of these twenty students, nineteen were learning to read and spell, thirteen were writing, and nine had learned arithmetic.[9] Over the next six years, the total number of students grew by ten. In his 1884 *History of the County of Peterborough*, Dr C. Pelham Mulvany described a school of

> about thirty children, which is presided over by Alfred McCue, an Indian teacher. All can read, and speak English. To induce them to attend regularly they are daily served with a good dinner. It is needless to add that, by this system of attending to the wants of the stomach as well as to those of the brain, there are few truants. The children are all members of the Band of Hope, and have pledged themselves to abstain from the use of intoxicating liquors. It is to be hoped that they will adhere to the good resolution adopted in youth, for there is nothing that demoralizes the Red man more quickly than the potent fire water.[10]

This initiative was a means of fostering temperance and was part of the broader goal of assimilating Indigenous Peoples into Christian settler society. The emphasis on abstinence reflected broader colonial views that linked societal issues among Indigenous communities to alcohol use, further reinforcing the school's role in shaping behaviour and identity in line with settler expectations. In this county history book, the author also stated that all the students could speak English, but Inspector Brown undermined this notion when the school was first inspected in 1885. His subsequent letter to the minister of education represents one of the first files related to the day school held in the RG10 archive. In it, Brown reported "that The New England Company owned 2,000 acres of land where the Indigenous Peoples reside. There is a brick mission house and a moderately sized frame school room. The community consisted of about thirty families, totalling 200 people, with sixty children of school age. These children receive their meals at the mission house. Rev. Edward Roberts serves as the superintendent of the mission, and the schoolteacher is an Indigenous person. While a few students are ready for the reading, a significant challenge remains: the children primarily speak their native language in daily life and study English at school. Additionally, the children in this area are noted for their remarkable singing abilities."[11]

Clearly, teaching English was a priority for this missionary-style schooling, but it was met with mixed results. The combination of food and singing lessons persuaded some students to attend, but other historical accounts indicate that it was difficult to increase attendance. A history of the New England Company published in 1885, explained that other factors were influencing the school: "This station is also under the care of the Company's missionary at Chemong, but a resident missionary and teacher being provided by the Methodist body, and the band having greatly diminished in numbers, the Company's expenditure at this station has for several years past been very small in amount."[12] The attendance challenges faced by the school were further compounded by external factors into the middle of 1800s, such as the declining population of the local Band and the limited financial contributions from the New England Company, which relied on the Methodist Mission to provide a resident missionary and teacher.

In the latter half of the nineteenth century, the community was not as supportive of the efforts to educate their students under the missionary program developed by the New England Company. There have been limited studies on the development of the New England Company and its Indian day schools, which also operated in the Grand River, Sault Ste Marie, and British Columbia regions during the same period.[13] Therefore, Brown's is the only schooling inspection report in the online federal archives regarding the New England Company's operation.

The New England Company was seeking opportunities in other parts of the world, so they decided to end their mission in Curve Lake in 1898. That year, the company sold 1,548.36 acres to the Department of Indian Affairs for only $1; this included the mission house or school building.[14] Community members were upset with the New England Company, as they had to lease their land from the organization. Chief Joseph Irons and Council passed a resolution to purchase the mission house for $2,250 to gain more control of the situation: "Indeed, Curve Lake First Nation had to purchase part of its own Reserve that had been set up in trust for its benefit!"[15] A more comprehensive overview of how this school developed in relation to other attempts by the New England Company in various Indigenous communities is needed to provide more details about this period. The New England Company, which represents the first attempt at schooling in the community, would subsequently be restarted by the federal government and Methodist Missionary Society.

The bulk of this book will focus on the period after 1899, due to the chronology of documents that began in that year and the direct involvement of the federal government, which started controlling education on reserve after the New England Company left in 1898. Therefore, the first file in the RG10 federal archives for the "Mud Lake Indian Day School" begins in January 1899, when Indian Agent McFarlane, who oversaw the Rice Lake Agency, wrote to the Department of Indian Affairs about the absence of a teacher at the Mud Lake Indian Day School. He explained that the previous teacher had been hired by the New England Company and that he "was not aware that the teacher was leaving until informed today by mail."[16] McFarlane requested that a teacher be found as soon as possible because the school could not operate without one. The Chief of Curve Lake, George Taylor, wrote to the Department with a request to hire William McCue to be the temporary teacher at a cost of $200 per year.[17] This request was based on a Council meeting where the community passed a unanimous resolution to hire a "member of our band, who holds a good 'teachers certificate' and has some twelve or thirteen months experience as a teacher."[18] The earliest documented files on this school indicate that the community had long advocated for control over their education, repeatedly petitioning the government for self-governance in schooling. These records show ongoing efforts to secure culturally relevant education, curriculum autonomy, and improved conditions for students. However, despite these requests, government policies often failed to support true educational sovereignty, resulting in continued external control over Indigenous schooling.

On the same day that Mud Lake Chief and Council passed this resolution, Indian Agent McFarlane wrote to the Department about his concerns regarding the hiring of an "Indian teacher": "I have received from the Indians in confidence that they would rather have a white teacher but that they did not like to oppose McCue for private reasons ... I would advise that a white teacher be hired with proper certificates. There is a good number of pupils in the fourth book and Mr McCue is appointed postmaster at Chemong and would have to neglect some of his work if hired as teacher ... There is a white teacher with a second-class certificate and good recommendations would take this school at $200 a year."[19]

The Indian agent controlled decisions about the day schools on reserve, and McFarlane overruled the decision of Chief and Council to hire an Indigenous teacher. The Department approved of this change and wrote to him: "The Indians do not seem to know their own mind, and they tell you in confidence that they would rather have a white teacher, – you may by your own discretion, if you have not already notified McCue of his appointment, and appoint a white teacher."[20] As a result of this approval, McFarlane decided to hire a White teacher named Lily Middleton, who only had a third-class certificate for teaching and less experience than McCue.[21]

After ignoring the community's hiring request, the Department also inquired about the percentage of the teacher's salary that the Band would pay: "With regard to the agreement relative to the payment by the band of the teacher's salary, I beg to say that while the Department is not in any way obliged to obtain such agreement, it would like to have the Indians consent to this money being taken from their funds."[22] In response, the Mud Lake Chief and Council submitted a clearly worded resolution that explained why they would not be paying any salary for a teacher of the department's choosing:

> We wish it to be clearly understood that we have no fault to find with Miss Middleton in any way. But the wishes of this band were expressed to the Department in a resolution dated Feb 4th asking that Mr. McCue be hired as teacher. The Department on the 8th Feb approved of the appointment, and authorized our agent Mr. McFarlane to appoint Mr. McCue. But for private reasons of his own, and because someone has gone behind the bands back, and told him something in "confidence," our agent ignores the approved

> wishes of the Band and proceed to do as he pleased, and therefore as we have not been fairly dealt with in this matter, we cannot become responsible for the Teacher's salary.[23]

This resolution was passed unanimously and outlined the knowledge Council had regarding the internal hiring process between the Indian agent and Ottawa. It appears that the Department agreed to pay for the teacher's salary and she remained at the school until the summer of 1900, when she resigned to attend teacher's college.[24]

After Miss Middleton left the school, McFarlane found it difficult to find a qualified teacher for such a low salary and began to side with the community. The Curve Lake Chief and Council again requested that one of their own members fill the position until someone suitable was hired. McFarlane wrote on 23 August 1900, that "the request that one of the Indians teach until a qualified teacher be good [*sic*] as there is some of the Indians in the Band well advanced. I would recommend that their request be granted."[25] The second Indigenous teacher, Daniel Whetung, was hired to teach from September to December or until a properly qualified teacher was secured.[26] Joseph Whetung, another community member, taught the next term and continued teaching until the summer of 1901.

In February 1901, the Curve Lake Chief and Council passed a resolution to create a new school. They wanted to build a larger "brick building fifty feet by thirty feet for school room and a hall room which is needed very much."[27] This two-storey building would allow for a Council meeting hall on the upper floor and a schoolroom on the bottom. It was also agreed that construction costs could be paid with their Band funds. Indian Agent McFarlane supported building the new school, as the current one was not meeting the population's needs.[28] Chief Irons wrote a personal letter to the Department, explaining that the cost would be around $1,000 and expressing hope that the Department would send tenders for contractors.[29] Instead, the Department argued that the size of the building be reduced to forty feet by twenty-five feet, as only twenty-five out of the fifty registered students attended the school regularly.[30] The plans also had to be inspected and approved by an architect hired by the Department. The resulting markup submitted to the Department showed the two-storey building along with a much higher price.

Originally, the reserve was only willing to pay $1,000, but after estimates were submitted to fit the school with heating through a furnace and piping system, additional furniture, and further specifications required by the Department – including a "teacher's podium" – the estimated cost that was approved was $3,200.[31] The community funds paid this larger price entirely, even though the Department made all the decisions about hiring contractors, negotiating prices, and making design choices. Construction of the new school was completed on 3 December 1901.[32] Later that month, Chief Irons and Secretary Daniel Whetung wrote to the Department about essential items missing from the building. They said the contractors had "done shameful work, as we Indians have very little money and have no money to spend on extravagance, we don't mind paying for a thing what it's worth ... All we are asking is to have the combined building furnished with all the necessities both Inside and outside."[33]

They argued that the school was missing essential components including piping for heat, seats and desks for all students, and additional brick or concrete around the furnace to insulate the children from the hot metal. There were additional concerns about the work on the roof and whether it would support the weight of snow over the winter months. The Department refused to respond to these requests, as they argued that the community had already been notified about where to supply these materials. As the community was never involved in the tender discussions for buildings on reserve, the government had full control over who was chosen, even if that person was unsatisfactory. At a Mud Lake Council meeting, Chief Irons and Secretary Whetung passed a resolution to demand the government's assistance in furnishing the school. It said: "We now ask as our guardian to see that seats and desks are furnished for the combined school and council house that the necessary fences are built for all of which the money was granted."[34] Indian Agent McFarlane did not grant approval for the final work to install the desks until February 1902.[35] Throughout the next year, the Mud Lake Chief and Council regularly had to pay for additional upgrades, including painting, installing a new water pump and school bell, repairing fences, improving drainage around the school, and making other general repairs.[36] These school repair expenses were paid directly from the Band funds without any support from the government. The reliance on Band funds to cover these costs, rather than government-provided resources, highlights the financial strain placed on the community as they worked to sustain and improve the school's infrastructure. The Chief and Council's actions show a deep commitment to education and a recognition of its importance for their community. Their willingness to allocate limited Band funds for essential school repairs and upgrades reflects their belief that a functional and well-maintained educational environment was vital for the children's learning and the community's future. By prioritizing infrastructure improvements, they demonstrated that education required more than just instruction; it needed proper facilities and resources to be effective. Their efforts also suggest a desire for self-reliance and agency in providing for their community's educational needs, even in the face of systemic neglect and inadequate support from the government.

Rather than submitting a community resolution to appoint a new schoolteacher in the fall of 1901, Indian Agent McFarlane submitted an extract of his annual report. This file explained that the Mud Lake Band passed a motion to "hire a white male teacher after the summer holidays if the male teacher is not too high in salary."[37] This motion was not signed by any members of the Mud Lake community, yet it permitted McFarlane to search once again for a White male teacher to replace the school's Indigenous teacher. Until August of that year, McFarlane tried, unsuccessfully, to secure a White teacher who wanted to teach at the school. He was once again forced to hire an Indigenous teacher, Alfred McCue: "As I could not secure a white teacher for the school, I have got the best Indian teacher that I could find."[38] The Department reluctantly approved the hire, but the assistant secretary emphasized the temporary nature of the appointment, writing, "I beg to say that his services are only to be retained, as you have already been informed, until a white teacher can be secured."[39] The Department clearly prioritized settler teachers as part of its broader colonial agenda while simultaneously undervaluing the contributions of Indigenous educators like Alfred McCue, even when they were better qualified and available. Only in the worst-case scenario – when no other teacher could be secured – would the Department approve of an Indigenous person operating the school on the reserve.

Alfred McCue taught at the school for over eight years (1901–09) due to the support of the community and Chief and Council and the Department's repeated failure to find a qualified teacher trained to their specifications.[40] During this period, the community was also tasked with paying for increases to the teacher's salary, which rose from $200 to $300, despite this being a federal responsibility. The Chief and Council sent several notices to Indian Agent McFarlane indicating that they should not have to pay for the difference in salary, but these memos were never enforced.[41] The Department unilaterally chose to increase the yearly rate regardless, as they wanted to hire a more expensive White teacher who would not accept only $200 a year.

By 1908, the school building's inadequate construction was becoming apparent. When the water was high during the spring, the school's cellar flooded, creating a muddy basement floor. The water also damaged the basement walls, creating a situation that could worsen. As a result, Daniel Whetung paid out of his own funds for both the labour and cement to stop the flooding and requested reimbursement from the Department of Education.[42] Mud Lake Chief and Council also approved the payment of $75 from reserve funds to fix the issue, but the Department was reluctant to send the money.[43] They wrote to Indian Agent McFarlane, "You should state whether you authorized it or whether it was undertaken by Whetung solely upon orders from the Council of the band."[44] The Department did not trust the Indigenous population living in Mud Lake to spend their own funds, which were kept in Ottawa.

Daniel Whetung was incensed by the Department's decision not to pay "my little account." He argued that without the concrete basement, continual flooding would cause additional damage to the walls and lead to unclean and unhealthy conditions in the school. This water could eventually erode the school's foundation, placing the building at risk. Whetung stated: "*The Indian Department must think that this Band of Indians are all fools and don't know how to carry on their own business. If they are? They are much mistaken. For there are Indians here who know as much about carrying on business as some of the membership of the Indian Department* [emphasis in the original]. And if you could show me one instance where this Indian Council ever tried to defraud the Indian Department. I would speak differently I have been easy with this council by waiting for my payment from the Indian funds."[45] Whetung's statement underscores the frustration and indignation felt by the community at the paternalistic attitudes of the Indian Department. By highlighting the Council's integrity and business expertise, Whetung challenged the prevailing stereotypes that depicted Indigenous Peoples as incapable of managing their own affairs. His pointed remarks also revealed the inherent inequities in the system, where decisions about essential repairs and financial obligations were often delayed or dismissed by the Department despite the immediate and pressing needs of the community. The refusal to settle his account strained relations and symbolized the broader disregard for Indigenous agency and self-determination in managing their own resources and infrastructure.

Whetung's correspondence reflects his mounting frustration with the Indian Department's refusal to approve payment for critical repairs. He warned the Department that if they did not pay the bill by the end of February 1908, he would "have to look for some authority to assist me in collecting."[46] Whetung criticized the Department for their lack of trust in Indigenous Peoples to manage "business" and pointed out the absence of any valid rationale for withholding payment, especially since the funds in question came directly from Band resources. The Department's justification – that the Indian agent had not authorized the expenditure – further fuelled his frustration.

In a follow-up letter on 1 March 1901, Whetung challenged the Department's logic, asserting: "I don't see why the Indian Department cannot pay this account supposing they are not responsible does not the [Indian] act say the Indians could see their money at any time for improvements to buildings on the reserve and is not this a great necessary improvement. Why should not the Indian Department pay this account when they are paying the schoolteacher $300 a year salary without the consent of this band?"[47] His argument underscored the inconsistency in the Department of Indian Affairs' approach to financial oversight when they could allocate Band funds without consultation for teacher salaries but were unwilling to approve essential infrastructure improvements. This exchange again reveals the systemic paternalism of the Department of Indian Affairs, where community priorities were routinely dismissed or obstructed under the guise of bureaucratic control. At other times, when the community needed money for essential repairs, the Department delayed funding, especially if a local Indigenous person had made the repair. This bureaucracy not only put students at risk but also worsened the relationship between the government and Indigenous Peoples at this time.

Finally, the Department escalated the concern to the chief accountant who said the payment could be made if "an architect be employed to inspect the work and report whether it was properly done, and if charges are reasonable."[48] The Department did not believe Indigenous Peoples had the ability to construct buildings or repair them on reserve, but the architect found that "the work has been done well and the price I consider fair and reasonable."[49] This inspection, which cost the Department an additional fifteen dollars, was a direct result of their refusal to take Whetung's account seriously. Only after the architect's confirmation did the Department acknowledge the validity of the work and the severity of the problem. The added expense and delay exemplify the systemic barriers faced by Indigenous communities in addressing critical infrastructure needs, as their expertise and integrity were routinely dismissed without external validation.[50]

In the spring of 1909, a school inspection by Inspector Ramsden would end Alfred McCue's teaching career at Mud Lake Indian Day School. The report lambasted the progress of pupils on reserve and said that since 1901, McCue "had failed to make a success of the school." The school inspector reported that McCue lacked the proper equipment, and his "method of teaching in this school is not along modern ideas."[51] The inspector continued: "The Indians are dissatisfied and careless about sending their children to school, but, if a qualified teacher, who is interested in his work, is given them, I am sure that a noticeable improvement could take place. There are over 25 children of school age on the reserve and it is too bad they should grow up in ignorance. They have a good school building and if the salary were raised a good teacher could be secured and I would suggest that Mr. McCue's service be dispensed with after June 30, next, and the school reopened after the summer holiday with a new teacher."[52] This report reflects critically on McCue's teaching methods and the systemic challenges Indigenous educators faced, including a lack of support, resources, and training necessary to meet the expectations imposed by the government. Ramsden's suggestion that raising the salary would attract a "qualified" teacher further highlights the Department's prioritization of settler teachers over Indigenous ones. The decision to remove McCue ultimately stemmed from broader biases against Indigenous teachers, as well as the colonial emphasis on assimilative education methods that disregarded the cultural and structural barriers faced by communities like Mud Lake.

Based on this report, the Department instructed Indian Agent McFarlane to search for a new schoolteacher. It is not clear if these findings were sent to McCue or if he was allowed to defend himself as, within a month, he was no longer the teacher. This information was also not passed to Chief or Council; instead, the government decided internally to raise the annual salary of the school to $450 per year to attract new graduates from the nearby Peterborough Normal School.[53] The annual salary had been increased by 50 per cent to attract a non-Indigenous teacher with training, yet no graduate from the Peterborough Normal School was willing to "go to the Reserve."[54] The lack of interest from qualified candidates underscores the Department's failure to address systemic issues that made teaching positions on reserves undesirable, including isolation, inadequate salaries, and the paternalistic structures that limited local agency.

While the Department was busy searching for a suitable teacher, Curve Lake passed a resolution to keep Alfred McCue. On 28 June 1909, Chief Joseph Whetung and Council said, "There [*sic*] schoolteacher Alfred McCue to remain here and teach school. The good people of Mud Lake reserve heard there was going to be a change, so they passed this resolution holding their former schoolteacher [–] hope you will kindly approve the same. We will wait for your reply at an early date."[55] The resolution reflected the community's trust in McCue and their desire to retain him as their teacher despite the Department's criticisms. However, the Department took over a month to reply, writing to Indian Agent McFarlane: "Mr. McCue has tendered his resignation and the same has been accepted, steps have already been taken with a view in securing a successor. Furthermore, the Department is of the opinion that, in view of the friction has lately existed between the teacher and certain members of the Band, a change of teachers will be in the best interest of all concerned. For the foregoing reasons the Department cannot approve this resolution, and you will be good enough to advise the Indians accordingly."[56] This response not only dismissed the community's collective decision but also highlighted the Department's disregard for local agency in educational matters. The vague reference to "friction" suggested an attempt to justify their refusal without directly addressing the community's support for McCue. The Department's insistence on overriding the resolution illustrates the broader pattern of undermining Indigenous governance and autonomy, prioritizing its own agenda over the expressed needs and wishes of the community.

Clearly, the government did not consider the perspectives of Chief and Council, who had democratically passed a resolution to keep McCue as the school's teacher. Moreover, even on the most urgent and personal matters, the Department always interacted with First Nations communities through their Indian agent. This person filtered what information would be received regarding the school and ultimately made crucial decisions, such as the hiring of teachers, of their own accord.

Similar conversations about the use of Indigenous teachers occurred throughout Canada during this period. Martha Walls recently researched six Mi'kmaq teachers from Quebec who moved to New Brunswick to teach in Indian day schools between 1900 and 1923. The research highlights how the "network of power" between the Department of Indian Affairs and the bureaucracy of schooling institutions was linked.[57] However, Walls argues that these teachers acted as "change agents" – individuals from Indigenous communities who participated in protesting or resisting colonialism. The local reserves petitioned for Indigenous women to teach in their communities as they could still speak Mi'kmaq, which was seen as beneficial for civilizing purposes and as a means for retaining some parts of their culture. The Indigenous teachers, Walls concluded, "imparted to students the federally ordained day school program and as they reached into communities to facilitate a broader 'civilizing agenda' through such seemingly mundane actions as teaching sewing and knitting, these teachers did the bidding of the colonialist state. More important, however, are the ways in which these teachers subverted state policy. By using and teaching the Mi'kmaw language in the classroom, and by refusing to yield to DIA authority, they challenged the very essence of the Canadian colonialist project."[58]

The government recognized that Indigenous teachers would always impart some of their own cultural traditions and so worked to remove them from Michi Saagiig Anishinaabeg territory. These disputes would continue between church organizations, the federal government, and the elected members of Chief and Council. This chapter has illuminated the critical roles played by the New England Company in establishing and operating the Curve Lake Indian Day School. From the creation of the reserve to the formalization of education systems, these institutions imposed European educational methods on Indigenous communities, aiming to assimilate Indigenous students into the emerging Canadian state. The early classes laid the groundwork for the Indian day school system that would proliferate across Canada by the late nineteenth century. Through these schooling efforts, European ways of education became tools for religious conversion and land division, fundamentally altering the lives and cultures of the Anishinaabe. The archival records, such as those detailing teacher appointments, school inspections, and community resolutions, reveal a constant struggle for control over education. Indigenous voices advocating for their own teachers and better school conditions often clashed with the colonial authorities' decisions. The story of the Curve Lake Indian Day School is one of resilience and resistance, highlighting the community's persistent efforts to maintain its cultural identity amidst external pressures to conform to Eurocentric norms. As we move forward in this book, we will continue to explore these themes of cultural imposition, resistance, and the ongoing impacts of colonial education systems on Indigenous communities. The history of the Curve Lake Indian Day School provides a profound understanding of the complex interplay between Indigenous agency and colonial control, setting the stage for a deeper examination of the broader implications of colonial educational practices.

CHAPTER 4

Mismanagement and Mistrust: The Methodist Missionary School in Curve Lake

Without the consent of the Curve Lake Band Council, the federal government requested that a Methodist missionary visit the community and provide recommendations on the school and a potential parsonage in which a teacher could live. Reverend George W. Henderson visited the community during the summer of 1909 and made several statements about the school and the way of life in the community.[1] Henderson was impressed with the "pretty good type of the race" who had tidy homes and created a mission house, church, and school facility all with minimal help.[2] He noted the church was "the best looked after and neatest Indian Church I have seen."[3] Henderson was confident that this location would be ideal for a new Methodist mission. He consulted with the Chief and his brother and said they were "both reliable men and Christians" who were enthusiastic about the idea.[4] The current teacher had been dismissed by the Department, and the community had already bid him farewell, clearing the way for the new mission. The Methodist Church was the only service held on the reserve, and it had the community's full support. During winter evenings, they gathered congregations of about 100 to 120 people, with fifty-five members belonging to the Methodist Church. They also held class and prayer meetings. Henderson believed that the situation was clear-cut: if the necessary arrangements could be made with the Department and the right person found, the mission could be successfully established.

Henderson was a loyal advocate of missionary work and wrote to the general secretary of the Methodist Society to share his views. Throughout the letter, Henderson tried to convince the Department that the Methodist mission should be in charge of the school because of its established influence in the community. The mission already had a strong base of supporters and had secured the funding for local initiatives, including healthcare. Henderson also assumed that the Chief and his brother were on board. However, they had written privately to the Department requesting that the current method of education continue. Ultimately, the request by Reverend Henderson convinced the Department to allow the Methodists to hire a teacher for the school and allow them to live in the former New England Company mission house.

The Methodists hired Mr George Cork, a sixty-nine-year-old married man with a forty-five-year teaching career who had earned a first-class teacher's certificate in June 1862.[5] The Department was reluctant to give the position to Cork because of his age. They wrote: "His retention in the position will be dependent upon the success he makes of the school. The Department would have preferred a younger man and expected that you would have been able to secure one, as it is considered doubtful whether a man of Mr. Cork's advanced age will be able to adapt himself to prevailing conditions."[6] The government was aware of the difficult conditions in a remote and underfunded Indian day school and believed that Cork's age would impede his ability to teach the students adequately. It also appeared that the government preferred a younger man so that they could stay in the position longer and use more updated methods of teaching. While Curve Lake First Nation was not notified of this hire until the first day of the school year, they welcomed Mr George Cork into the community. In a Council resolution passed on the first day of school, they said, "Mr. Cork of Toronto is accepted as a teacher to start school today for the term of one year at the salary of $300 per annum."[7] This resolution ensured that the expense of the teacher for the community would stay the same despite the Department's advertised pay of $450 per year. In an internal letter, the Indian agent agreed that the "increase of $150.00 in the salary being paid the present teacher of the Chemong

Indian School will be paid by the Department, only $300 to be charged to the funds of the band."[8]

On the day that Cork arrived in the community, he sent a handwritten note to the Department explaining some of his concerns. Cork mentioned that he had received a warm welcome to Curve Lake from Chief and Council, but his boarding facility was in a "bad state of repairs."[9] He also noted a pressing need for the Department to officially recognize him as the new teacher: "What I am writing for now is concerning my credentials. They have not heard of my appointment, and I came without anything to show by what I authority I came. The chief very delicately spoke to me about it today. Please write to Chief Whetung concerning my appointment."[10] The hiring of Mr Cork was clearly not relayed by the Department, and the confusion regarding the operation of the school, while it appeared to be quickly solved, demonstrated a concerning practice regarding the turnover of schools to unauthorized individuals.

This arrangement with Cork and the Curve Lake community would only last until March 1910, when he was asked to transfer to another Methodist school. At the request of the general secretary of the Methodist Church, Rev. Dr Sutherland, he was asked to exchange positions with the teacher of the Georgina Island reserve. George Cork was disappointed with this news as he had only been at the school for eight months but believed he had established a good rapport with the community. He wrote to the Department, asking if they could intervene and keep him at the school: "I like it here, and Chief Joseph Whetung informs me that the people are well pleased with my work. Then again, I am not a preacher and prefer not to have any responsibility regarding religious work except Sunday School work. While feeling that it is hardly fair to make the change without my consent, I shall bow to the decision of the Department."[11]

These comments were based on the perspective of Mr Cork, but it appeared that the reserve was responding favourably to a teaching approach that did not focus entirely on Christian education. Moreover, a letter from Chief Joseph Whetung to the Department of Indian Affairs reiterated the positive work of Cork: "The members of my band appreciate Mr. Cork (Toronto) for his excellent work and good qualifications as teacher of Chemong Indian School."[12] Whetung also said that the community wanted Cork to stay until the next term in September 1910 and hoped the Department would make a "suitable reply."[13] In a rare response, the secretary of Indian Affairs, J.D. McLean, wrote directly to Chief Joseph Whetung instead of sending his messages through the Indian agent. He explained: "I beg to inform you that arrangements have been made for the transfer of Mr. Cork to Georgina Island and Mr. Prosser, teacher there, to the Chemong school, to take effect on the 1st of April, next. The Department trusts that Mr. Prosser's services will be satisfactory and that he will receive the hearty cooperation of yourself and the Indians of the reserve, as without this the greatest good cannot be accomplished."[14]

In the first decade of the twentieth century, Curve Lake Chief and Council requested specific teachers in their community whom the Department only accepted as a last resort. Instead – and without the permission of the community – the Department repeatedly changed teachers in direct opposition to the wishes of Chief and Council. The changing of teachers in the middle of the school year was less than ideal for the educational progress of the students.

By the fall of 1910, the community of Curve Lake had had enough of the new teacher, Mr John Prosser, and sent several concerning messages to local officials. In a letter addressed directly to the Peterborough school inspector, the new Chief Daniel Whetung demanded something be done about the terrible teacher they were sent.[15] His letter indicated that he had reached out to provincial officials first before going to the local federal Indian agent, illustrating the blurred lines between the responsibilities for education. He wrote: "Sir, I would like you to come up and inspect our school teacher. I think you will find that he is not [qualified] as a teacher – How is it that we cannot get a good teacher like you white people – We pay the teachers as much as you whites. Pay your teachers [illegible] is the Department of Indian Affairs at Ottawa to be blamed for [illegible] Are our guidance they ought to send us the best quality teacher [illegible] intend for us to know something."[16]

Whetung firmly believed that racism was the primary reason Curve Lake struggled to secure a qualified teacher for the community. The nearby White community of Peterborough had established a normal school for teacher training and a full school board. Chief Whetung's letter

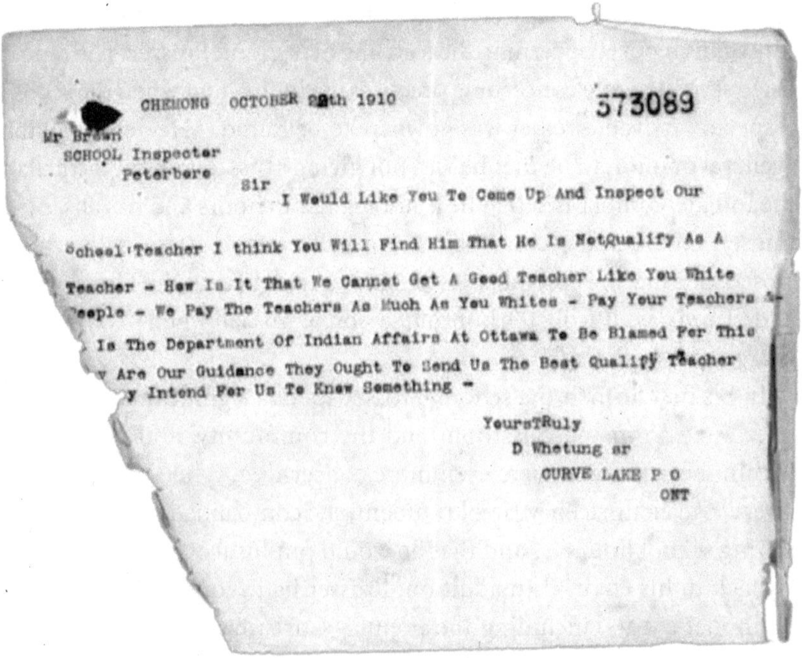

CHEMONG OCTOBER 29th 1910 573089

Mr Brown
SCHOOL Inspecter
Peterbore
Sir
I Would Like You To Come Up And Inspect Our
School Teacher I think You Will Find Him That He Is NotQualify As A
Teacher - How Is It That We Cannot Get A Good Teacher Like You White
People - We Pay The Teachers As Much As You Whites - Pay Your Teachers
Is The Department Of Indian Affairs At Ottawa To Be Blamed For This
Are Our Guidance They Ought To Send Us The Best Qualify Teacher
y Intend For Us To Know Something -

YoursTRuly
D Whetung sr
CURVE LAKE P O
ONT

Figure 4.1
Typed letter dated 29 October 1910, from D. Whetung of Curve Lake to the school inspector, expressing concerns about the qualifications of teachers sent to the community and questioning the role of the Department of Indian Affairs in providing quality education.

prompted action not by the Department but by the provincial government, which forwarded the letter to the minister of education and then the deputy minister of education, A.G.U. Colquhoun, who finally sent the message to the Department of Indian Affairs. Ultimately, J.D. McLean responded by asking the Ministry of Education in Ontario to inspect the school, stating that once the "inspector's report is received the Chief's complaint will be dealt with."[17] In the meantime, Chief and Council passed another resolution demanding that Prosser be removed and a qualified teacher be found to replace him. In response, Prosser wrote to the Department requesting money for attendance prizes and a "truant officer" to force students into school.[18]

Finally, on the last day of 1910, the school inspector, Mr Ramsden, submitted his report concerning the teaching of Mr John Prosser. The report listed several highly concerning practices, including that when the school inspector arrived, Prosser was nowhere to be found.[19] He described the "general opinion to be that he was not giving satisfaction. In particular, the Indians complained that he is not regular in hours and has absented himself on different occasions, one for half a day to attend sale, school closed, one day in September last to show a trick bear at the Lindsay Fair and fifteen days during the hunting season of this fall when his wife took charge of the school."[20]

In his first term at the school, Prosser spent a significant amount of time away from the classroom and the community, and his actions within the classroom were even more concerning. When the inspector interviewed a thirteen-year-old student, she complained that "he sleeps during school hours … and that he would put his feet on the desk and layback in his chair."[21] In addition, Prosser had refused to participate in annual events, including the popular Christmas concert, deciding to leave the community as soon as the holidays started. A further concern was that Prosser "has had no clock since summer holidays, having been broken and stored away in the cupboards, they also claim that he has no watch. The schoolroom had a general untidy appearance, seats being piled up and in disorder. The attendance register is poorly and carelessly kept."[22]

These critical concerns were reinforced with another resolution, which Curve Lake First Nation sent with the school inspector. The chief school inspector concluded: "I fear he is indifferent and lazy and that it would be in the best interests of the Department to allow him to devote all his time to the education of his trick bear."[23] This "trick bear" was a circus animal that was trained by the teacher and lived nearby in the mission house.

Despite these serious grievances with the quality of education on reserve, the Department decided to keep him for another six months to finish the rest of the school year. They wrote to Prosser stating, "The Indians of the Mud Lake Band have expressed their dissatisfaction at your lack of qualifications and the methods of teaching followed by you in the Chemong School and, as you have not succeeded in obtaining the confidence of the Indians, the Department is of the opinion that it would be to the interest of all concerned if you would give up this school by the 30th June, next."[24] The Department also provided the option to keep Prosser on the Indian day school teaching list in case another position became available. This indicates that, despite the disastrous teaching inspection, the Department was still willing to employ this teacher at other Indian day schools within the system.

This message drove Prosser to respond and defend himself and his teaching abilities. He stated that every claim "could be proved false," and the community was not receptive to his teaching style because they preferred Mr Cork, who had been switched for his position on Georgina Island.[25] Prosser requested that the chief inspector return to the community to hear his side of the story. He also provided "proof" of these claims by enclosing a signed list of sixteen students that said: "We the undersigned pupils of Mud Lake Day School desire to say that we never saw Mr. John Prosser asleep in our school in our lives."[26] Chief and Council wanted Prosser to be replaced with a suitable and more qualified teacher in the community.

At the request of Prosser and the Department, in February 1911, Chief Inspector Ramsden conducted another investigation into the teaching quality in the community. When Ramsden arrived at the school this time, Prosser emphatically denied all accusations and said that "he loses none of the school time in the attention he bestows upon his trained bear."[27] During this visit, and with Prosser in the classroom, the students denied that he fell asleep during any previous lessons. However, during Ramsden's visit to the community, Chief and Council passed another resolution in favour of having a certified teacher for the school. Ramsden noted, "I may say that I am always favoured getting as good teachers as possible but pointed out to the Band was the difficulty the Department was experiencing in getting qualified teachers to remain for any length of time on some of the different Reserves."[28] He also stated that Prosser was doing much better than during his last visit and instead recommended that "he can do well if he applies himself and I think the Department should write him and tell him he is on trial for the last time and that it is expected that he will do his very best to increase the attendance by persuading the parents to interest the children and by working agreeably as possible with the council and members of the Band."[29] The Department agreed with this recommendation and permitted Prosser to continue teaching the community "on his last chance" until June 1911. They told him that it would be "manifestly unfair to the Indians to keep you on if satisfactory results are not obtained" by the summer term.[30]

After he was given this warning, in two separate letters written in the spring of 1911, Prosser accused Chief Daniel Whetung and members of his Council of being his "enemy" and undermining his schooling efforts. He wrote that any "Indian Reports were rubbish," and that Whetung forced him to spend money in his store, or he would "fall into immediate danger of losing any school."[31] He requested again that a truant officer be sent to the community to help his attendance records, as many students over fifteen were no longer attending.[32] Indian Agent McFarlane refuted these claims, writing to the Department, "I do not know as to the accuracy of his statements about Whetung. For I think, Whetung was instrumental in working the opposition to him."[33] The teacher, who had already received a negative review, was now accusing the leader of the community without any proof.

While Prosser was technically hired by the federal government, the Methodist Church ran professional development through teachers' conferences. In May 1911, Prosser was invited to the Mount Elgin Institute (residential school) for a conference with all the Methodist "Indian Teachers." The focus of this conference was on themes that included "how to make the Indian a good Citizen, Remnants of Paganism, Why should we educate the Indian, Indian home life, How far can Indian Missions be made self-supporting, Possible cooperation between White Work and Indian Missions."[34] It is not clear whether Prosser attended this conference, but it was mandated for any "Indian workers," and the church agreed to cover the costs of travel and accommodations. These conferences would provide additional rationale for implementing educational changes to the curriculum.

By June 1911, Chief Daniel Whetung had had enough of passing resolutions that were dismissed. He wrote to the Department of Education in Ontario requesting more information about uncertified teachers:

"We have a school teacher here now sent by the Indian Department of Ottawa. This teacher has neither certificate or even a permit how is that he could be allowed to teach[?] As I understood that the government was work stric[t] (than former years) to see that the teachers were qualif[ied] to teach."[35] Chief Whetung reiterated Inspector Ramsden's reports, which found significant issues with the teaching methods used by Prosser. Whetung argued that Prosser showed several errors on the blackboard "that would be sufficient to prove that the teacher was not qualif[ied] to teach in any school (white or Indian School)." Chief Whetung stated: "I am always very anxious to see the young here to be well educated the people could tell you that I often urge them to send their children regular to school."[36]

The Department of Education immediately forwarded the Chief's letter to the Department of Indian Affairs, who responded later that June that "the necessary action will be taken by this Department."[37] It's apparent that no action was taken by the Department, as the next file in the federal archive is a letter from Prosser seeking permission to go on a fall hunting break during the first half of November.[38] In fact, the Department contacted Prosser in December 1911 to say that "if you care to remain on temporarily as teacher. The Department will, however, take steps to secure the services of a duly qualified teacher for this school early in the spring."[39]

In February 1912, Prosser submitted his resignation to the Department to avoid being formally let go. He was cognizant of the Department's role in protecting his career and wrote to express his gratitude: "My qualifications and services here have been much better than represented by my enemies. Many thanks to the Department for their kind consideration and regards when I was in the hour of danger. If the Department permits one to complete the seven years, they respect my work as a Methodist missionary, and I will do the very best I can to promote the children of this school. I have a son who pass the entrance and is now in his second year at the high school. He can speak the Indian language quite perfectly and might someday be of use to the Department."[40] His acknowledgment of their assistance "in the hour of danger" suggests that he relied on their backing to maintain his position despite criticisms. By emphasizing his qualifications and his son's fluency in the Indigenous language, Prosser appears to be appealing to the Department's interests, possibly to leave a favourable impression or to secure future opportunities for his family. This highlights the complex dynamics between missionaries and the Department, where personal ambitions were closely tied to the colonial education system.

Despite the grievances against his teaching, Prosser was permitted to stay until the end of June 1912 – nearly two years after the Department first received a report about him. Mr Prosser believed the community was against him and that his only defense was the Department that protected him in his "hour of danger." Furthermore, it appeared that his son, who lived at his mission home, was the most successful student as he attended the nearby high school and learned the Indigenous language from the community. His son was even allowed to teach the final month of June, as Mr Prosser wanted to attend the Methodist Conference in Cobourg.[41] His only qualification for being a teacher was his attendance in the local high school, reinforcing the notion that a White student was a better choice for a teacher than a qualified Indigenous community member.

In June, the Department of Indian Affairs received multiple correspondences from Prosser and debt collectors about outstanding money he owed. He believed the Department owed him wages until the end of summer despite his leaving in the month of June. A collection agency wrote to the Department indicating, "a balance on a suit of clothing and I understand the J.H. Prosser is going to leave the school and go to some other part of the province. I would appreciate it if you would facilitate any effort in compelling Mr. Prosser to pay his honest debts."[42] The Department refused to pay Prosser any more money or settle his debt and instead sent multiple letters reminding him that he was no longer employed.

The Department only began a search for a new qualified teacher once Prosser was completely gone. Chief Daniel Whetung's father, Daniel Whetung, Sr, made clear his community's desire for a teacher in a letter he sent to the Department in July 1912. He wrote: "If you could write to our agent Mr. Macfarlane, Keene, and ask him to advertise for a teacher,

(I think a female teacher would suit better for this place, as Male Teachers are always want[ing] to find something else to do besides teaching). I just [thought] if we advertise right now we would have more chance to get a teacher while there is a vacation."[43] These inquiries were warranted given the problems in the past in securing a teacher, and the recommendation for a female teacher would disrupt the decade-long chain of male teachers.

Whetung Sr's request was forwarded to the Methodist Missionary Society, and they secured the application of one female teacher with a second-class teacher's certificate. Miss Jane Armour was qualified for the position and wrote in her application that she had been teaching for "nine years at the Ryerson Indian School," so she was aware of the requirements for this position.[44] The Methodist Society believed "conditions at the Chemong School are not suitable for a lady" and directed her to apply to another school in the Muskoka region of the province.[45] Miss Armour responded: "You did not state the nature of objectionable conditions in the Chemong School. However, I may state if it be in regard to discipline and general management that I have never experienced the slightest difficulty in these matters … I feel certain I should [find] no difficulty."[46]

Based on this letter and her experience with other "Indian Schools," they offered the position to Jane Armour. She was to begin teaching in September 1912 at a rate of $400 a year – $50 less than the previous male teacher with no experience or teaching certificate.[47] Unfortunately, the agreement fell apart at the very last moment when the Methodist Society found another male teacher instead.

This new teacher had just completed his bachelor's degree but had no educational training. He also requested a salary of $600 and was "personally known" by the Methodist Missionary Society.[48] The Methodist Society argued that "no qualified teacher can at present be obtained for that position at the salary which has previously been paid."[49] The Department disagreed as they had believed that Jane Armour was going to be hired at the rate of $400. They wrote back, "Kindly explain why Miss Armour did not take the position[?]"[50] This debate continued as the Methodist Society said the offer was only conditional and they had not heard from Armour since the original offer. They reiterated that no teacher could be secured at the lower price point the Department offered.[51]

By the start of November 1912, the school had not reopened, nor had they been able to secure a teacher while the government and church organizations debated the cost. With pressure from Chief and Council, the Department increased the salary to $550 per year and offered a free residence to the male teacher the Methodist Society had recommended.[52] While this occurred, the newly elected councillor Alfred McCue – who was a former Indian day school teacher – passed a new resolution with the Mud Lake Council. This resolution instructed McCue to serve as the teacher at a salary of $300 or half the cost of the proposed male Methodist teacher.[53] Even Indian Agent McFarlane recommended that the Department approve this resolution, as "Alfred McCue taught this for a number of years and had a better education for a teacher and gave better satisfaction than any teacher they have had on the reserve since being dismissed."[54] McFarlane reiterated the community's wishes and showed once again that they had better experiences with people who knew them rather than unknown missionaries who provided constant problems.

The Department agreed to let McCue teach the remaining month of the term but stated that a new White teacher named Mr H.C. Buffam would be hired and begin his duties in January 1913.[55] Buffam's salary was nearly double that of Alfred McCue's, yet he requested a raise the following September. He asked for $700, but the Department only agreed to a salary of $600.[56] It was also noted that half of this money was from Band funds while the Department funded the other half.[57]

The first inspection conducted during Buffam's term found more problems with the building than his teaching style. Inspector G.E. Broderick reported that the school property was far from satisfactory: "Although the building is substantial and aesthetically pleasing, the interior planning neglects the needs of the school. The classroom is much too small to accommodate the enrolled pupils, poorly ventilated, inadequately lit, and improperly heated. With around thirty children crammed into a space half the needed size, lacking ventilation and heated by a stove, the situation poses a significant health risk to the community."[58] He said that the "closets [washrooms] are among the worst ever seen, located too far away, offering no privacy, and in a filthy condition."[59]

The school had only been in operation for twelve years when the inspector deemed it ready for significant improvement. Daniel Whetung had originally requested a larger schoolroom in 1901, but the Department of Indian Affairs had denied the request. The school building was completely unfit for the growing population and showed how underfunded building costs led to larger problems in the future. The report indicated that the new teacher was "earnest and efficient" and was in a "very satisfactory condition" given the school's circumstances.[60] While the closets could be quickly cleaned, the size of the building would continue to impact the quality of education received. This issue could have been easily remedied if the Department had listened to Daniel Whetung in 1901.

On his second inspection in February 1914, the inspector found that the school had been closed for two days to clean up from a community event. The Department requested that Buffam explain his rationale for closing the school and asked if the education was being affected on reserve. Buffam: "I regret to say the school closed on these occasions but even if the school room were not used in this way, it would be impossible to teach the next day owing to the cleaning up and the commotion of running in and out. I wish to add that Mr. Agent McCamus did not come here these two dates to visit the school but to be present at these functions, at the latter of which he lowered himself to dance with the natives in the hall after they had been forbidden by the Chief. The task of raising their standard of morality is already too difficult without our Agent setting them such an example."[61] Buffam's response justified the school closures and criticized Agent McCamus for participating in the community events, framing his actions as undermining school operations and the Department's broader goals of moral "improvement." His remarks reveal the paternalistic attitudes common among educators and officials at the time, viewing Indigenous cultural practices and gatherings as obstacles to progress and morality. Buffam's disdain for McCamus's involvement further highlights tensions within the colonial administration. Differing attitudes toward engagement with Indigenous communities often clashed, creating divisions that impacted the functioning of schools on reserves.

After his first year of teaching, Buffam was extremely concerned about the low attendance at the school. Out of a registered thirty-eight names, the average 1913–14 school year attendance was only twenty-one.[62] He had reported these students to the truant officer and the Indian agent, who both provided warnings to the parents. In addition, he attended Council meetings where he urged "parents to send their children, but without the desired result."[63] He requested that the Department advise him on improving attendance in the school. To fix the issue, the Department approved the school being moved to the old church on the reserve to provide more space for education. That summer, the community approved a $300 grant to remodel the old church and turn it into a functional school.[64]

Attendance continued to plummet at the start of the First World War. The new Indian Agent McCamus wrote to the Department in the spring of 1915: "I beg to say that the children are not attending as they should. They are not interested in their studies as they are in their play. They are bright as any children in the country and yet they do not get on as they should. The foundation of the trouble, I would say lay in the system followed in employing the teacher."[65]

He blamed the Methodist Missionary Society, which operated away from the community; consequently, the Department had no authority to change the methods used by the teacher. These ideas were reinforced by McCamus's monthly visits to the community and by another teacher in Hiawatha First Nation, who had more success with the attendance of students. That teacher was female and not directly associated with the preaching duties of the Methodists, so she was able to respond to the changing World War conditions. McCamus believed the Methodist Missionary Society had become "indifferent" and were no longer capable of enforcing any policies that the federal government created. The Department told the Indian agent to "inform Mr. Buffam that the Department will expect him to conduct this school in the interests of the children under his charge and he should endeavour to obtain the goodwill of their parents and do all in his power to secure the hearty cooperation of parents and pupils. You may also inform Mr. Buffam, if necessary, that so long as he remains in the service of the Department, he will be expected to carry out any suggestions for the management of his school made by the Department through you."[66] This directive reflects the Department's frustration with Buffam's inability to effectively engage with the community and address the systemic issues affecting the school. The emphasis on obtaining parental goodwill and cooperation highlights the Department's recognition, albeit limited, of the importance of community involvement in education. However, the rigid expectation for Buffam to follow departmental suggestions without question underscores the hierarchical and bureaucratic nature of the colonial education system, where local agency and teacher autonomy were secondary to federal control. McCamus's critique of the Methodist Missionary Society further illustrates the disconnection between religious organizations and the communities they were tasked with serving, revealing a lack of accountability and adaptability to local needs during this period of significant social and economic upheaval during the First World War.

On several occasions, the Department instructed teachers to persuade parents to support schooling efforts, as they realized that children would more likely follow their instructions than those of a truant officer, Indian agent, or teacher.[67] The letter from McCamus above also explicitly details that the federal government was in charge of educating Indigenous students and that management decisions would be made by the Department itself, namely by the Indian agent, rather than by individual teachers. This action did not result in an increase in attendance; the next month, only thirteen students out of a possible thirty-six attended.[68]

In June 1915, the Mud Lake Chief and Council passed another resolution that attempted to remove the teacher. In Mr Buffam's defence, he told the Department the community had voted to dismiss his services, but it was only because "the mover of the resolution has three little girls all over school age who have never been sent an hour to school, who wander almost as wild as Indians ever were."[69] He also explained that the other causes were "petty and unworthy. I have striven ever since I came here for the welfare of the Indians."[70] He believed the Band had no power to dismiss him as their teacher, as the Methodist Society had selected him. As this letter was received at the start of the summer holidays, Buffam remained the teacher until the following 1 October, when he resigned.[71] Indian agent R.J. McCamus was thrilled with this news. He told the Department he "has not been a success as a teacher. I sincerely hope his successor will take a greater interest in the children."[72] McCamus reiterated his position against using the Methodist Society to hire any teachers for this community: "I must say that I have grave doubts about the wisdom of that system. I think if the Department would engage the teacher through their own supervisors or through a school board of the members of the band with the assistance of the agency ... I have had a great deal of worry over this school. For the last year, there has been an agitation in the Band to put the teacher away. The parents take a kindly interest in the education of their children, and it has been discouraging to see them make so little progress. Mr. Buffam is well qualified but not well adapted."[73]

Neither the community nor the Indian agent believed that the Methodist Society could produce a teacher capable of meeting the demands of this school. The Department, on the other hand, was unwilling to hire a teacher itself and would only put pressure on the Methodist Society to find a suitable teacher. Assistant deputy and secretary J.D. McLean told the general secretary of the Methodist Church that "the Indians of this reserve are intelligent and advance[d] and take a lively interest in the education of their children and have intimated their desire to have a suitable and competent teacher placed in charge of their school."[74] In September 1915, the Department begged the society to secure a teacher by a particular date and said they would otherwise have to find one. McLean stated, "Unless they do so by the 15th instant, the Department will have to make the appointment."[75]

The Methodist Society secured Mrs Zella May Hanes to teach at the school in 1915. She was the first female teacher officially hired, and she had both a second-class teaching certificate that she earned in the nearby Peterborough Normal School and over a decade of teaching experience.[76] She was only hired after the Department confirmed that she was indeed married, and that her husband was employed.[77] Indian Agent McCamus wrote, "She has at least some of the qualifications for a successful teacher."[78] The Department did not request input from the community to see whether they were on board with hiring another Methodist Society–appointed teacher.

In her first year, it appeared Mrs Zella May Hanes gained support in the community as she used new methods to instruct the students. She helped organize a "Farm Fair," which was the first of its kind on the reserve. The Department's agricultural representative was invited to attend and said the fair was a "success."[79] Students grew vegetables and were awarded prizes based on the size of their produce; additional prizes were given in other categories, including art and drawing. After this event, the Department received a letter from Joseph Whetung, who stated that his son and "a great many other children say Mrs. Hanes is best teacher they have ever had. Before she came as Teacher the children had no proper training and more."[80] Arthur Whetung also sent a letter to the Department recommending the work of Hanes, who "had a great interest in Indian Children in trying to educate them and is doing all she can to make them understand the ways and rules of life."[81] He also noted that she should stay in her role for a least a few more years "for the changing of teachers after being here one or two years is of no way in which to give our Indians boys and girls an education."[82] The community wanted a teacher who would stay and develop a relationship with the students to help them learn throughout their education.

In the first school inspection conducted during Hanes's term, R.H. Abraham noted the average attendance was only twenty-six of the forty-five pupils on the roll.[83] He recommended that another truant officer be deployed and observed that "some of the Indians complain the teacher is no good, and that is why they do not send their children to school."[84] Finally, he described the state of the building: the blackboards were falling apart and the bathrooms "ha[d] only boards between them. Immoral conversations take place between the pupils of both sexes."[85] These concerns continued to escalate over the next year, during which Hanes continued to be the teacher.

During the fall of 1916, Chief Daniel Whetung telephoned the Department to make several complaints about the teaching style of Mrs Hanes. In a memorandum sent to the Indian agent, the Department explained that the Chief wanted to have more say in the educational content of the school, including the religion that was being taught.[86] The Department instructed Indian agent R.J. McCamus to "state what the trouble is amongst the Whetung's about the teacher."[87] Chief Daniel Whetung responded to this request by writing a two-page letter to the local school inspector – and, by extension, to the Department – describing his grievances with Hanes and the quality of teaching within his community. Since the release of Alfred McCue in 1909, there had been four teachers from the Methodist Society, each of whom had had difficulty running the school.

Chief Whetung was adamant that Hanes be removed as the teacher and recounted two problematic incidents that had occurred at the school in the past week. Hanes "wrote on the blackboard 'whore' and taught the children that one of our ladies who has long been prominent in church and is now organist was that kind of women."[88] Further, she "hit a small boy about twenty five times on the head and knocked him off his seat."[89] As a result of Hanes's teaching methods, the school continued to struggle with low attendance. Whetung was angry about the treatment of his community in the school and explained that the father of the boy who was abused was in the "trenches in France" while the mother wanted to "have the teacher arrested for striking him on the head."[90] Community members feared "being mixed up in court trial of some kind or that the children might be blinded or deafened by the being struck over the head."[91] Whetung commented, "Therefore, we cannot understand how the Methodist society could have this woman here unless they were in total ignorance of the kind of person she is."[92]

These concerns led to a massive rift in the community between those who supported her teaching style and those who would never send their children to the school again. The dispute became so severe that Indian Agent McCamus made a request to move the reserve out west.[93] McCamus argued that the economy was failing because of low hunting and fishing opportunities and "unsuitable land" for farming purposes. McCamus explained that the Council approved an inquiry into purchasing "two or three thousand acres where the young men of the Band could go."[94] He stated that the Mud Lake Band, along with the other Mississauga reserves, including Rice Lake, Scugog, and Alderville First Nation, could buy a block of land out west, potentially solving several of these problems. The Department did not believe his farming proposal and noted: "The project would probably involve a great deal of trouble and expense and it is very questionable involve whether this would entail any benefit to these Indians. The scheme simply seems to have been conceived through a spirit of unrest existing among a number of dissatisfied members of the Band, and I would therefore recommend that no action be taken in connection with it."[95]

While the proposal was seriously considered, the government was worried that they would only move to the western land and then "begin to petition for departmental aid in the way of seed grain, implements, etc."[96] They also argued that their statistics showed that the land in the community was perfectly suitable for farming and that the ongoing disagreements over the school were the true reason for some community members wanting to leave. Mrs Hanes's teaching style almost pushed the community to break apart and seek opportunities elsewhere.

Chief Daniel Whetung believed the only solution to these constant hiring issues was for the community to establish its own school board; this would allow the proper vetting of candidates and ensure that the community had an annual vote on who would teach at the school. This had been promised to Whetung on a visit to the Department, and he explicitly asked for this authority in December 1916.[97] Council approved a resolution to ask the Department for "an organization of a school board here for the betterment of the Day School."[98] Chief Whetung requested that the community be given the authority to "organiz[e] a school board on the same system as they have in the Brantford reserve as promised to me by you when I was there in November."[99] Whetung was aware of other Indigenous schools within the province and had learned that the Brantford reserve had organized their (approximately twenty) day schools into a separate school board, indicating that, in some cases, Indigenous Peoples could have some aspect of control.[100] He argued that this system would allow the Band more power in determining who the teacher would be and could avoid the issues that came with obtaining a teacher through the Methodist Society. Indian agent R.J. McCamus agreed with the creation of the board, as he thought "that it would give them an increased interest in the education of their children and cause them to feel that they had something to do with the school."[101] However, the Department refused to approve the creation of the school board on reserve. They believed that the Regulations for Indian Children contained "all the regulations necessary for carrying on the day school on this reserve."[102] The Department refused to allow Indigenous Peoples any authority over the Indian day school on reserve, and this continued to cause significant issues among the community

Reverend J.H. Arnup, the assistant secretary of the foreign missions for the Methodist Society, shared these concerns. He informed J.D. McLean, assistant deputy secretary of the Department of Indian Affairs, about the months-long quarrel between community members. Arnup and McLean's correspondence reveals that Mrs Hanes's teaching methods were causing issues on the reserve, but she denied Chief Whetung's accusations. The Methodist Society sided with Whetung and recommended "her resignation or removal, as I think her usefulness there is at an end."[103] However, Arnup did request, "If you can give her another chance somewhere else it would be a God send to her."[104] Although she had failed as a teacher of this "Indian Band," she would still be considered a suitable hire for other positions in the Indian day school system. Finally, the Methodist Society recommended the Department hire "a good competent man that would teach the school, preach, act as Indian agent, all in one and give him a living salary. It would be the best that could be done for church and state."[105] They also refused to listen to Chief Whetung's request that the community have its own independently operated school board, dismissing the idea of Indigenous self-determination in educational matters. Instead, they insisted that church and state retain full control over the school, ensuring that community members would have no formal input into decisions that directly impacted their children's education. This disregard for local autonomy highlights the systemic barriers Indigenous leaders faced in advocating for greater involvement and agency in managing their own educational institutions.

The Department also received the recommendation of Indian Agent McCamus, who expressed concerns similar to those of Chief Whetung. In particular, he described the tenuous relationships between the leadership of the community and Hanes, who, from the very beginning, had caused "troubles." McCamus explained that on her arrival to the community, she purchased a few items from Chief Whetung's store without paying him back. This feud was ongoing, as she regularly ordered goods from stores in Peterborough rather than participating in the local economy, which sustained several community members. Indian Agent McCamus also argued that her husband, Mr Hanes, caused many disturbances in the community as he was no longer employed and his "wife was supporting him." McCamus also explained the Whetungs' differing views of the teacher. He argued that Joseph and Arthur Whetung had no children in the school and were, therefore, not as knowledgeable as Daniel Whetung, who had several immediate family members in the school. Within the community, the families supported Chief Whetung's perspective regarding Mrs Hanes. Based on these perspectives and the declining attendance rates, McCamus "strongly recommend[ed] that she be removed as soon as possible otherwise I fear there is serious trouble ahead of her."[106] The Department agreed and decided to remove Hanes over the Christmas holidays to stop the community's disputes.

Mrs Hanes did not leave quietly and sent several of her own complaints about the actions of the Whetungs to the Methodist Missionary Society. She argued that the family of Chief Whetung were the only ones against her, and this was a result of her husband, who had been in several disputes at the local stores: "Mr. Hanes has had considerable trouble with Mr. Whetung Sr. and his son, Chief Whetung, and feels he can endure it no longer. He has been to town to see a lawyer about it. And as advised has decided to enter a case against the Whetungs' for assault on November 30th and also for untrue and bad things they have been saying about us."[107]

She also threatened to file her own lawsuit against the Whetungs for the "lies" they had told about her teaching methods. The Methodist Society forwarded the letter to the Department of Indian Affairs and asked for clarification regarding whether they or the government should ask her to resign. The Methodist Society argued: "I am not aware of the anything in official regulations or in the administration of Indian Affairs which gives the representative of the Missionary Society any right to ask for the resignation of a teacher appointed by the Department in an Indian school. Developments since December 8th make it still clearer that anyone lacking legal authority in Indian Affairs would be ill-advised to attempt a settlement of affairs at Chemong."[108] They believed that the Department of Indian Affairs should make any final decisions regarding Mrs Hanes's release, particularly given that the legal case was already underway. Additionally, they requested that the Department force her to resign so that the Methodist Society could be absolved from any blame, despite the fact that they recruited and hired Hanes in the first place.

While these discussions were going on between the Department of Indian Affairs and Methodist Society, Mrs Hanes was still trying to defend herself against the claims made by Chief Whetung. This time, she admitted the word "whore" was used in the classroom, but it was only because a student mispronounced the word "abhorrent."[109] She stated that all the students laughed, and she had to explain what the word meant, as students would not stop chuckling. Hanes also argued that her lawyer had instructed her to sue the Whetungs for slander but believed "matters had quieted since then." Finally, she accused Chief Whetung of stealing a water pump from the mission house where she lived; she stated that Whetung had done this in retaliation and said that the Department is "not going to do anymore around here without first asking us."[110] Hanes believed that she should keep her job, but Chief Whetung should be removed as the leader of the community, as he would just cause trouble for the next teacher.

Chief Whetung indirectly responded to these accusations by sending more information about the quality of teaching in the community. He sent a letter on 2 January 1917, along with a newspaper clipping that described Mrs Hanes. The local paper reported that "the Chemong schoolteacher had seemingly been the cause of the trouble by writing the worst name that can be applied to a woman and explained its difference to a similar sounding word to small children."[111] It appeared that the story had reached the media due to court proceedings, and Whetung demanded that Hanes be removed immediately and her second-class teacher's certificate be revoked. When the Department failed to make a decision on the school, Chief Whetung closed and locked the school to prevent it from being opened in the new year. Other community members came forward in January to share their dissatisfaction with the school closure. Some members blamed Chief Daniel Whetung for instigating the fight, while others wanted Hanes to be removed immediately.

A constable of the region also sent a note that said Whetung and his brother had been charged as a result of the assault that occurred against Mr Hanes when they tried to remove him from the community.[112] Neither the Department nor the Methodist Missionary Society sent instructions regarding what was to be done with the school, so it sat vacant until the end of January 1917, when a school inspector finally completed a full investigation.

Inspector Parker conducted the investigation and forwarded a letter to the highest levels of the Department of Indian Affairs, including Deputy Superintendent Duncan Campbell Scott. When Parker visited the reserve, he spoke with Mrs Hanes, as he preferred to "hear the teacher's side of the trouble before listening to the Indians."[113] However, he noted significant discrepancies between Hanes's story and what she had previously written to the Department. He believed she had caught herself in "church and ladies aid gossip" rather than fact and concluded:

> It was plainly evident from Mrs. Haines [*sic*] remarks that no matter what she may have said she certainly believes Miss Whetung to be immoral. But apart from this it would appear that the writing of such a word on the board in front of a class of children was very unwise. The result has been that the majority of the Indians resent such conduct on the part of the teacher and refuse to send their children to school. I regret to say that Mrs. Haines [*sic*] shows a rather vindictive spirit in her remarks of the school and I could plainly see that to leave in her charge of the school would be useless.[114]

Even without speaking with the Indigenous community, the school inspector had the same concerns the Chief had forwarded over two months earlier. It was apparent that Hanes had lost community support after calling a community member the "worse name you could call a woman." The slow investigation allowed Hanes to remain the teacher until March 1917, when a proper replacement was found.

The Methodist Society wanted some guarantees from the Department of Indian Affairs before appointing another teacher. They feared that since the Department had sided with the Chief, it would embolden him.

They indicated he had an "attitude of personal antagonism to the present teacher but an assumption of authority and a disregard of legal rights which, if persisted in, could not fail to affect injuriously the position and efficiency of any teacher who might be appointed."[115] The Department promised to speak with Chief Whetung about his attitude toward authority on the reserve and to explain the relationship between the church and state regarding education. They wrote to Chief Whetung: "A tendency is evident on your part to act at variance with the Department, which is a condition of affairs that cannot be countenanced. It should not be necessary to remind you that it is absolutely essential for the Department to exercise full control over its affairs in the different agencies; and I am quite sure that, with a little thought, you will come to a realization of this fact."[116]

They also threatened the democratically elected Chief, stating that if he further attempted to take control of the Band affairs without Department consent, "disposal from the Chiefship would have to be considered."[117] Even when the Department sided with the Indigenous community, who had justifiable complaints, they made threats and asserted that the government of Canada, not any individual Chief or Council, was in charge of all educational decisions. The paternalistic relationship between the government and Indigenous Peoples at this time meant that only the government had the power to make significant community decisions.

Chief Daniel Whetung provided the Department with his rationale for deciding to close the school himself. He explained that when Mrs Hanes shared the word "whore" with the students, she used his daughter's name as an example.[118] Chief Whetung wrote, "Now, Gentleman at the Department of Indian Affairs, I will leave that to you to see how you would feel if some lady called your daughter a whore, that is a very dirty business for a schoolteacher."[119] Whetung also explained that since community members knew his daughter to be the organist in the church, they did not want to send their students to school with a teacher who would tell such lies. He said, "Us Indians, especially here on this reserve we are trying to raise our familys to be good. The best we know how so we they will not forgot when they grow up."[120]

The community was on the verge of an internal breakdown because of the schooling issue. On one side of the argument were people who had supported Mrs Hanes, including William Knott and Joseph and Arthur Whetung.[121] They were pitted against Hanes's detractors, including Chief Daniel Whetung, his father, the parents of students, and the members of the Mud Lake Council. Letters sent to the Department indicate that the schooling problem was just one of several issues the community was dealing with due to unclear government policies. Arthur and Joseph Whetung had long-standing grievances over not being provided land within the reserve. Arthur wrote: "I am one of the original Indian Descendants of the treaty Indians ... and should have 50 acres of land given to me according to the Indian Act. Indians are to *be given land for free* [emphasis in original]."[122] He believed Chief Whetung was improperly enforcing the Indian Act, and the difference of opinion regarding the schooling issue had exacerbated these concerns on the reserve. William Knott requested that the Department investigate the claims before any new decisions were made in the community.

The Methodist Society was able to find a suitable replacement for Hanes in the spring of 1917. The Department approved hiring Mr Arthur Buie, who was in the second year of his bachelor's degree at McMaster University, held a second-class non-professional certificate, and had some model school training. In addition, he was twenty-four years old and had spent two years as a teacher in Ontario's provincial schools. He was also the first candidate not to be raised in a Methodist family, as they wrote: "Having in mind the present conditions at Chemong, Mr. Arthur Buie is the type of teacher whom I should be glad to see placed in the position. You will note that he is not a Methodist, which may enable him to dissociate himself more completely from both parties to the recent trouble there."[123] As a result of his qualifications and the difficult position, they also permitted him a salary of $600 per year.[124] Mrs Hanes and her husband were asked to leave both the school and mission house so that Buie could move into the facilities by the start of May 1917.

In May, the *Peterborough Examiner* reported on a "Case Tried at Chemong Village" as Mr and Mrs Hanes were unwilling to vacate the reserve. As a result, Indian Agent R.J. McCamus issued an arrest warrant for the couple as he had this authority on reserve.[125] As the arrest occurred on the reserve, McCamus acted as the magistrate and fined the couple $10 for trespassing in the community.[126] Joseph Whetung and William Knott sent newspaper clippings and letters of concern from the community.[127] These individuals told the Department of Indian Affairs that Chief Whetung and members of the Council were planning to visit Ottawa to cause "troubles" for the Department.[128] The Department replied that "there is no necessity for their making this trip" and that any of these significant concerns with the school could be "adjusted through correspondence."[129] Despite the trial that occurred on reserve, the Department was still unwilling to meet face-to-face with the community to help seek a resolution for issues regarding the constant rotation of teachers. A letter from the Department of Indian Affairs, which was sent to Indian Agent McCamus, rather than Chief Whetung, admonished McCamus: "If you were aware of this proposed visit, you should have notified the Department."[130] The Department was highly concerned that a group of Indigenous Peoples would arrive in Ottawa from Curve Lake to discuss the ongoing problems with their educational system.

After being denied a visit to Ottawa to discuss these ongoing issues, Chief Daniel Whetung wrote to the Department to address these and other serious concerns: "It is not altogether the school trouble that is bothering us. But there is such a hostile feeling among the people we fear they may be at war amongst themselves before long."[131] He explained that Joseph Whetung had created a separate council in the community and started calling himself Chief although he had not been elected. He had also organized a small group of individuals who were spreading "lies and discontent" among the community. Unfortunately, this letter is missing parts that outline Whetung's recommendation. It says, "We think and advise the Indian Department that strong measures be taken to stop this [missing] -one, if a riot is to be avoided. [missing] that Joseph Whetung be made to plain [missing] -stand that he is not recognized."[132] Chief Whetung believed that unless serious action was taken, the community was at risk of falling apart and that this was ample justification for him to visit Ottawa immediately. He said: "I sincerely hope that the trouble among the people may be stopped. My whole desire is and has always been for peace and quietness as many of our boys are in the trenches and some are wounded, and some killed and there is plenty of trouble without the people fighting amongst themselves."[133] Despite the urgency conveyed in his letter, the Department's response was slow and inadequate, offering no clear resolution to the escalating tensions within the community. The lack of documentation regarding the promised inquiry further worsened these issues, leaving Whetung and the community without recourse or support.

Several different pressures, including the fact that many community members were away fighting in the war, compounded the schooling issue. Whetung requested that the Department conduct an independent investigation and said he would abide by any request they made. In response to these concerning remarks, Deputy Superintendent Duncan Campbell Scott agreed to "send an officer of the Department to the reserve at an early date to hold an inquiry."[134] No further references to this investigation or its results were ever submitted to the RG10 federal archive. The lack of documentation raises questions about whether the investigation was ever conducted or if its findings were deliberately omitted. This absence underscores the broader challenges of accountability and transparency within the Department of Indian Affairs, particularly in addressing disputes and concerns raised by Indigenous leaders. Whetung's willingness to cooperate with the inquiry further highlights his commitment to resolving the issue through formal channels despite the systemic barriers and delays imposed by the Department.

While these investigations continued, the new schoolteacher, Arthur Buie, began to supply teach from April through June. Upon the first school inspection, it was reported that attendance had jumped to thirty-three students out of a possible thirty-six and that Mrs Hanes had taken all of the teaching manuals when she left.[135] The Department also reported "that [Buie] has been doing good work there and he gets on well with the Indians, and the Department would be glad to have him remain."[136] Buie had only been contracted to supply teach the Mud Lake Indian Day School until the end of June, as he was to enter his third year at McMaster University in September 1917. In July 1917, the Canadian government passed the Military Service Act, which implemented conscription for able-bodied men. That same month, Buie wrote to the Department and said, "Owing to war conditions I have decided to remain at Chemong another year provided conscription does not take me."[137] His rationale for this decision was likely influenced by the fact that men enrolled in university were likely to be enlisted in the service. The Department accepted his offer to remain and provided him a $600 salary for the entire school year of 1917–18.

When the school opened in September 1917, it became clear that Buie was fleeing from conscription.[138] In an urgent telegram, School Inspector R.H. Abraham wrote: "Schoolteacher at Chemong School … opened school yesterday … and left in the night without notice … advise placing Alfred McCue Indian as temporary … teacher has taught before."[139] Buie had vanished after the first day of class, leaving the community without a suitable teacher. Once again, Alfred McCue was called on to fill the supply teacher role in the community's time of need. As a last resort, and purely because of his Indigenous identity, the Department paid him only $400 rather than the advertised $600.[140] By this time, Alfred McCue had over a decade of experience with this school, yet even in an urgent situation when no other options were available, he was paid 33 per cent less than a White teacher. The Department only agreed to this option "temporarily" and stressed the need for the Methodist Society to find "a qualified teacher."[141]

As the First World War continued, it was impossible to find another teacher, so McCue stayed on into 1918. Indian Agent McCamus reported, "I have been quite pleased with the way Mr. Alfred McCue is getting on and he is doing much better than I expected."[142] Once again, the Indigenous community member (Mr McCue) kept the school running while the Department and the Methodist Society failed to secure a qualified teacher. The Indian agent's only concern was that McCue might leave in the spring, as the salary of a trapper was much higher than his teaching salary. He recommended that McCue's salary be raised to "at least five hundred dollars" to retain his services throughout the year. The Department agreed with this recommendation and increased his salary to $500, which was comparable to other economic opportunities on reserve. In his first end-of-year report, Inspector R.H. Abraham found that although thirty-five students out of a possible thirty-seven were present on the day he attended, the average was only sixteen pupils.[143] This discrepancy suggests that many students were frequently absent, likely due to economic pressures or family responsibilities tied to wartime conditions. Children were often required to contribute to the household through work or other means. The irregular attendance highlights the broader challenges faced by reserve schools during this period, where external factors such as war, poverty, and systemic neglect by the Department impacted education outcomes.

Another inspector, Broderick, recommended in May 1918 that "a properly qualified, well-trained teacher having the missionary spirit" replace McCue.[144] While Broderick's attempt to remove McCue in favour of a more "qualified" teacher failed, McCue himself resigned in August 1919.[145] His resignation marked the end of a tenure defined by perseverance amid limited resources and external support, underscoring the essential role that Indigenous educators played in keeping schools operational despite systemic barriers and the indifference of colonial authorities.

Broderick also recommended enforcing the full extent of the attendance law on students who regularly missed class.[146] In response, the Department, for the first time, recommended that three children from the Taylor family be placed in a residential school.[147] It said that "if the father refuses to sign these applications the children may be placed in school under the regulations."[148] While there had always been attendance issues in the school, this was the first time students would be sent off reserve to deal with truancy.

Broderick also criticized the "attempt to convert an ill-constructed, cast-off church into a school building."[149] He called the building a "wretched failure" that was insufficient in every manner and said that "it would be difficult to have conditions more favourable to immorality."[150] Broderick described the physical condition of the building as being "every way most unsatisfactory [and] They are a positive discredit to those responsible for the moral and educational welfare of the children of the community."[151] He recommended that a new building be "erected immediately" with adequate heating, lighting, and ventilation. Moreover, the mission house used as the teacher's residence was getting old, making it difficult to attract the "right type" of teacher. Broderick wanted a new school as soon as possible as "there is no language too strong in condemnation of this building."[152]

In August 1919, Indian Agent McCamus wrote to the Department with a different concern regarding the school: several families were planning to leave the reserve as their children wanted to receive education according to the "new ways" with teachers whose credentials attested to their qualifications.[153] Later that month, the Methodist Missionary Society and the Department of Indian Affairs agreed to hire Mr Wesley Watson. Watson had graduated from Queen's University and then attended the Ottawa Normal School before teaching in rural schools throughout the province for twelve years.[154] As a result of his postsecondary experience and teaching abilities, he was offered the position for $700 a year – nearly double the salary paid to McCue.[155]

Watson, who was sixty-one years old, taught for just over a month before the school closed again. This time, Indian Agent R.J. McCamus reported that an outbreak of diphtheria had caused the school to be closed.[156] It is not clear whether the illness was, in fact, diphtheria or the Spanish flu, nor is it clear how many community members had been infected. The Indian agent opined that "while [Watson] is a good teacher, he is an old disruptive man and not fit for the work."[157] Around the same time, Watson wrote to the Department to report, "One of my girl pupils was buried today, which is very sad."[158] He also explained that his wife was old and sick, and he could no longer afford to travel back and forth to the hospital in Peterborough for her to have regular healthcare.[159] He requested that the Department provide him a "little money to help my wife in her sad condition" but stated that he could no longer teach the school when it reopened. The Department agreed to pay the rest of his quarterly salary but would not receive any other correspondence from him.

This time, even the Methodist Missionary Society recommended that Alfred McCue undertake the teaching duties at the school for the winter 1919 term until a replacement could be found. Once again, McCue's reliability and willingness to serve the community made him the default choice despite the Department and the Methodist Missionary Society's ongoing search for a replacement. His return highlights his critical role in maintaining education on the reserve, even as the authorities continually undervalued his contributions. The Methodist Missionary Society continued searching for a replacement despite several failed attempts. Another Methodist minister, Harold J. Bell, visited the community and wrote to the Department in 1920: "The people of the reserve urge me to ask you to take whatever steps are necessary to secure a teacher, and if any arrangement can be made by which Mr. McCamus can be allowed to make the selection, the difficulty of securing one may be lessened."[160] McCue's temporary reinstatement underscores the systemic challenges in staffing reserve schools, where the broader indifference of colonial authorities left communities dependent on local solutions. Despite their repeated efforts, the Department and the Missionary Society's inability to secure a long-term teacher highlights their lack of commitment and planning, leaving McCue and the community to shoulder the burden of ensuring the continuity of education. His presence during this time bridged significant gaps and demonstrated the community's preference for a teacher they knew and trusted, starkly contrasting the authorities' persistent search for an external replacement.

Church officials believed that the local Indian agent, in this case R.J. McCamus, was better suited to select a qualified teacher who understood the community's concerns. Compared to the centralized church in Toronto, the Indian agent had more daily interactions with the school and could, therefore, understand what the community needed. While the Spanish flu had ended by the early spring 1920, McCamus reported that the community had become "completely discouraged over the school business."[161] During his entire time as the Indian agent, the community had not had "one good teacher" who was willing to stay and educate the students over many years. He again shared that several members of the reserve were looking into moving "to a white settlement in order to have their boy connected to a good school."[162] In a separate letter sent the next month, McCamus advised: "The people are anxious to have a good teacher for their children and would be satisfied to get even less Department money, if necessary, in order to pay the extra salary."[163] He recommended that the salary start at $900 to attract a teacher who would be qualified and capable of moving to the reserve for an extended period of time.[164]

In response to these urgent requests, the Methodist Missionary Society hired a woman named Lillian Jessup, who had just graduated from Queen's University; she started at the school in May 1920.[165] McCamus seemed to be satisfied with this new arrangement. In October 1920, he wrote, "Miss Jessup of Chemong is doing excellent work and having a good influence, every child of the school is on the roll."[166] Another positive report about her teaching was submitted the following summer in 1921. McCamus wrote: "We have not had anything like as a good a teacher in Chemong since my appointment and I would strongly recommend that the Department give Miss Jessup a substantial raise in her salary and try and retain her services."[167] He further said that the "Chemong school is currently overwhelmed, necessitating the presence of two teachers. The primary class alone has over 30 students, each requiring individual attention, a challenge that few teachers could manage. Furthermore, Miss Jessup has a significant positive influence on the village community. Her previous teaching experience at the fort in Winnipeg has given her valuable insight into Indigenous character, enhancing her effectiveness in her role."[168]

After this report was submitted, Jessup may have returned to university or left for another job as she was no longer the teacher in the fall of 1921.[169] A July 1921 resignation letter, presumably from Miss Jessup (there was no signature), reiterated McCamus's concern regarding class size: "The reason for asking that two teachers be employed was not that I would have less work but more time to do better work. There are now enrolled twice as many pupils as have been before and more will begin in the fall."[170] The author felt this task was too large for a single teacher who could only focus on a dozen pupils with "the others running wild in the woods."[171] Those students in particular, were more "interested in their gardens than their schoolwork."[172] This letter highlights the systemic contradictions faced by reserve schools during this period. On one hand, truancy officers were sent to enforce attendance, and parents were threatened with residential school if their children did not attend. Yet, when attendance increased, the schools were ill-equipped to accommodate the growing student population due to chronic underfunding and understaffing. This irony demonstrates the broader failure of government policies, which prioritized control over Indigenous education rather than ensuring adequate resources and support for meaningful learning. The increasing class sizes, coupled with limited resources and the competing economic demands on students' time, made it difficult for teachers to engage all pupils adequately. Jessup's resignation reinforces the chronic neglect by the Department to address these structural issues, leaving both teachers and students in untenable situations. The remarks about students' preference for gardening over schoolwork also reflect the complex realities of reserve life, where subsistence activities were often prioritized over formal education, especially in the absence of meaningful support from the education system.

Miss Ethel Browne, who had no teaching qualifications, was hired by the Methodist Missionary Society to reopen the school after the fall 1921 term.[173] She continued to teach at the school until the end of 1922 when McCamus submitted a report about her work. He wrote, "The Chemong school, I am sorry to say has not so good a showing in attendance as it did under Miss Jessup."[174] It seemed that Browne was a capable teacher, but she did not "take a personal interest in them" and, therefore, was not authentic enough to effectively engage the community.[175] In other words, teaching ability was not always sufficient to secure a teacher's position, as they also had to work with community members to earn educational support. The Indian agent reiterated that this school was at maximum capacity for a single teacher, and it required someone with knowledge of the education of Indigenous students to be successful.

Browne shared these concerns and requested to be transferred in November 1922. She asked if there were a vacancy in a "two-roomed" schoolhouse, such as in Rama First Nation, where there would be more than one teacher and the ability to live within the building.[176] Miss Browne, as a teacher within the Indian day school system, was aware of the conditions on other reserves and requested to be sent there of her own accord. She argued that the number of students she was required to teach was not worth the salary she was receiving in her position at Curve Lake. Specifically, the additional living expenses, including having to pay rent for the mission house, and more than four trips a year into city centres for supplies was "above what one can afford to pay according to the salary received here."[177] In Indian day schools with a teachers' residence in the building, the teacher's living costs were significantly reduced. The difficulty of reaching the nearby town of Peterborough during the winter months also contributed to Browne's reluctance to stay on at the school. Despite these significant concerns, both the Department and Methodist Missionary Society agreed to employ Miss Browne at the Indian day school for another year.

The community continued to deal with outbreaks of diphtheria, measles, and the flu, which worsened attendance in 1922. The school was closed for an early winter break in 1922 in the hope of stopping the spread of the illnesses, but the epidemics continued to impact students well into April 1923. Indian Agent McCamus said that, as a result of school closures, "a good many of the children did not like Miss Browne. She does not seem to be able to win their confidence and affection as Miss Jessup did."[178] McCamus had now made several references to the superior qualities of the previous teacher and that summer would recommend her to the position again. He wrote to the Department in June 1923, "I may say that Miss Jessup is a much better teacher for Chemong as she takes a great interest in the moral welfare of the people. I understand she is available."[179] To solve the attendance issues, McCamus believed the community required a teacher who understood their needs and could be trusted with their children.

As Miss Ethel Browne did not like living on the reserve and Miss Jessup had a strong rapport with the community, it seemed natural to switch roles. The Department of Indian Affairs contacted Miss Jessup and offered her the position at a salary of $750 per school year with an additional bonus of $15 that was now mandated by the government of Ontario.[180] Unfortunately, the Methodist Missionary Society reported "that Miss Lillian Jessup has accepted work in connection with the Toronto Public School Board and feels that she cannot undertake the work at Chemong."[181] As this correspondence was received in mid-September, the Methodist Society decided to contact "an Indian on the Reserve who had qualifications, and was willing to undertake this work."[182] It wasn't clear if this candidate was once again Mr Alfred McCue, but the Department outright refused the request to hire an "Indian." They wrote to the Methodist Missionary Society: "The Department cannot approve of the permanent appointment to the Mud Lake School of any teacher who is not properly qualified. The enrolment and attendance are such that no efforts should be spared to secure a satisfactory teacher as a permanent incumbent."[183] Notably, the policy of hiring "properly qualified" teachers was only enacted when an Indigenous person was suggested for the job, as Miss Browne herself was not a qualified teacher.

Despite the school year being well under way in other parts of the country, the Department refused to have a supply teacher from the community open the school. They once again relegated the duty of finding a qualified teacher to the Methodist Missionary Society. At this point, the search for a teacher who would last more than a few terms in the community had continued for over a decade.

In September 1923, Chief Daniel Whetung wrote about his significant concerns regarding the education provided by the department. The community, he said, "has been without a teacher of any qualifications for a good number of years and as a result – I regret to say that not a single child has accomplished much as to pass the examination for high school in the last 50 or 70 years. I understand the government is spending money to advance Indians! Why not spend it in this section! We are willing to pay more for a qualified teacher and no other kind will do. We have from 45 to 55 children school age and what is the average?"[184]

The community was tired of their children receiving inadequate education, and the children were too discouraged to attend regularly. Chief Whetung understood that the Methodist Mission Society was in control of hiring the teachers. Still, he offered a new solution that could accelerate the process: "I strongly suggest that the Indian Agent be authorized to advertise in the local paper of Peterborough and secure a good teacher which he is capable of doing."[185] He was adamant that this advertising method could secure both a local and qualified teacher from the nearby normal school and help improve the quality of education for the community. Chief Whetung included this personal anecdote at the end of his letter: "I had to go away from my reservation to get what little education I have and I am sending one child away from home now to be taught by a qualified teacher is this going to continued? I hope not. I hope that there will be a different system of securing a teacher."[186]

Whetung offered his own personal experience, suggested suitable solutions to this ongoing problem, and expressed a clear desire to improve the quality of education for his community. The Department coldly responded to these significant and personal concerns by reiterating, "As this school is conducted under the auspices of the Methodist Church, the authorities of that church have been requested, and are endeavouring to obtain a qualified teacher."[187] The Department also did not respond to his request for an advertisement to be taken out in the local paper and instead waited until the Methodist Missionary Society found someone to fill the position.

In late September 1923, the Methodist Missionary Society hired Miss Edna Harris, who had no teaching qualifications, for the position. They wrote to the Department indicating that although she had attended a teaching collegiate for three years, an "illness prevent her from writing on Normal Examinations."[188] Miss Harris did have experience teaching in "Indian" schools, as she had spent the last year teaching at Brandon Industrial (Residential) School in Manitoba.[189] The Methodist Missionary Society continued to find unqualified teachers to fill the position in Mud Lake instead of taking Chief Whetung's advice to hire someone from the local normal school. As this application was received at the end of September, when school was supposed to start, the Department of Indian Affairs approved of her hire at a rate of $700 per year plus $15 a month in provincial bonuses.[190]

Within a few months, Miss Harris was overburdened with her community responsibilities. Reverend Barner from the Methodist Missionary Society visited the community and told the Department that too many students were in the one-room schoolhouse: "There are at the present time twenty-eight children in the primary class, and an average attendance of forty in the entire school. They suggest that next year two teachers be appointed; that the teacher in the senior room be a man and he act as a missionary teacher."[191]

The community had already expressed their concern about this issue to the Department numerous times, but upon receiving this news from a reverend, they decided to investigate. By December 1923, the Department had obtained another report from a commission of the Methodist Missionary Society, which said: "At Mud lake it was apparent to the commission that the services of two schoolteachers are required, as the number of pupils attending the school is far greater than can be properly instructed by one teacher. The Chief and several members of the band spoke to the Commissioners with reference to the necessity for another teacher."[192]

A week later, the Department also received a report from the provincial school inspector who suggested that another male teacher be hired, "who would take an active interest in the work and stimulate attendance. It is reported that the second class could be carried on in a building close at hand."[193] With this overwhelming support for another teacher – plus the community's provision of a building suitable for the purpose – there were no obstacles to securing another classroom.

After receiving this information, the Department decided to also seek the services of another teacher with the Methodist Missionary Society; this resulted in more problems. Assistant Deputy and Secretary J.D. McLean wrote to the society in December 1923: "The Department is now in receipt of information which prompts us to take immediate steps to secure the services of a male teacher for the senior classroom."[194] McLean suggested that while it would be the church's responsibility to find a residence for the new teacher, they could conduct the classes in the nearby public hall. This arrangement would place the onus on the community or local church to hire and house the teacher and establish new classrooms without federal support. By the end of January 1924, the Methodist Missionary Society wrote to the Department, "I have not been able to secure anyone and would now advise that if the Department has in mind anyone who would take the position."[195] McLean reiterated that it was the church's responsibility to find a suitable teacher and noted that the Department had "no applicant that would be suitable."[196] He also mentioned that the Department would be willing to use the second teacher as a "principal" of both classrooms and that this information could be included in their search. A principal was typically a senior teacher who both taught and helped operate the school. Neither the church nor the government provided further information for the remainder of the 1924 school year.

In the spring of 1924, Indian Agent McCamus again desperately stressed the need for another teacher on the Mud Lake reserve. He wrote to the Department: "Miss Harris of Chemong is working to her limit and I wish to say that if the Department cannot procure a second teacher. I would recommend that Miss Harris be given an increase of salary, she is really working *very* hard and doing good work and she deserves an increase [emphasis in original]."[197]

As neither the church nor the government could secure another teacher, the entire responsibility of operating the overpopulated school was placed on an unqualified teacher. Harris even submitted her own report to the Department, indicating that there were fifty-five students enrolled and that she had "been greatly handicapped because of the large attendance and small quarters and not sufficient school equipment."[198] In addition, she was making less money than a male teacher, with a much larger workload. The Department responded that it was Miss Harris's job to teach this school and that another teacher would be secured by the summer holidays. J.D. McLean wrote to the Indian agent that "in the meantime we are not prepared to grant any increase in salary to the present teacher."[199]

That same month, Harris fell ill and could not complete the term. Chief Daniel Whetung sent an urgent telegram to McLean. In it, the Chief explained that Harris was unavailable to teach but that he was able to recommend a qualified teacher.[200] Whetung had travelled to the Windsor Hotel in Peterborough to send the message and stated that a qualified teacher named Arthur Smith from nearby Young's Point was willing to teach for the rest of the year. He required a salary of $100 a month or $1000 a year but could begin immediately.[201] Whetung waited at the hotel until he received a telephone call from the Department confirming the appointment for the community. In this time of need, Whetung was able to secure a qualified teacher without the constraints of the slow bureaucracy that had tried to hire a male teacher for over a year. The Department was forced to accept the hiring of Smith at the rate of $100 a month for the rest of the school term and informed the Methodist Church of this change.[202]

The remaining two months of school proved that the hiring of a qualified teacher by Chief Whetung yielded better results than those of the Methodist Missionary Society or the government. Indian Agent McCamus assessed the new teacher twice and noted: "This school is a very heavy one, but Mr. Arthur Smith proved himself quite capable of handling it. He is a very efficient teacher and is willing to accept the position for another term, and I would strongly recommend that his services be secured as soon as possible."[203]

The report from McCamus also explained that Mr Smith had nine years of experience in a school with attendance as high as seventy, so he could manage many students at once. On his second visit, McCamus wrote: "Mr. Smith is an excellent teacher and can handle the school with ease even with every child on the reserve in attendance."[204] Chief Whetung also said that they were "greatly pleased with his work" and that Smith was perfectly capable of handling the large class size.[205]

Smith continued to teach into 1925 without any complaints or concerns from the community, Chief Whetung, or the Indian agent. In Mr Smith's quarterly report, it was revealed that he was still doing excellent work, and only one concern seemed to persist. Indian Agent McCamus wrote: "One of the Chief holdbacks of Chemong is the determination of the parents to stick to their own language, with a few exceptions. They are quite jealous of it and will not favour the use of English by the children when at play."[206]

This report indicated that students who attended the school were forced to learn in English, but the parents – and perhaps Mr Smith himself – allowed the use of their Indigenous language while playing. This was never a concern in the letters sent from Chief Whetung or community members as they were focused on obtaining a qualified teacher. The Department never explicitly responded to McCamus's concern, but his report indicates the intent of the school was to have children who could only communicate in English and not in the language of their family. To encourage the use of the English language, McCamus requested that the Department offer a small prize to encourage the "best attendance … or the best reader of each class – or best in arithmetic – writing – any branch."[207] The prizes were never awarded, as attendance dropped almost to zero for the last two weeks of class; students instead worked with their parents on the land in the nearby "fruit district."[208] The teacher appeared to have no concern about the summer starting a little early, and he agreed to teach again during the 1925–26 school year. Despite his success, Smith could not prevent the students from using their Indigenous language outside the confines of the classroom. McCamus believed that the parents exacerbated this problem and were the sole reason for students not progressing to higher grades. Smith's success in the school, compared with the previous decade of teachers, indicated that this system of allowing the students to speak their language was much more effective in earning community support for education.

Smith received so many good reports that the superintendent of Indian education recommended that an Indigenous student be sent back to school in Curve Lake rather than a public school in Lakefield, Ontario. He sent a memo to Duncan Campbell Scott indicating that Curve Lake's new teacher had "full qualifications (second class professional) and has taught at this school two years with success." He quoted a public-school inspector report that said: "The pleasant relationships between teacher and pupil are commendable. The general management is commendable. Mr. Smith, in my judgment, is a good man for this school. He has a happy way of managing his pupils. They respond to his teaching and progress is being made."[209]

Considering these positive recommendations, the Department requested that Mr Ryerson Whetung's son not be sent to the nearby public school in Lakefield but be sent to Mud Lake instead. They argued that the school on reserve was of an equal or better quality than the school in a nearby White town.

This brief period of "commendable" schooling, largely driven by the efforts of Chief Daniel Whetung, ended when the Methodist Missionary Society disbanded in the summer of 1926. While the first two decades of the twentieth century saw the restart of the Indian day school system in Curve Lake, they also established a new working relationship between church officials, Indian agents, teachers, Chief and Council, and community members regarding the quality of education on the reserve. This period marked a shift in governance and oversight, shaping how education was administered and controlled within the community. This system would slowly spread throughout the country, with over 304 similar Indian day schools in operation by 1920. These patterns of underfunding, unqualified teachers, and paternalistic treatment of Indigenous Peoples by the government would continue in the late 1920s as a new religious organization took over the operation of the school. The relationship that was established between the community and the

New England Company and, later, the Methodist Missionary Society was unstable and led to significant issues with both the teachers' quality and the needs of the growing population. The early classes were also clearly a failure: students struggled to progress to higher levels of education, and community members' repeated complaints concerning teaching behaviour were never adequately dealt with. In addition, Indigenous Peoples were now clearly within the lowest classes of priority for quality education, as they could not compete with rising teaching salaries throughout the First World War period. Education in this school had only focused on providing the basics. Yet, even this small goal was rarely achieved as untrained teachers had full control over the quality of education being received.

CHAPTER 5

A Legacy of Neglect: The United Church of Canada's Indian Day School

During the summer of 1926, the Methodist Church underwent significant changes, including creating a new identity under the banner of the United Church of Canada. This newly formed organization would now oversee the Curve Lake Indian Day School until its closure. The United Church would follow the same path as its predecessors, providing the bare minimum requirements of education to Indigenous Peoples as a means of assimilating them into the growing church. Their focus on rote memorization, English language learning, and the removal of Indigenous culture continued to impact the community in harmful ways. Maintaining the school in Curve Lake would become an even larger challenge as systematic racism and external factors – including the Great Depression and the Second World War – made even the daily operation of the school a challenge. Over the next two decades, the United Church would fight to maintain control over Indigenous education in Curve Lake despite their continual inadequacy in providing quality schooling. In response, Curve Lake First Nation's leadership and community would do everything possible under the Indian Act to challenge the church's control.

The new tenure of the United Church of Canada signalled the end of the employment of Mr Arthur Smith, who resigned in the summer of 1926 due to ill health.[1] In response to his resignation, Chief Whetung once again wrote to the Department and urged them to find a qualified teacher and to advertise the job in the *Peterborough Examiner*."[2] The Department promised that they would search for a suitable candidate but noted that selecting a new teacher for the school was now under the United Church's purview.[3] The Department also told the United Church that "Chief Dan Whetung, of Curve Lake, is an intelligent Indian and he takes an interest in this school," and stressed the need to hire a qualified teacher at a rate of $85 to $100 a month.[4]

Over the summer of 1926, the conservative member of Parliament (MP) for Peterborough West, Edward Peck, wrote to the Department of Indian Affairs regarding the quality of education on the reserve. Peck, who had been elected in both the 1925 and 1926 federal elections, sent a letter on official House of Commons letterhead to Duncan Campbell Scott about the "condition of education in the Reserve," which was technically within his jurisdiction as MP. He wrote: "They have, at present ... a teacher who does not appear to be qualified to [t]each the children more than elementary subjects. Mr. Whetung states that ... he has had to send his oldest boy to another school. There are a number of children requiring education in the Reserve, and it would seem desirable that a teacher, fully qualified to train them and bring them on, is necessary. Kindly let me hear from you in the connection with the matter."[5] Peck's intervention reflects a growing external awareness of the shortcomings in reserve education and the reliance on informal channels of advocacy to prompt action from the Department of Indian Affairs. His letter, while framed in paternalistic language, acknowledged the unmet educational needs on the reserve and highlighted the limitations of the current teacher's qualifications. The mention of Mr Whetung sending his son to another school showed the lack of confidence within the community regarding the education system on reserve, where families felt compelled to seek alternatives elsewhere. Peck's involvement suggests that concerns about education were becoming political issues, drawing attention to the systemic neglect by federal authorities in addressing the disparities faced by Indigenous students.

The letter specifically addressed the experience of Roy Whetung, who was being sent to the nearby school in Lakefield. This appeal by the MP demonstrated that the community of Curve Lake was now taking its concerns about education to its federal representative in an effort to be heard. Scott never responded to the letter, but J.D. McLean, the acting deputy superintendent, wrote to Peck and told him that the church was looking for a suitable teacher to replace Mr Smith.[6] Soon thereafter, the United Church wrote to the Department to announce that they had secured the teaching services of Mr Morgan Lewis and to request that the nomination be sent to the community as well. While the church said Lewis was qualified, a nearby pastor, and of "good character," they did not mention his specific credentials.[7]

Within a month of the school's opening, Chief Whetung sent another message to the Department about the education on reserve. He explained that over the last thirty years, the population had doubled on reserve and, as a result, they had "over sixty children of school age."[8] This rapid population growth had overwhelmed the school, leaving it overcrowded and unable to serve the community's needs. Chief Whetung emphasized the urgent need to add another room to house the higher grades, pointing out the detrimental effects of the current conditions. He also stated that "the bigger children get discouraged when they do not get along in school as well as they ought to. As there are too many children and worse of all too many grades in one room. The last two teachers we had resigned on account of nervous breakdown."[9] This overcrowding hindered effective teaching and learning, making it difficult for students to progress academically. His message underscored the pressing need for immediate action to prevent further harm to students and teachers and ensure that education on the reserve could meet the community's growing demands.

Chief Whetung was "willing to do anything reasonable" to secure another room for the class, including lending the council hall until a new school would be built.[10] That fall, the school inspector, R.F. Downey, suggested the addition of images to increase attendance: "The interior of the school building is quite bare and unattractive. A few pictures would do much to brighten it up."[11] These minor solutions indicate that both the federal government and the United Church provided the bare minimum to maintain the operation of the school.

The Department requested further information from Indian Agent R.J. McCamus to determine if another teacher was required. He wrote, "The present teacher is a young inexperienced man and not so able to handle the school as the former teacher" given that over fifty students were in attendance.[12] McCamus believed the community required either "two teachers or otherwise a very competent one with experience" for the school to function. He also recommended that the council hall Whetung had suggested could be a suitable location for another classroom and would just need "blackboards, a teacher desk and chair, and the ten desks for children."[13] With these arrangements in place, the Department of Indian Affairs asked the United Church to find a second teacher for January 1926.

The United Church did not look very far. They quickly nominated Miss Viola Lewis, the first cousin of Morgan Lewis, for the position. Viola Lewis had only "physical training," a second-class interim certificate, and one year of teaching experience.[14] The church was influenced to hire her by the current teacher and by Rev. J.E. Todd, who argued that she came from a good family and would make a strong hire. In the meantime, the Department received an application from a qualified teacher named Jean Scott, a recent graduate from the Peterborough Normal School who had earned both junior matriculation and a second-class certificate.[15] Her references were also more impressive as they came from the Peterborough Normal School rather than from a minister. Instead of hiring a more qualified teacher, the United Church decided to offer the position, which was to begin immediately, to Viola Lewis at a rate of $80 per month.[16]

Throughout the rest of the 1926 school year, both Mr and Miss Lewis received positive teaching reviews from the community. In June 1926, Bert McCue, the acting secretary of the Curve Lake Council, sent two positive letters to the Department about their work and recommended them for jobs in any school board. McCue wrote that Viola Lewis had "been highly satisfactory in every respect ... she possesses natural ability as a teacher and disciplinarian which together wither her ladylike manner and good character give added dignity to the profession she represents."[17] Bert McCue offered even stronger praise for Morgan Lewis: "His services have been highly satisfactory as shown by the fact that the school has attained a standard along education lines, excelling that of any other time in the history of the school."[18] But the new Indian agent, Vincent Eastwood, cautioned that "unless something is done in connection with a raise in salary we are going to lose both these teachers."[19] The Department decided to provide a $5 raise for Viola Lewis and to wait to hear from Morgan Lewis about what was needed to convince him to stay.

Morgan Lewis, a fully qualified teacher with two years of experience running a successful school as principal, could negotiate additional perks to stay with the community. He told the Department that he required additional pay and a "fair rental price" for the United Church mission house on reserve. He also asked for extra funds to repair the house, as it was part of the missionary society. Finally, he requested "a fresh water supply to be provided. At present time I have to depend on the hospitality of our neighbours for theirs."[20] In response, the Department offered a different resolution. Instead of increasing his pay, the Department would allow Lewis to live in the mission house for free but would not supply additional funds to fix the building. They also stated, "The Department is not prepared at the present time to authorize the drilling of a well, and it is thought you can continue the same arrangement to obtain a supply of water as you are at present doing."[21] Lewis agreed to these terms, but the Department's offer indicates its unwillingness to provide added benefits to teachers who worked successfully within the Indian day school system.

While Morgan Lewis continued to work at the school, Viola Lewis resigned at the end of the 1929 school year because she was going to be married.[22] To replace Miss Lewis, the Department sought the services of Miss Jean Scott, who had applied three years earlier and was more qualified. Acting Assistant Deputy A.F. MacKenzie told Indian Agent Eastwood to contact Scott immediately.[23] The application had been kept on file for over three years, and as Miss Jean Scott had not been able to find a job, she accepted the position to reopen the school in January 1930 at a rate of $80 per month.[24]

The first teaching reports for the spring of 1930 were mixed. Indian Agent Eastwood reported that Morgan Lewis "had taken over the difficult problem of teaching in a school where children receive their instructions in an adopted language and has had every success in giving these children a general education and qualifying several of them for higher school education, the first occasion on which this has occurred at this reserve."[25]

The Department believed that Lewis was successfully helping the students progress to higher grades while the Indigenous families were providing guidance in their own language. While the language issue was still a concern to Indigenous community members, this progress into high school had not been seen previously within this reserve.[26]

On the other hand, Jean Scott received an "unsatisfactory report" as her discipline and class organization did not meet the current standards.[27] This report was disputed by Indian Agent Eastwood, who said that the school inspector unfairly punished her for children leaving their seats for various items during class time. He insisted that each time he visited Scott, he found that she was interested in the work; he recommended that Scott be given until Christmas to improve.[28]

The Department managed to maintain the services of Miss Scott, but Mr Lewis resigned from the position in the summer of 1930 for unknown reasons. To replace him, the Department agreed to hire Miss Thelma Carveth, whose application had been forwarded by the Indian agent. She had been teaching since 1927 in a large rural school and had earned a first-class teaching certificate from the Peterborough Normal School.[29] As a result of her first-class certificate and reference from a school inspector, Carveth was hired at $95 per month.[30] The new duo of Carveth as principal and Scott as assistant teacher received mixed reviews in October 1930. The school inspector noted that Carveth "is young but quite enthusiastic and should succeed … In an Indian School like this one it seems to me that there should be a male Principal."[31] The inspector said that Miss Scott was "somewhat disappointing" and should be let go so that Miss Carveth could remain – but as the assistant instead of the principal. The Department responded to these complaints by removing Scott and hiring Miss Bertha Long to replace her.[32]

The constant rotation of teachers would continue to impact the Curve Lake Indian Day School well into the 1930s. In the spring of 1931, Carveth and Long received positive reports about their teaching, and the community now had "7 entrance pupils" who were getting ready for high school. The school inspector requested that both teachers stay another year, but this was not to be. The principal, Miss Thelma Carveth, resigned in July 1931 and stated, "very unexpectedly my application which has been in for a vacant position in our public school for two years has been considered. Rather than let pass this opportunity, I have thought it best to give up my present one although I regret doing so very greatly."[33] She had only been teaching in Curve Lake in hopes of receiving a public school posting when one became available. During the summer of 1931, Indian Agent Eastwood hired a principal to replace Carveth; he lasted four days before resigning after seeing the living conditions of the mission house.[34] Clearly, the underfunded system created significant challenges in keeping qualified teachers, as the housing facilities were woefully inadequate compared to those offered to teachers in other places.[35] The United Church had not improved the teachers' residence, and the building desperately needed repairs and clean running water. There was a constant rotation of young, inexperienced schoolteachers spending a few years on reserve and then moving to more profitable jobs in the nearby cities. Unless teachers could be paid a higher rate – one closer to those offered in urban areas – the Indian day school had no chance of securing qualified teachers for a sustained period.

The inspection files of the Curve Lake Indian Day School reflect the ongoing control the Department had over even the smallest details of the operation. Several files in the archives reveal that even the most basic items needed to operate a school, such as chalk, paper towels, and a clock, had to be approved and paid for by the Department of Indian Affairs.[36] This strict control over the materials available in the classroom reflected the federal government's intentions and ensured that all items in the facility were accounted for. When items were requested to address situations such as the unsanitary conditions of the closets (washrooms) in the classroom, the response from Ottawa was often delayed. In the late 1920s, Inspector R.F. Downey indicated that "the present school building, the community hall, a church and two closets complete the property. The buildings are in a good state of repair, except that the closets are in an unsanitary condition."[37] He explained that the community hall had been fitted to serve as two classrooms, but "Miss Lewis has the greater number of pupils, and her classroom is the smaller. A re-adjustment of the number of pupils in each room might prove beneficial."[38] This recommendation was evidently not approved, as the fall inspection of 1927 also noted that the "closets needs attention before winter sets in."[39]

The Department stated that the Indian agent "will be good enough to see that these closets are thoroughly cleaned out and placed in a good state of repair at an early date. No unnecessary expense would be incurred."[40] A year later, the Department sent another reminder: "I have to request that you will arrange to have these closets thoroughly cleaned out and placed in a good sanitary condition. If any repairs are required, you should have some made. You should keep all costs in this connection as low as possible."[41] Once again, in May 1929, School Inspector Downey wrote, "Something should be done to correct the unsanitary condition of the closets which are in a disgraceful condition at the present time."[42] Once again, the Department asked that the Indian agent fix the closets and that "this work should be carried out as low a cost as possible."[43]

The community was stuck in a cyclical maintenance system: they would request money for repairs, which were then underfunded, leading to further disrepair and a need to request even more money to fix the dilapidated buildings. While the community repeatedly urged the government to do whatever was necessary to fix the school and mission house, they did not have authority over their funds. The decision of whether and how to meet these needs was made solely at the government's discretion. The impacts of this situation were far-reaching: not only did the significant structural issues of the school facility create an unpleasant learning environment for the students, but, in tandem with the unfavourable living conditions in the mission house, they also exacerbated the issue of transient teachers. As the community had no authority to override the decisions of government officials on these matters, the government continued to provide the bare minimum of education on the reserve at the cheapest possible price.

The Department's policies for procuring essential educational materials in the classroom perplexed the Indian agent. In January 1928, the federal government clarified how classroom supplies should be procured going forward. They explained to Indian Agent Eastwood: "All classroom material is supplied to Indian day schools through the Government Stationery Office here. The teacher should prepare, in due time, a requisition for his requirements, and this he should hand to you, and you should certify and send to the Department … In the future, the Department cannot pay accounts covering the cost of materials of this nature supplied to the school, and you should inform the teacher accordingly. The account which you forwarded in payment of two boxes of chalk will be paid."[44]

This policy was tested later that year when "emergency funding" was required to supply teachers with materials. In the fall of 1928, the Indian agent had paid $9 for three reams of paper ($3 per ream) without using the new protocols for obtaining material through the Department. The paper was required to administer examinations to students at the Indian day school. The Department wrote a scathing letter, stating that the agent had paid more than double the amount that the Government Stationery Office paid for paper ($1.45 per ream), and wrote, "Until we have a full explanation regarding the purchase of this paper, the Department is not prepared to pay the account."[45] Indian Agent Eastwood explained that the teacher at the Mud Lake reserve "ran short and needed this material immediately for examination paper for the last quarter and did not realize his supplies were so low until the day before the writing of his tests. In regard to the price of three dollars per ream this is the price quote at both the stationery stores in this city and the only place it could be obtained."[46]

The Department agreed to pay for the "emergency purchase" but reminded the Indian agent that this would not be done in the future and that the teacher should be shown a copy of the procurement policy, which had been sent to Eastwood earlier for "his future guidance."[47] The Department persisted, stating, "It is noted that he required the foolscap for use as examination paper, but it is not understood why it was necessary for him to purchase such a large quantity."[48] These letters between Peterborough and Ottawa indicate the government's priority – the cost of paper rather than the quality of education. This slow bureaucratic process for procuring supplies also impacted more significant upgrades to the school. In urgent situations, Indian Agent Eastwood continued to incur costs without the Department's permission. In the winter of 1928, for example, the furnace urgently needed repair: "cold air [had] come up into the classroom and it was necessary that this expenditure be incurred without taking the time to refer it to the department."[49] In another case, Eastwood stated, "I found it necessary to have the black boards at the Curve Lake Indian day school re-finished. I ordered Taylor of the Mud Lake Band to do this work … as Taylor was in need of funds and the work was necessary, I paid him direct as is shown on the attached voucher."[50] These examples provide insight into the autonomy of the Indian agent in using the funds of the Department for critical building or school needs. The letters from the Department to the Indian agent also reveal the ongoing negotiations and justifications required to request additional funding for reserve schools. In the case of Curve Lake First Nation, the correspondence suggests that Indian Agent Eastwood was consistently advocating for increased funds despite the Department's overall reluctance to allocate more resources. This dynamic highlights the tension between local officials pushing for better school conditions and a federal system resistant to increased spending.

Serious issues with the heating of the school persisted and caused significant problems. Eastwood wrote to the Department about this urgent matter in February 1929: "The wood burning stove which supplies the heat to the school room at Mud Lake day school has burned out and is beyond repair. Temporary measures have been taken to provide heat but these are not satisfactory as the stove fills the school room with smoke. It will be necessary for us to purchase a new one … In the meantime I am writing for authority to make a purchase. I have had two heating men up at the Reserve and they claim the stove is beyond repair. This stove is from 20 to 25 years old. The same condition applies to the church, although not quite so urgent."[51]

Eastwood provided a reasonable explanation for the replacement of the stove and had attempted alternative measures before reaching out to the Department. He had to give this information to ask for more money. Despite the critical need to heat the school during winter, it would take Ottawa more than a week to reply. In early March 1929, the Department responded, "You may arrange for the purchase and installation of a new stove of a type that would be satisfactory to heat this school. If possible, you should obtain competitive prices and make the purchase from the firm quoting the lowest price."[52]

This expectation characterized all funding proposals submitted to the Department for this school. If and when an item broke in the school, the Department always chose to replace it with the cheapest possible option.

Indian Agent Vincent Eastwood, like other Indian agents at the time, had agency in determining when or where funds under their jurisdiction would be used. For example, it took more than two years after the schools' inspections for Eastwood to finally request help to remedy other issues at the school, including the closets. In the summer of 1929, he wrote: "The whole building at the present time requires some brightening up and cleaning up, inside and out. A coat of paint on the floor of the Senior room and the woodwork throughout the whole interior painted would make a much cleaner and brighter school. Many of the window-panes need putty and the window and door frame are in need of a coat of paint."[53] Eastwood explained that the current teacher was willing to do this work at a cost of $2.50 a day; he stressed to the Department that "at a small cost I think a coat of paint where needed would be well spent and preserve the building. Also, the reglazing of the windows would make the building easier to heat."[54] Although Eastwood had made arrangements for this necessary work, the Department was adamant that no funds be spent until a detailed spending plan was submitted.

Nearly a month later, Eastwood finally provided a detailed quote for the cost of materials to improve the school. He stated it would cost around sixty dollars to do most of the work on the school and again stressed the need to improve the condition of the building. He wrote: "The floor downstairs has never been painted. It is soft wood, it would be necessary to paint this and the wainscotting. The ceiling needs an additional coat to brighten it up. The room upstairs has a hardwood floor, the woodwork needs painting. All outside the building is in a very bad condition. It would be necessary to paint all windowsills and woodwork also needs re-glazing."[55]

This message, along with earlier letters that highlighted issues with "unsanitary" closets and a broken furnace, show the significant state of disrepair.[56] The entire building was falling apart, and the Department wanted to find the cheapest solutions to fix the problems. J.D. McLean approved the request for sixty dollars to fund this renovation but noted it should be "completed at as early a date as possible" because it was now the end of August, and school would be restarting shortly.[57]

The issue surrounding the stove in the school was not mentioned again during that winter. Because of the delays in the process, the Curve Lake Chief and Council decided to step in. Chief Daniel Whetung wrote to the Department in May 1929, stating, "A resolution was passed ... for this council to buy a new furnace for the school and repair the furnace in the church out of the funds of the band."[58] Therefore, the furnace that was supposed to be paid for by the federal government as an essential component of their fiduciary duty to education was instead funded by the Band itself. It was only after Chief Whetung agreed to pay to correct the problem that Indian Agent Eastwood obtained a quote for $598 for both the church and school furnaces. In September of 1929, Eastwood noted that "it has been rather difficult to get local plumbers to supply a quotation during this busy season and hence the reason for delay, but the furnaces have been not urgently required ... You authorized me to purchase the equipment but as the cost is as high as it is, I thought best to inform you."[59] Eastwood notified the Department but not the Chief and Council, who had already agreed to pay any price to supply a furnace for the school. Instead, this letter delayed the furnace installation, underscoring that the Department and not the elected Council oversaw any financial decision.

A.F. Mackenzie had now been promoted to acting assistant deputy and secretary of the Department of Indian Affairs and so had the authority to make the decision on spending. He reiterated the philosophy of the Department to seek cheaper options: "The department would like you, if possible, to obtain quotations from other firms in Peterborough or elsewhere for supplying and installing a furnace in the school."[60] He clarified that the "Indian Education" funds would pay for the repairs to the furnace in the school while the furnace for the church (in the same building) would be paid for by "band funds."[61] This overrode the Chief and Council's decision to pay for both of the furnaces from their funds to expedite the replacement. MacKenzie further instructed the Indian agent, "You should give this matter your prompt attention in order that, if it is decided to install new furnaces, the work can be completed before the extreme cold weather sets in."[62] Eastwood replied two days later, indicating that he would immediately seek additional quotes on the furnace and reiterated that "the supply of good body wood is practically exhausted at the Reserve and the caretaker inform[s] me that it is impossible to sustain the heat necessary for the comfort of the pupils."[63]

These problems had been identified over seven months ago, and now that the winter was approaching, the Department was forced to look for a solution.

Eastwood was preoccupied with the delayed painting and resealing of the school. He wrote in the same month that "in order to keep these outhouses for the use of the pupils only, we are purchasing a padlock. These places have been used by the general public at large, which I do not think proper. A very satisfactory job has been made on these places."[64] Labour returns submitted in September 1929 indicate that several students were employed to complete the painting work for twenty-five cents a day. This practice raises questions about the use of student labour in maintaining the school infrastructure. While the modest payment may have been seen as a means of providing some compensation, it also highlights the lack of adequate funding and professional labour allocated for such tasks. The reliance on students to perform essential maintenance reflects the systemic neglect of Indian day schools, where the responsibility for upkeep often fell to the community itself, further burdening students who were already navigating the challenges of an underfunded and overcrowded education system. In the meantime, more serious concerns, such as a lack of quotes to replace the furnace, would result in even more issues that would impact the operation of the school.

On 5 October 1929, Eastwood sent an urgent telegram to the Department with an ultimatum. He wrote that the "school furnace [must] be installed or necessary to close the school [–] present furnace unusable."[65] The Department had received multiple reports from school inspectors, their own Indian agent, and the Chief and Council of the community and yet refused to act quickly to fix the issue. They sent a letter, not a telegram, three days after receiving the message stating: "The department requested Mr. Inspector McGookin to look into the matter and to make a recommendation … I am now authorizing you to deal with the matter while Mr. Inspector McGookin is there. You will please secure his advice … Upon the return of Mr. McGookin, instructions will be directed to your concerning the furnace in the church building. Please show this letter to Mr. McGookin."[66] The Department's reliance on bureaucratic procedures and the deferral of responsibility to Inspector McGookin exemplify the systemic inefficiencies that plagued the administration of

Indian day schools. While students and teachers endured harsh conditions with an unusable furnace, the Department delayed substantive action, prioritizing administrative protocol over the immediate needs of the school community. This incident illustrates the broader pattern of neglect and disregard for the welfare of Indigenous students in the federal education system.

This caused another delay in replacing the furnace; the inspector's report was not submitted until the end of October 1929. Inspector McGookin confirmed what had already been explained multiple times by multiple parties over nine months: "I examined the building which was originally built for a community hall and is not altogether suitable for a school. These Indians are clamouring for a new council hall, but if any building is anticipated, it should be a new two class school, and the present structure turned over to be used as a Council Hall."[67] Upon inspection by McGookin, the school furnace was found to be not only entirely useless but also hazardous to the building, having been in use for twenty-five to thirty years. The inspector also reported, "both teachers are providing excellent service and that students are making steady progress, though attendance remains irregular, particularly during the fall and winter months, due to families moving around."[68]

This scathing report from Inspector McGookin reaffirmed several issues with the school building and noted that teachers from the Indian day school were attending additional training in the nearby town of Peterborough. During this period, Peterborough operated one of the only teacher-education facilities in the province, and the nearby teacher's convention was a justification for closing the school in order to inspect it thoroughly. Despite the work of the teachers to improve the quality of education, the school still struggled with having too little room to meet the demands of the growing population. It was also clear that the furnace was still in utter disrepair and was a danger to the pupils in the facility.

As the provincial government hired the inspector and he would regularly visit other rural facilities, he was seen as a "trustworthy" person to make the determination about a similarly sized furnace. Finally, in response to this report, the Department agreed to pay for a furnace at a cost of $244; it was purchased in November but was not in operation until early December.[69] Indian Agent Eastwood wrote to the Department:

"I looked over this furnace on Saturday, December 7th, and find it satisfactory. I inquired of the teacher and Chief as to how it was taking care of the heating of the school and they were very much pleased with it."[70] From the Department's perspective, the furnace dispute was now over. Still, in the same letter, Eastwood also requested safety equipment for the furnace that would regulate the temperature in the basement and within the classroom.

Another teacher, Miss Margaret Gardiner from the French River area, was finally recruited by the United Church. She had over fourteen years of experience teaching and, in her application, wrote that she was "rarely ever lonely whenever there was real work to do and the big world of nature around me."[71] Her experience in remote areas, coupled with that of teaching in a large one-room rural schoolhouse for most of her career, convinced the Department to hire her at a rate of $95 per month. Still, her only qualification was that she was a nurse with a first-aid certificate.[72] Within the first month of her hire, Indian Agent Eastwood stated, "Every effort has been made to better the school attendance. There are some band members who will not send their children. These we have appealed to in every way."[73] Eastwood recommended that the annuity payment paid to reserve members be withheld from members "guilty of permitting truancy of their children. This is only time collections of fines imposed can be made without trouble in doing so."[74] While this recommendation was never instituted, it indicated that the government was willing to break treaty obligations if parents withdrew students from an inadequate education.

Chief Whetung wrote to the Department in December 1931 to express serious concerns with Miss Gardiner. He explained that she was not a qualified teacher and had made "very unsatisfactory" progress. Disconcertingly, the seven students who were about to write their high-school entrance exams were failing.[75] In addition, he wrote: "I am proud of the way our school had been getting on the last few years and it would be too bad to keep her on; as the pupils have lost interest in her, I for one as others would like if you could see your way to make a change as soon as possible for the interest of the children."[76]

As was their pattern, the Department did not believe the words of the Chief and chose to secure another report from the local school inspector before making any decisions regarding the removal of the teacher. Indian Agent Eastwood called the school inspector, R.F. Downey, and confirmed his thoughts about the teacher: "I am somewhat fearful of the value of Miss Gardiner's services in the senior Classroom" as several members had complained to Eastwood over the lack of progress.[77] The school inspector also said that "she over emphasizes such exercises as singing to the detriment of studies, I also think she is not progressive."[78] Downey did not believe that "singing" constituted his definition of "progressive education" and wanted to focus on the traditional regimented studies. The Department was nonetheless reluctant to remove Gardiner until a suitable replacement could be found. It reminded the Indian agent: "It must be kept in mind that at Indian day schools, the extra-curriculum activity is nearly as important as the classroom exercises."[79] Superintendent of Education Russell Ferrier requested a full report from all parties to make a final decision on the matter.

Gardiner responded to these accusations with two lengthy letters detailing her side of the situation with the school inspector. She stated that the accusation was a "stunning blow," and that she was aware that the school inspector did not like her teaching methods.[80] She argued that it was unfair to only listen to his side of the story and insisted that the Department visit the reserve to see the source of the disagreement. She wrote: "I have felt that I could do much to try to help raise the moral standard of the children, for God knows they need it."[81] Gardiner positioned herself as a saviour whose priority was to help improve the morality of Indigenous children. She also did not like being compared to Mr Lewis who had used "individual teaching" as a method to help the students progress better.[82] She accused Chief Whetung of not listening to her concerns regarding classroom space and stated that it was unfair that she had to "pay Whetungs' so much [rent for boarding] when there are so many who need help ... while there is so much waste here."[83] The letter was rambling and accusatory; it ended with a footnote mentioning that Gardiner had not shared this information with anyone and requesting that the Department keep the letter confidential.[84]

Gardiner sent her second letter directly to the superintendent of Indian education, Russell T. Ferrier, and again rambled through various accusations against the Chief, students, school inspector, and the previous teacher. She was still upset about the unfavourable teaching review and said: "I cannot understand *why* [emphasis in original], unless that someone has been reporting things that are absolutely one-sided."[85] She said that Mr Morgan Lewis had left most of the senior grades behind in classes such as language, geography, and history and they required additional lessons to catch them up. Lewis had prioritized other subjects and "individual learning" techniques he had learned at teacher's college. Miss Gardiner also blamed the entire community for the immorality she felt pervaded the reserve: "There is much immorality here and help is greatly needed in church and Sunday School … I don't dance, play card, etc., but I have not once in any way interfered with those who do nor mentioned such pleasures in S.S [Sunday school] or day school."[86] In this manner, Miss Gardiner reported on the reserve for having "whiskey, tobacco and immorality," as almost all students over the age of fourteen smoked cigarettes.[87] She argued she was the only one "quietly trying to … give them a decent Christian life" and this was evidenced in the hour-long Christmas concert that many people told her was the "best one ever held."[88] Gardiner also disputed the claims made by the Department that Chief Whetung cared about education and was progressive for his time. She said, "Mr. Whetung may be a 'very progressive Indian' but he and his family do nothing to help in uplifting in any way."[89] After being in the community for just a few short months, Miss Gardiner was sending damaging accusations to the Department.

Unfortunately, any insight into the Department's perspective on this issue has been lost, as Eastwood was required to telephone the superintendent of Indian education. During that phone call, they decided to remove Gardiner, but Eastwood wrote: "I think Miss Gardiner should have special consideration for reasons as stated by telephone."[90] Superintendent Ferrier wrote to Gardiner in January 1932 to indicate that a new teacher would replace her as soon as possible. However, he also said that "it is entirely probable that you are not wholly responsible for the difficulties that have arisen."[91] Miss Gardiner responded with a last attempt to save her position by explaining more of the work she had done after hours. This included working with a group of fifteen girls in "memorizing the commandants and a good number of bible verses to win a bible."[92] She also mentioned how she was "in a home visiting a sick girl one day last week" when she learned she would be fired. The parents of this student and a few others had told Miss Gardiner that they would submit a petition to keep her for the rest of the year. She felt "that the people ought to be allowed to speak sometimes. Otherwise, how shall they ever get any sense of responsibility."[93] She insisted that she cared about the welfare of these children and would like another inspector to evaluate her performance and listen to the people.

Removing the teacher in the middle of the school year angered several community members who had children about to take the high school entrance exam. A petition was signed by thirty-one members of the Band, who wanted to keep Gardiner until the school year ended in June.[94] They insisted that she had been treated unfairly by school inspectors and warned that their children would not make "any headway that is if another teacher was appointed."[95] The group said that Miss Gardiner had been helping some sick students and conducting regular Sunday school lessons, which had never been done before. The petitioners included the families of McCue, Taylor, Jacobs, and Knott. The Department also received another handwritten letter addressed directly to Russell Ferrier about wanting to keep her as the teacher.[96]

In response to these mixed reviews of the teacher, Ferrier travelled to the community to conduct a full investigation on 27 and 28 January 1932.[97] In a memo for the Curve Lake file, he wrote: "I visited the Mud Lake Indian Reserve, with a view to straightening out difficulties at the school there. Miss Gardiner has given quite good service but is very difficult to get along with and the reserve is divided in its allegiance to her. This is affecting the attendance and the work of the school generally and I believe that some parents of Entrance pupils – of which there are 7 – are really concerned about their progress. The arrangement that Miss Gardiner should leave today and be replaced on Monday by Mr. Rome was confirmed."[98]

The superintendent rarely visited the school on reserve, as he was responsible for all the country's residential and day schools.[99] So when the superintendent did visit he met with several leaders of the community and recommended that although Gardiner had been forced to resign, she could be rehired in September at another school. He also indicated that this situation was to be blamed on both the Indian agent and Indigenous leaders in the community who disagreed over the teacher. He wrote: "Care will be taken in the future to see that members of the band do not agitate every time there is a little complaint. Both factions understand the serious effect of dissension."[100] Ferrier was adamant that any concerns over education could be settled within the reserve without government interference, which was both time-consuming and costly.

The new teacher, Mr Rome, introduced physical activity and sports to the community both on and off the reserve.[101] Indian Agent Eastwood wrote: "He has organized seasonable games on the reserve amongst the school children and the older members. This has promoted a better feeling and is of interest to all. The hockey team played a number of games with the villages near the reserve and did quite well. There are number of boys just past school age with nothing to do in the winter months and Mr. Rome has endeavoured to get them interested in something."[102] It was hoped that the teacher's efforts to seek opportunities to solve "disputes" through sport would curtail the community's fighting over the school.

The community of Mud Lake was not satisfied with the school on the reserve, as evidenced in a memo submitted the following year, which detailed the visit of Chief Daniel Whetung to Department headquarters in Ottawa. This trip concerned the "educational needs for the reserve" and the associated physical buildings, which were not meeting the community's requirements. The memo noted that Chief Whetung made them aware of the ongoing issues.[103] Whetung told the Department they were using the council hall as two classrooms, but that it was advisable to vacate that property as soon as funds became available to build a suitable school. The old school on the far side of the church had quality lumber that could potentially be reused to save costs. The Chief believed that the site of the old school building was a good location, as it was somewhat removed from the highway. However, the memo noted that the Department should not agree to a request as they had already invested in a new furnace, painted it, and maintained it in good condition. Plans for the 1931–32 budget included a new two-room school.

This information was found on an internal document called "memo for file" within the Curve Lake school records, and it is not clear if this finding was relayed to Chief Whetung. The building used to educate students was never designed to house them; it was instead a former community hall. The government believed they should not have to pay rent on this building as they had repaired the furnace. Repeatedly, the federal government ignored its fiduciary responsibility, the treaties (Treaty 20 and the 1923 William's Treaties), and the BNA Act by providing inadequate resources to this community and favouring the cheapest piecemeal options available.

After this visit to Ottawa, Chief Daniel Whetung and Council began sending monthly resolutions to the Department in which they offered to pay for additional services for the upkeep of the building with community funds. The first special meeting memo indicated that Council had passed a resolution "to hire some person to clean and scrub out the school closets, one double & two single closets once each month or when necessary."[104] The Department rejected this resolution but asked for further clarification regarding who would be employed and at what cost. The Department's request for a per-annum breakdown of costs is indicative of the control it wielded over all funds – even those that rightly belonged to the community. Chief Whetung clarified both in May and September of 1930 that they would pay a person from the reserve a fee of eight dollars to clean and repair the school closets.[105] These pleas to repair and maintain the closets clearly went unheeded, as School Inspector McGookin outlined these ongoing issues in his September 1930 inspection report: "The two closets are in a very bad condition and past repairing. They have been in use for the school, community dances, and fall fairs for many years and are most unsanitary and dilapidated. I would recommend that two new closets be built as soon as funds are available, this fall if possible."[106]

Upon receipt of this inspection, the Department authorized Indian Agent Eastwood to create new closets and remove the old ones from the property.[107] Again, the Department made clear its priority: "All expense[s] in the erection of the new closets should be kept as low as possible."[108] This issue may not have occurred if the Department had agreed to regular cleaning, which the Chief and Council had requested nearly four months earlier. In addition, it demonstrated once again that the Department trusted the words of the provincial school inspector over the Council members who lived on the reserve. The closet repairs were completed that fall – over two years after this significant issue was first reported.

The slow process by which even small issues with the facility were addressed served as an impetus to create a more sustainable school building. Another memo was added to the Curve Lake file after Chief Daniel Whetung and Indian Agent Vincent Eastwood jointly visited the Department in Ottawa the following year. They both remarked: "Two classrooms are required. One should be considerably larger than the other, so that it could be used for school concerts and other functions."[109] As a result of the Chief's second visit – this time accompanied by an Indian agent – the Department agreed to seek out funds "for the new building at the coming session of parliament."[110] Despite this apparent progress, the commitment to action remained conditional, as the request for funding was still subject to parliamentary approval. This delay highlighted the continued reliance on bureaucratic processes that often prioritized financial and administrative considerations over the community's immediate needs. While the Department's response marked a step forward, it also demonstrated the recurring challenge of translating verbal agreements and documented memos into tangible improvements for Curve Lake and other Indigenous communities reliant on the federal schooling system. This ongoing dependence on Ottawa's decisions reinforced a slow, incremental change pattern that frequently left pressing issues unresolved for years.

This call for a new school also coincided with an increase in attendance; there were now sixty-one students in the school. In addition to the new building, nine more desks were required to meet the school's growing needs.[111] The reports for the following three years do not discuss renovations or the promised new building in significant detail. The topic of school facilities was eventually addressed again in January 1934, as another report from the Department of Indian Affairs made it clear that the Mud Lake school building was still in a state of disrepair and this problem extended beyond Mud Lake to the entire day schooling system. School Inspector McGookin stated: "The Mud Lake Indian Day School needs painting inside and out. It has become dingy and neglected looking. This applies in some degree to most of our day schools on the reserves I visit ... the buildings are rapidly reaching the state where renovation will be costly."[112] Despite the urgency of this report and the clear need for additional repairs across the system, that spring, Indian Agent Eastwood only requested two additional brooms, at a cost of seventy cents each, from the Department of Indian Affairs.[113] The stark contrast between the systemic neglect highlighted by Inspector McGookin and the minimal requests from Indian Agent Eastwood reflect the profound inadequacies in addressing the needs of day schools. The failure to prioritize meaningful investments in infrastructure perpetuated an environment of neglect and disrepair, where the bare minimum, such as requesting brooms, took precedence over critical renovations. This inaction reflects the broader systemic indifference of the federal government, which routinely deferred or dismissed the urgent concerns of Indigenous communities, leaving schools like Mud Lake to languish in unacceptable conditions.

Over the remainder of 1934, tensions between the community and the Department of Indian Affairs reached a boiling point. After repeated inspections criticized the school building's structure and equipment, a new school was recommended. A handwritten note from the "Mississauga of Mud Lake Band Council" requested action on a resolution moved by Councillor James McCue and seconded by Councillor Albert Whetung. The resolution read: "As the present school classrooms are held in our council hall, which is unsuitable in every way for this purpose and there is not sufficient accommodation for the number of pupils attendings schools. We request the Department at Ottawa grant us a proper school for this reserve and return to us our council hall for the purpose it was originally intended."[114] This formal resolution reflects the broader systemic failure of the Department of Indian Affairs to provide adequate educational infrastructure, forcing communities to repurpose vital spaces at great cost to their governance and cultural activities. Despite repeated inspections and clear recommendations, the community continued to face delays.

Indian Agent Eastwood was receptive to these concerns, relayed this information to the Department, and offered additional context that supported the case for building a new school. He wrote, "At the present time there are 63 pupils attending school on the reserve. Mr. William Rome conducts the senior classroom on the ground floor with an attendance of 26 pupils. Miss Long has a junior class with 37 pupils on the second floor. The building not being designed in the first place for a school, has a great many disadvantages."[115] Eastwood also explained that "every foot of space is used," and the "lighting is very poor and in the winter months it is difficult for the children to see the blackboards after two o'clock."[116] The physical building was in such a state that "the whole building needs repairs. Several large cracks have appeared in the walls within the last year … the building is not suitable for the purpose it is now used for."[117] At the end of his letter, Eastwood stated his belief that the construction of a new school had been cut from the Department budget as a result of the "past difficult years" but was adamant that he had already explained this "matter very thoroughly with Mr. Ferrier at that time and this may be on record."[118]

On the same day that he relayed the resolution of the Mud Lake Council, Eastwood sent an additional letter to the Department outlining a separate and immediate concern regarding the school. He explained that the principal, Mr Rome, was now improvising and practising regular fire drills because, during school hours, there were thirty-seven young pupils on the second floor of the school, but only one exit that led downstairs. In the case of a fire, the only other means of exit entailed a fifteen-foot drop from a window. He requested that either a suppression system or a fire escape be installed and that, at a bare minimum, a chemical fire extinguisher be installed at the door.[119]

Within five days, the Department responded to Eastwood, explaining that it could not cover the costs of a new school building but would investigate fire-prevention measures. Secretary of Indian Affairs A.F. Mackenzie wrote: "The Department will have no funds during the coming fiscal year, 1935–1936, to provide the cost of erecting a two-roomed school for the Indian children on the Mud Lake reserve, and it will therefore be necessary to continue the use of the council hall. The need for a new school building will not be lost sight of, but its erection will depend upon Parliament providing funds for the purpose."[120] Again, the urgency of the community's needs was acknowledged but action was repeatedly postponed due to budgetary constraints. While the Department assured the community that their concerns had not been forgotten, their insistence on waiting for parliamentary approval effectively stalled any meaningful progress. In the meantime, students and teachers were left to endure overcrowded, unsafe, and unsuitable conditions.

Interestingly, Mackenzie contradicted himself a few paragraphs later in his response to Eastwood: "As this building will be required for school purposes for a considerable period, it will be necessary to take precautions for the safety of the children, in case of fire."[121] The government knew that the inadequate school facility would continue to be used for an additional unspecified time period despite the serious safety concerns. Focusing on fire-prevention measures instead of addressing the root problem highlighted the Department's tendency to apply short-term fixes to systemic issues. This approach ignored the broader impacts of inadequate facilities on the students' education and well-being. For the Curve Lake community, the council hall's continued use disrupted its intended function and reinforced a sense of disregard for the community's governance and cultural priorities. These delays and half-measures deepened frustrations and widened the gap between the community's needs and the Department's willingness to act.

It would take another four months to sort out the additional details and costs of the fire prevention plan, but the Department finally agreed to purchase a fourteen-gallon chemical fire extinguisher, which was to be placed at the foot of the stairway and a "25-foot ladder built and kept on hooks on the side of the building, for emergency use."[122] The Department's philosophy regarding Indian day schools was apparent in A.F. MacKenzie's instruction to the Indian agent: "No unnecessary expense should be incurred in building the ladder."[123] Even in cases where the safety of children was concerned, the Department provided as little funding as possible to meet requirements. The Department's continuing pattern of attempting to fix issues by the cheapest means possible again forced the community to find their own solutions.

The Curve Lake Chief and Council sought alternative solutions after finding the Department unwilling to support building a new school. In May 1935, Chief Daniel Whetung and all the councillors passed another resolution. It read: "If the Department of Indian Affairs cannot see their way clear to build a new school this year. We the mud-lake council would propose the removal of partition wall between the senior classroom and the council chamber making it into one large room, and more light. This council is willing that the Department use these rooms until such time they are in a position to build a new day school which we hope they will be able to do so in the near future. We also recommend that the outside brick wall and door steps into the school be repaired."[124]

Council also attached a hand-drawn sketch of the current school layout and indicated in the letter that the main wall should be taken down for additional space. After already giving up their council hall to meet the demands of the growing school, the community decided to try to create a better space on their own.

The Department was reluctant to spend additional funds to meet the community's requests and attempted to bargain with Chief and Council over the repairs. They requested that all "work … be performed by Indian labour." They also stated that while they would pay for the removal of the partition wall, the other costs would have to be paid for by Council: "It is thought that the Band would agree to providing the cost of shingling the roof and painting the building, from their own funds … If the council do not agree to authorizing the cost from their funds, the Department would have no funds this year to paint the building or reshingle the roof."[125]

In this instance, the Department attempted to alleviate their fiscal responsibility to pay for day schools on reserve by negotiating to have school-repair costs paid for with community funds. Indian Agent Eastwood responded that "the council appear to loathe to spend any money on this building," as it was not meant to be a school and was in a constant state of disrepair.[126] As a result of the community's rejection of this negotiation, the Department decided that "classroom activities can be carried on under present conditions of the coming school year (1935–36)," as they no longer had funds for any of the requested repairs.[127]

Indian Agent Eastwood would not request another update on the new school to the community for a year. In September 1937, he wrote to the Department to remind them of "the promised new school at Mud Lake reserve, the urgency of which you are already acquainted with. You will recall this was in the estimates of 1930–31 and was postponed at that time on account of the depression. I have not put this in the estimate again,

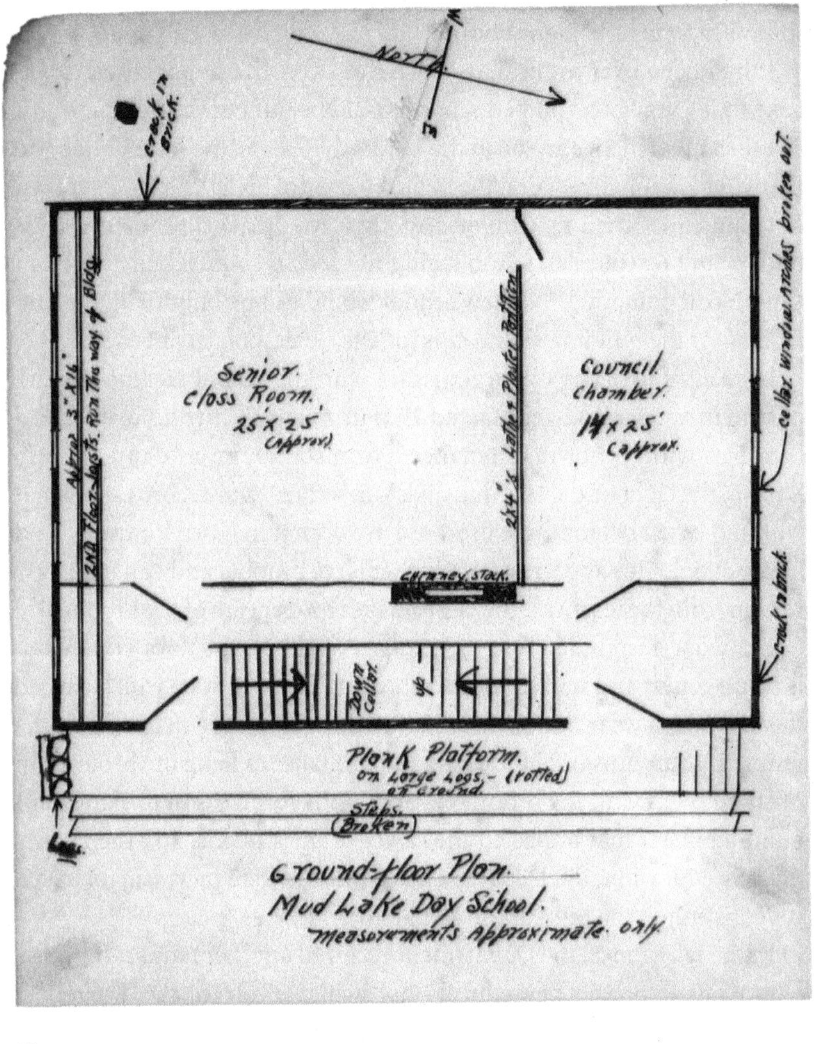

Figure 5.1
Architectural floor plan of the Mud Lake Indian Day School, 1935, showing the senior classroom, council chamber, and central plank platform, as part of early twentieth-century educational infrastructure.

but hope it was not been lost sight of. When I was at Ottawa last year with the councillors from Mud Lake, we were assured at that time that something might be done about it."[128]

It had been over seven years since the Department promised Curve Lake that a new two-roomed school would be built in their community. There is no evidence in the archive that the Department responded to Eastwood's reminder, but on the digitized copy of his letter a hand scrolled note illustrates the Department's apathy: "Mud Lake 2 roomed school, understand 65 (pupils), school being housed in council hall at present time. No action now."[129] A new school would not be built that year, and repairs for the building would continue to be desperately needed.

Instead of focusing on larger issues with the school facility, the Department increasingly contacted Indian Agent Eastwood over trivial concerns with minor maintenance. For instance, in June 1938, Phillip Phelan, the chief of the training division, wrote: "Our records show that within the past 18 months 14 brooms have been purchased for use at Mud Lake School. This appears to be a rather large number and you might ascertain from the teacher if the janitor takes proper care of the brooms."[130]

Eastwood responded that the expense spent on the floor was due to it being rough and had a considerable number of knots, which caused the brooms to wear out quickly. He continued, "I hope to cut down the number of brooms used by asking the caretaker to hang the brooms up or stand them with the broom part up."[131] In comparison to significant building issues that impacted the safety of the students and the quality of their education, the Department's concerns were increasingly trivial yet constituted the bulk of the Department's focus.

In the fall of 1938, the Department received another request from the school inspector for a new educational facility at Curve Lake. The report stated: "Fifty-eight pupils are now attending Mud Lake Indian Day School and this taxes the capacity of the two classrooms. The need for additional accommodations is still present ... With this additional space [the teacher] can carry out the instructions of other subjects now on the curriculum."[132]

The Department had now heard from the Indian agent, Chief and Council, and multiple school inspectors that a new space was required. The need for a new facility was also reinforced by the 1938 provincial curriculum being implemented in Ontario. This curriculum increased the number of subjects and, therefore, increased the space required for additional activities.

In December 1938, almost a decade after the community first requested a new school, Superintendent of Welfare and Training R.A Hoey wrote to Indian Agent Eastwood. Hoey explained that provisions were being made to create a new school in the 1939–40 fiscal year.[133] He also enclosed a building survey that provided recommendations on whom should build the school, how many students it should hold, and whether it should contain accommodations for the teachers.[134]

Eastwood quickly responded with all the necessary information. He obtained a $9,000 quote for the building, including indoor plumbing, a large basement, and classrooms with enough space for eighty to one hundred pupils. Eastwood secured engineering plans, a suitable location 160 feet from the shore of Buckhorn Lake, and a potential site for a well.[135] He stated that "the labour available at the reserve is unskilled … I think it essential that the building be carried out by contract, with Indians employed where possible."[136] He believed that the Curve Lake community could not do the work themselves and preferred the services of a nearby construction company. These paternalistic discussions were not shared with the Chief and Council. Finally, Dr Harold McGill, the director of Indian Affairs, initiated the construction process on 3 February 1939.[137]

During the construction process, the Department vetoed plans to dig a well to provide fresh water to the school. Instead, it opted for water coolers that had to be filled at a nearby well, which the government did not own. They argued, "The cost of this well would involve considerable expenditure which our funds will not permit at the present time."[138] Despite some changes to the original plan, the construction neared completion in November 1939. Indian Agent Eastwood reported: "All who have seen it are very pleased with the school and all members of the Band are quite proud of it."[139] A month later, in December 1939, the school opened after the final desks had been secured and the coal transferred from the old school's basement to the new one.[140] The final price of the school amounted to $11,048.98.[141]

Within a month, issues with the quality of the new school building became apparent. On the first day after the winter holidays, there was

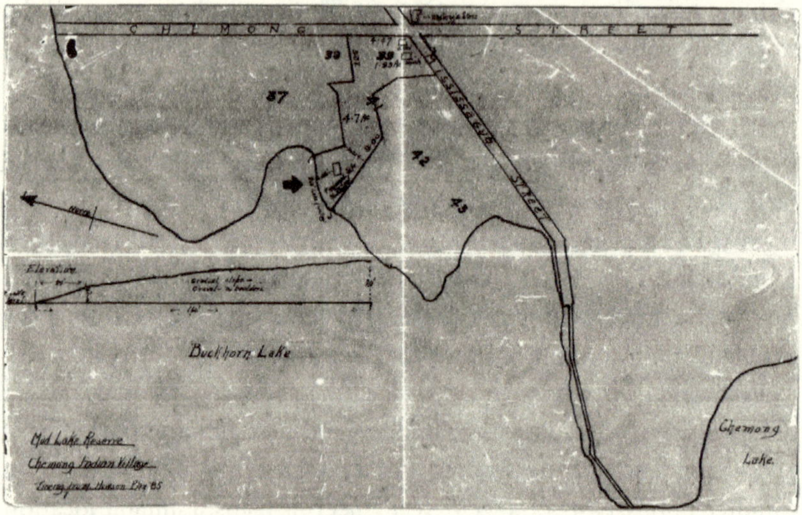

Figure 5.2
Survey map of Mud Lake Reserve, illustrating land divisions, elevation details, and proximity to Buckhorn and Chemong Lakes, with the school location marked by an arrow. Building Location, Mud Lake Indian Day School, 1938.

"an odor emanating from the chemical lavatories in the new school."[142] Eastwood investigated the smell and informed the Department that W.R. Turner of Peterborough (a plumber off reserve) may have installed the new septic system incorrectly. This led to the smell spreading throughout the entire building, and Eastwood noted it was "quite noticeable in classrooms during the day."[143] On the same day, under separate letterhead, Eastwood outlined a significant issue with all of the blackboards: "The black boards at the new school have become loose from the wall to which they were fastened. Every section has become loose and three or four of these are curved outwards about an inch. It makes it difficult for the teachers to use the boards in this condition and I thought I should advise you in order to have the matter rectified by the contractor."[144] These glaring deficiencies in the construction and oversight of the new building raised questions about the contractor's workmanship and the Department's accountability in ensuring quality standards. The odour from the septic system and the warped blackboards disrupted the school's daily operations, creating an environment that was not conducive to learning.

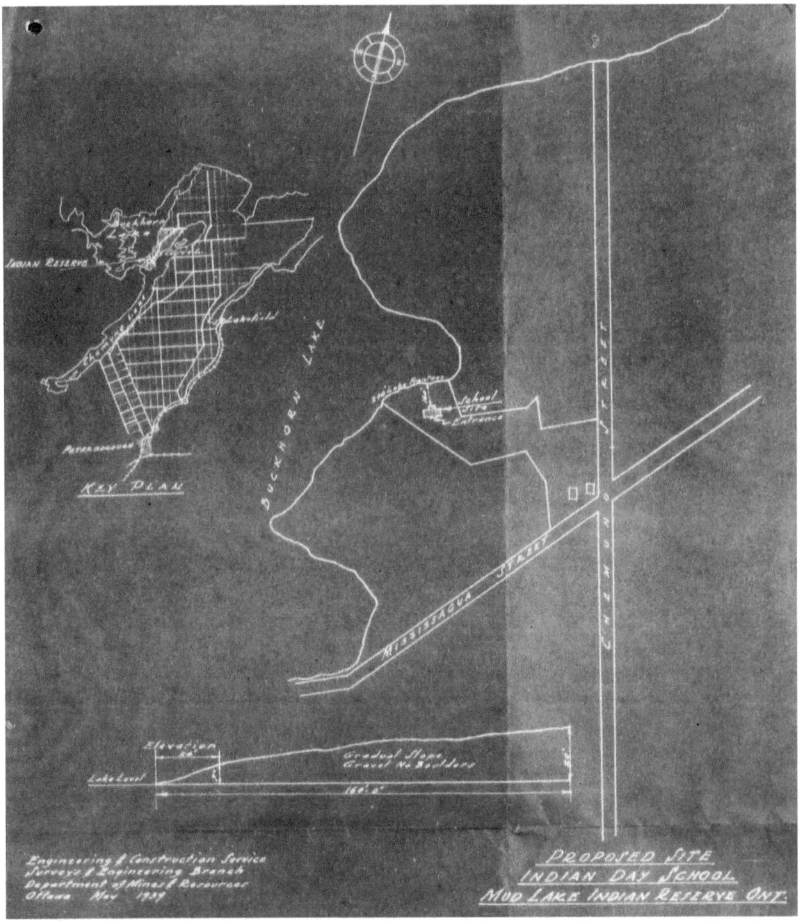

Figure 5.3
Proposed site plan for the Mud Lake Indian Day School, detailing land divisions, key elevations, and proximity to Buckhorn Lake, created by the Engineering and Construction Service. Proposed Site, Mud Lake Indian Day School, 1939.

For the teachers and students, these issues added to the growing frustrations with a system prioritizing cost-cutting and expediency over the community's needs.

Eastwood's detailed reports reflect his persistent efforts to advocate for immediate repairs, but they also underline the systemic neglect that allowed such substandard work to pass inspection. The Department's

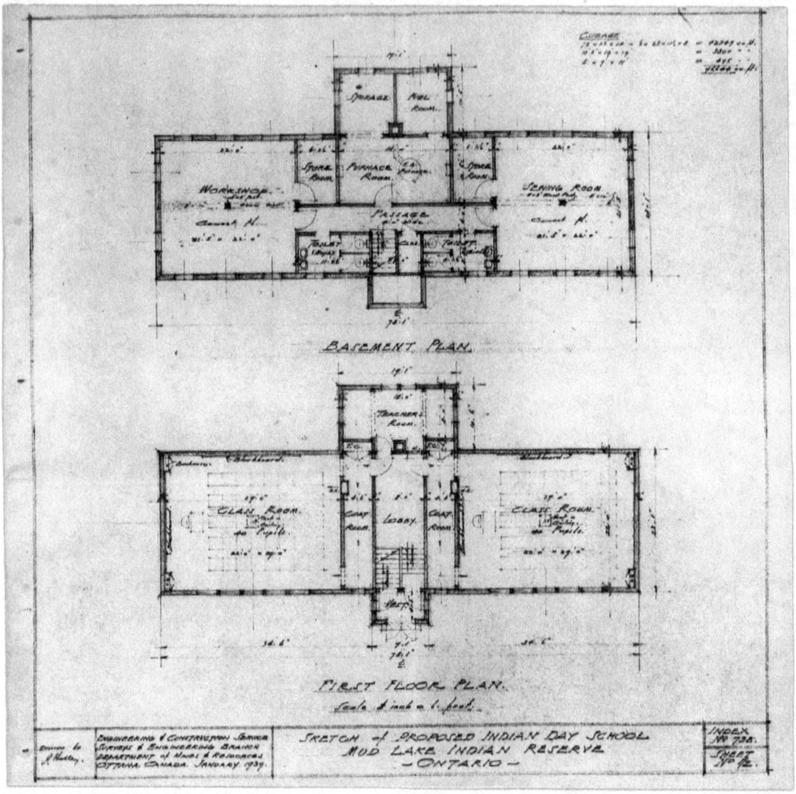

Figure 5.4
Architectural plans for the proposed Mud Lake Indian Day School, showing detailed basement and first-floor layouts, created by the Department of Mines and Resources. Mud Lake Indian Day School Interior Proposed Sketch, December.

reliance on off-reserve contractors, like W.R. Turner, further compounded the problem, as it demonstrated a lack of engagement with the community and its capacity to address local needs more effectively. These recurring issues in the new school building served as a stark reminder of the challenges faced by Indigenous communities in securing safe and functional educational spaces.

While the Department had previously stated that they would feel more confident if outside contractors, rather than labourers from the reserve, built the school, the state of the new facility suggests that this confidence

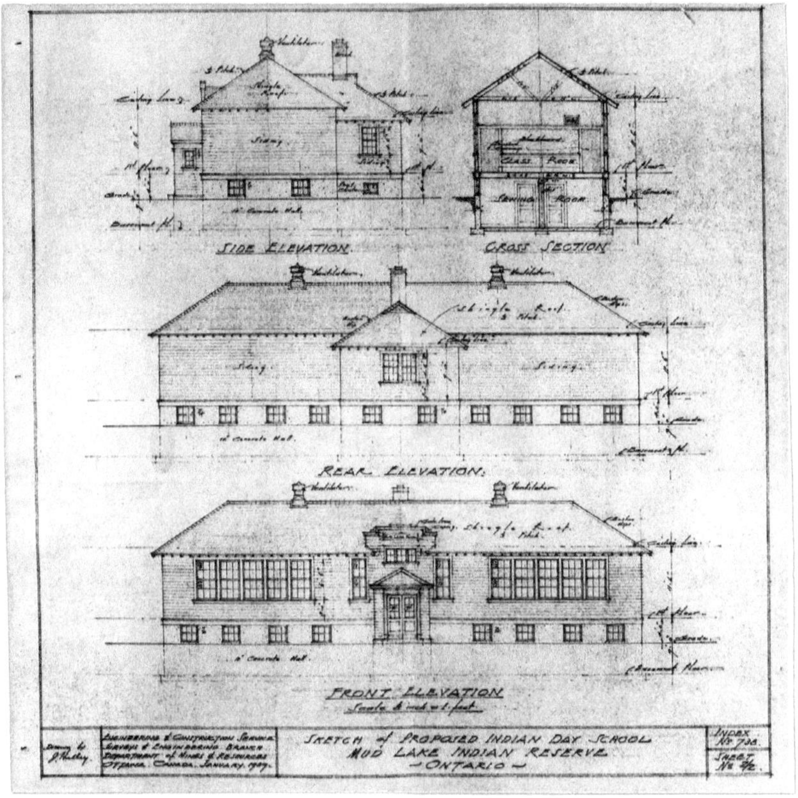

Figure 5.5
Elevations and cross-section plans for the proposed Mud Lake Indian Day School, illustrating architectural details and building dimensions, created in January 1939. Mud Lake Indian Day School Exterior Proposed Sketch.

was unfounded. The construction work was shoddy, and the project was over budget. The building quality issue was passed up the chain of command until it reached director of Indian Affairs Dr McGill, who confirmed that "installations were done in accordance with the specifications of the manufacturer's direction and that the contractor is being asked to remedy the faults."[145]

While the Department absolved itself from responsibility and blamed the manufacturer for the issue, the problem worsened at the new school. A few weeks later, Eastwood explained: "The odor throughout the

Figure 5.6
Photographs of the finished Mud Lake Indian Day School, showcasing the front facade, side view with community members, and interior classroom, taken in 1939.

school has become so overpowering that I have instructed the teachers to close the toilets and have had the two outhouses from the old school fitted with boxes and moved to a satisfactory location near the school as a temporary accommodation … I had this work done as I was concerned about the health of the pupils and the danger of having the strong odour penetrate into the considerable amount of fibre board that is used through this school."[146]

The weather exacerbated the issues with the toilet system: no significant changes could be made until the ground thawed and the road to the reserve became more accessible in the spring. The first few months of the new school's operation were marked by even worse conditions than those in the outdated council hall.

Internally, the Department of Indian Affairs scrambled to seek a solution to this issue after the chief engineer revealed that the Curve Lake Indian Day School toilet facilities had been a "test case" for a new septic system: "The desire to obtain an inexpensive indoor system for use in larger Indian Day Schools where a piped water supply is not available, it was decided by the Indian Affairs officers to try the system at the Mud Lake School as a test case. Enquiries are being made by this service to determine whether the failure of the Mud Lake system is due to the design of the equipment or to the manner in which it was installed."[147]

This information was not shared with the community or Indian Agent Eastwood. This test endangered the health of Indigenous students attending the school. Once the director, Dr McGill, learned of this experiment, he sent the following order: "No type of chemical toilet now manufactured, is satisfactory for installation in any residences. From the description of the toilets installed for observation in the Mud Lake Reserve school, it would not seem that any result much better than that noted, could be expected."[148]

It was not until June 1940, over six months later, that a contractor from the Canadian Sanitation Company arrived to rectify the issue. To do this, the contractor dug several septic pits around the school that would divert the waste into larger holding tanks. Indian Agent Eastwood was skeptical that this would be a long-term solution to the issue but wrote, "I hope and trust this arrangement will work satisfactorily."[149] This significant concern was buried rather than dealt with properly.

Smaller issues, such as the absence of a school bell, were also noted during the first months of the new school's operation. Chief and Council required permission from the Department to move the old school's bell into the new school, as it would cost additional money to install. This relatively minor issue was important to the community as "in most homes there are no clocks, and they depend upon the bell for their time and also for sending their children to school."[150] The bell also acted to divide the classes into set periods and as a warning in case of fire. More importantly, "ringing the bell for various causes has been a long established custom on this Reserve and the members miss the bell considerably."[151] The absence of the bell reflected the broader tensions between the Department's administrative control and the community's lived experiences and traditions. For the Chief and Council, the bell was more than a practical tool – it symbolized routine, order, and connection within the community. Its absence disrupted the school schedule and the rhythms of daily life on the reserve. Despite the seemingly minor nature of the issue, the delay in resolving it underscored the extent to which even minor requests were subject to bureaucratic processes, further alienating the community from decisions affecting their schools. The continued need to seek departmental permission for basic adjustments demonstrated the systemic disregard for local autonomy and the importance of preserving cultural practices in educational spaces.

Over the course of twenty years, members of the Curve Lake community contacted the federal government repeatedly regarding the significant structural and safety issues of a building that was never intended to be a fully operational two-roomed schoolhouse. After decades of broken promises, when the government did proceed with construction, it failed to consult the community regarding what important features should be included in the new school building. Worse yet, it hid the experimental nature of the septic-tank system from the community and never properly remedied the issue when the experiment failed. On top of these problems, the government systematically underfunded teachers' salaries and school materials. As a result, the community struggled to find and retain a good teacher who could help students progress to the higher grades. When the United Church took control, they implemented the same questionable hiring practices. They also continued to undervalue the contributions of Indigenous leaders on reserve who fought for more control over the quality of education being provided. Together, church and state worked hand in hand to maintain the day school in Curve Lake at the lowest cost available without any major concern for the health, well-being, or education of Indigenous students. By constantly undermining Council and stealing funds from the community, the government and church maintained the status quo, and they did so at a massive cost to Indigenous students.

CHAPTER 6

Beyond the Classroom: Educational Philosophies and Opportunities

The austerity measures of the Great Depression and the Second World War impacted both the pedagogy and type of education in the Curve Lake Indian Day School. By the 1930s, the economic impacts of the Great Depression, coupled with the presence of the newly established industrial powerhouses, including General Electric and Outboard Marine in nearby Peterborough, provided a new opportunity to assimilate Indigenous students. These companies were attracted to the area by inexpensive and plentiful land and by the tremendous amount of hydroelectric power generated by the Trent-Severn Waterway. Having tapped into this cheap and reliable source of power, the companies began searching for as many labourers as possible. Peterborough became an economic powerhouse and attracted thousands of immigrants from across Europe who were fleeing instability. These companies also began to rely on the local Indigenous labour as an additional skilled workforce. During the 1930s and 1940s, the Department of Indian Affairs refused to expand arts-based education and instead revised the curriculum and renovated school facilities to promote manual-training education. This short but important chapter highlights evidence that education for Indigenous people during this period was designed to create workers for the emerging Canadian economy.

A similar story of economic priorities over quality education also played out in British Columbia. As Sean Carleton explains, "Separated from the land, the vast majority of settlers, and an increasing number of Indigenous Peoples, had little choice but to live by selling their labour power in exchange for wages to purchase goods and services from the emerging market economy."[1] This process was destructive for Indigenous cultures but generative for the "ongoing development of British Columbia as a capitalist settler society."[2] Without this process – removing Indigenous Peoples from the land, placing them into various forms of schooling, and retraining them to meet new societal needs – the development of Canada would not have taken place. Carleton argues, "the introduction of new methods of education … further disrupt[ed] Indigenous lifeways and compel[led] the growing masses into wage labour."[3] The Canadian government believed that Indigenous Peoples could be converted from wards of the state into productive workers who could contribute to the country's socioeconomic development. In British Columbia, this manual training "gradually implemented reforms as part of its strategy to use schooling to prepare children for participation in the capitalist economy."[4] We must recognize that this schooling policy was directly linked to larger goals within the Canadian colonial project. Carleton states that "colonial dispossession and capitalist development are dialectically intertwined, deeply enmeshed, and ongoing processes that require constant state legitimation through the invention and administration of various structures and techniques of rule, including education."[5] Education was often the cheapest form of dispossession, as evidenced by the federal government's refusal to provide more than the bare minimum to the school in Curve Lake. This pattern was not isolated to British Columbia but mirrored across Ontario and most of Canada. In Ontario, similar schooling systems prioritized cost efficiency and the assimilation of Indigenous children into settler economic frameworks, often at the expense of providing quality education or addressing community needs. The systemic underfunding and neglect of schools like Curve Lake reflect the broader national policy of using education as a tool for dispossession designed to erode Indigenous cultural ties while redirecting labour into the settler economy. Across Canada, the emphasis on manual training and basic education reinforced a system where

Indigenous children were prepared only for subservient roles within the capitalist economy, ensuring the continuation of colonial dominance while minimizing state expenditures. This widespread approach illustrates the deep entanglement of education policy with the economic and colonial objectives of the Canadian state.

One file from 1936 shares a story from early in William Rome's tenure, when he attempted to secure the services of Cyril Rice, the local supervisor of music for schools in Peterborough County, for the Curve Lake Indian Day School. Rice wrote: "I teach the schools all around Curve Lake school, and also teach the Indian School at Hiawatha."[6] As his services were to be partially funded through a grant by the provincial Department of Education, it would only cost $50 per year to have Rice visit Curve Lake for one hour per week to teach the ministry music course. The teacher and Indian Agent Eastwood both recommended that the Department of Indian Affairs fund the program, as "there is excellent talent amongst the children of this school."[7] The Department quickly vetoed this proposition: "Owing to lack of funds, the Department is not prepared to favourably consider this proposal."[8] The Department's refusal to pay for this program, which was already in place in other day schools and the nearby town of Peterborough, highlighted its unwillingness to pay more than the bare minimum for education on this reserve. A few months later, in June 1936, the Curve Lake Chief and Council, led by Daniel Whetung, responded by passing a resolution to allow the music teacher to attend each week if the Department would reconsider.[9] Again, the Department quickly replied that they had "no funds provided for this purpose."[10] Even though the provincial government had already paid $50 to implement this program in other schools, the federal government was unwilling to provide funds for this type of activity. This refusal was indicative of the broader disparity between the resources allocated to Indigenous and non-Indigenous schools across Canada. While provincial funding had enabled similar programs in settler schools and even in other nearby day schools, the federal government's decision to withhold support for Curve Lake demonstrated its ongoing prioritization of austerity over the well-being and cultural enrichment of Indigenous students. Music education, an avenue to foster creativity and preserve cultural connections, was treated as a dispensable luxury rather than a valuable component of a well-rounded education. The Department's rigid refusal also demonstrated its broader unwillingness to engage with or invest in programs that could nurture the exceptional talents identified within the Curve Lake community. This pattern of neglect reinforced systemic inequities, limiting opportunities for Indigenous children to access the same quality of education afforded to their non-Indigenous peers in neighbouring schools.

Compared with the previous three decades of teaching turnover, Mr William Rome's tenure as principal was uneventful. Rome remained the principal until 1938 and received many positive reviews of his teaching from the Department of Indian Affairs. One report noted that Rome had improved the school attendance to nearly fifty-nine pupils, and seven of those students were preparing to take the high school entrance examination.[11] Although archival records mentioning Rome are minimal, he was employed for nearly eight years as a teacher at the school without any major problems with the community or the Chief and Council.

As Rome was leaving, the Department managed to secure two first-class applications for the principal position for the first time. Mr Jack Cowling, who had earned a first-class teaching certificate and was taking summer courses at Queen's University, applied for the job through the Indian agent, whom he knew. Even though he was qualified and lived in nearby Peterborough, the Department instead hired Mr Stuart Mackey. The only difference between the two applications was that Mackey had spent the summer of 1938 at the University of Toronto learning the "new curriculum."[12] This specialized training, taught by Thornton Mustard, a progressive educator in Toronto,[13] promised more success in the rural schools of the province and was seen as a "progressive" way to educate students.

The new curriculum would be implemented across the province that year, so Mackey's knowledge provided an added benefit. He cited this benefit in his application: "I studied this summer in the class devoted to the administration and teaching problems met by a teacher in a senior room such as this. The application of new course of study to these grades was dealt with in the methodology classes. This is a unique advantage since, naturally, this study of our new curriculum could not have been done before."[14] At the age of twenty-four, Mr Mackey had four years of teaching experience; the Department deemed that he was ready to be a principal and hired him at a rate of $950 per year.[15]

Mr Mackey had to earn the support of the community as Mr Rome left on good terms, with five students passing the high school entrance exam. Upon his first review, Indian Agent Eastwood remarked: "At the beginning of school, a new teacher has a little difficulty gaining the confidence of his pupils. Attendance fell off but is now, I am glad to say, improving. Tuition grants were secured for one member of the Mud Lake Reserve attending Vocational School at the Peterborough Collegiate."[16] While Mackey initially had trouble, he appeared to be fitting into the community. Furthermore, this was the first time community members had earned tuition grants to attend high school in the nearby town of Peterborough.

After his first month at the school, Mackey wrote a detailed four-page letter to the Department about new pedagogical methods that could be employed in the day school. Indian Agent Eastwood had requested this information regarding a "plan for training handicapped children in the rural areas."[17] Mackey explained that there was now an organized system for educating such children "without removing them from their homes and school environment."[18] With the help of "special training units" sent to each school, the teacher could provide additional support to those who were struggling. Currently, two units responded to the different needs of "handicapped students." The first was called the "Opportunity Unit" and was for "pupils who are unusually backward in any or all subjects."[19] Mackey believed the community would benefit from these units and wrote: "I am justified in stating that opportunity units would be of greater value to our Indian School than to the average 'white' school."[20] He also noted that the other teacher, Miss Long, and the former teacher, Mr Rome, agreed with this perspective.

The other kit that was offered by the Ministry of Education was for "sight saving units," which were for children whose "eyes are defective." Mackey again wanted a few units sent to the school "because of the frequent occurrence of trachoma among the Indians."[21] Two students who were attending the Mud Lake school were already undergoing treatment for trachoma – a disease that may lead to blindness if left untreated. Mackey said the students were "in little danger, [but] it is conceivable that sight saving units might be of value in some future time."[22] Teachers at the Mud Lake school were, as was too often the case, trying to convince the Department to offer more support.

Inspired by an article in the *Canadian School Journal*, Mackey outlined his perspective on implementing these units for students classified as "backwards." He explained that "a word on the nature of the training given to backward children might not be out of place. The emphasis is placed on the fundamentals: reading, writing, spelling, arithmetic. Special direct teaching methods and materials are employed. After 12 years, an attempt is made to teach some manual craft sewing, knitting, wood carving, reed work, in simple forms give the children skills which enable him to hold up his head among the children who are learning more rapidly than he in literary fields."[23]

Mackey believed this teaching method could benefit all Indigenous students in the day schools and hoped the Department would support the $3 per unit cost of this "special training" for Indigenous students. Ironically, the method of teaching "backwards" students mirrored the traditional way of teaching Indigenous students to use the natural materials around them for their benefit. He also noted that the new "Auxiliary Class Certificate" taught these methods and offered more "value to a teacher of Indians than any other single course."[24] Mackey stated his willingness to take the course.

Mackey saw four advantages to using the units. First, students "would be thoroughly trained in the three 'R's,'"[25] after which "they would be mentally much healthier; their self-respect retained; their spirit unbroken by a continual sense of inferiority. This same feeling of inferiority is at the root of much actual mental illness occurring in later life."[26] He felt this would lead to the "handicapped" student's "renewed interest in school [and] would give the teacher a chance to inculcate the sensible health and living habits."[27] Second, he argued that a focus on these types of "backwards" children would benefit both the pupil and the entire community. The rest of the class would theoretically have more time to explore advanced topics once the slower pupils were removed from the learning. Third, he said that the approach would lead directly to the assimilation of the "Indians" as "it would improve the efficiency of our school materially." He argued that "increasing the school's efficiency would seem to be the apparent way to bring the end of Indian isolation a lot closer."[28] Finally, he said that putting these "backwards pupils" under the control of a male teacher would "present a much simpler disciplinary problem to a man than to a woman." These final comments indicate that Mackey "came to feel strongly about these points" of educating "handicapped students" and thought that, as a male, he could enact these plans successfully within the community.

The Department received this lengthy letter from Mr Mackey but decided not to purchase the lesson units or officially endorse this method for a variety of reasons. They argued that this teaching style would be better suited to the new two-roomed school that would be built on the reserve in the summer of 1939.[29] The Department also wanted to wait until Mackey officially received his Auxiliary Class Certificate.

During the Second World War years, the school continued to grow but was impacted by global conditions. As the new school opened in 1940, reports to the Department expressed the community's excitement for this new facility. The Curve Lake Chief and Council requested permission for the community to sponsor an official opening and the improvement of the school grounds with trees and shrubbery.[30] The community also requested that an official from the Department attend the school's official opening.[31]

In June 1940, the chief of the training division, Mr Phelan, was present at the opening of the school and congratulated all the students who had passed their entrance examinations.[32] Due to the success of the school and the number of men who had signed up for military service, the Department allowed the school to open in October rather than September.[33] This was a "satisfactory arrangement, as a number of families, especially at Mud Lake Reserve, do not arrive home from their summer work until the first of October."[34] During the war, when most of the men were away, the children played a significant role in harvesting wild rice and other fall crops. Changes were also made to Miss Long's salary, including a $3.70 tax per month for national defence and war certificates.[35]

In May of 1941, Inspector of Indian Agencies W.S. Arneil submitted a school report. The new inspector examined both the teaching and quality of Indian Agent Eastwood's work on the Mud Lake reserve. He said the attendance was good except during flu season but two families never sent their children to the school. Arneil wrote: "Definite promises were made by parents to Agent that children would attend regularly in future – their excuses for non-attendance were worthless. These interviews were well-handled by Mr. Eastwood and I feel his mingled appeal for their attendance coupled with the definite threat if not rectified will have the desired effect. School and lavatories were clean. School appears well managed."[36] In his role, Arneil had the authority to enter a parent's home and demand to talk about their children's school attendance. Moreover, threats could be made to remove students from the reserve and send them to a residential school. This report highlights the coercive power dynamics embedded within the education system on reserves. The use of threats to enforce attendance exemplified the lack of agency afforded to Indigenous parents in decisions about their children's education. The inspector's comments framed the parents' reasons for non-attendance as "worthless," dismissing any legitimate concerns they might have had, whether related to cultural differences, mistrust of the system, or practical challenges. The implied threat of sending children to residential schools occurred during the broader systemic violence of the era, where education policies were used as tools of assimilation and control.

Arneil's report also sheds light on the pervasive surveillance of Indigenous families by government officials. The ability of inspectors and agents to intrude upon private homes and compel compliance reinforced the colonial state's authority over Indigenous communities. Such practices further alienated parents from the schooling system, creating an environment where attendance was achieved through fear rather than trust or mutual agreement. This approach failed to address the root causes of absenteeism and deepened the cultural and social disconnect between the community and the imposed education system.

In the summer of 1941, Mr Mackey resigned from his role as principal, setting set off a wave of panic about securing another teacher, preferably male, in the middle of the war.[37] While the Department was still looking for a male teacher for the principal position in the fall of 1941, it did not ask the United Church if anyone was available. Instead, based on the recommendation of Indian Agent Eastwood, they promoted Miss Long to principal and hired Miss Anna Tate from nearby Bobcaygeon.[38] Although she had no teacher's certificate, she did have a senior matriculation in one subject and was the only teacher available in the entire region. The Department agreed to this arrangement based on Miss Long's ten years of experience. They also raised her pay to $95 per month, with Miss Tate earning $85.[39] No reports about the quality of the school were received in the years that Miss Long and Miss Tate operated the school. They remained the teaching duo until 1944, when a qualified teacher, Miss Shirley Hamilton, applied for the junior teaching position. The Department hired Hamilton but was never provided any documents or evidence regarding her teaching qualifications. Hamilton lasted in the school for less than a year and resigned during the summer of 1945.[40] The school continued to face enormous challenges in securing an adequate long-term teacher. Other than Miss Long, who had now been at the school for ten years, a constant rotation of teachers would force the government to change their schooling methods in the years to come.

The present-day Chief of Curve Lake First Nation, Keith Knott, was a young student during this time and remembered many of his earliest experiences with education, including Miss Long and Miss Hamilton as his first teachers. I interviewed Chief Knott in April 2024 in the former Indian day school, now a council room across from the older school building that was still an operating daycare. He attended his first year of school in 1943 at the age of six and recalled how his older siblings talked about the school before he was sent. During his childhood, Curve Lake was quite remote with only mud roads into the community and an ice road in the wintertime. The village had no electricity until the early 1950s, so his lifestyle centred around helping his family. A typical day would start with class at 9:00 followed by chores and, if he had time, some play afterward. He said, "There things you had to do, and you have to do it. No getting away from it."[41] He remembers there being two classrooms, one that went up to grade 4 and the other from grade 5 to 8. The class would always start with reading the alphabet, followed by the "three r's." Keith said, "they used to call it reading, writing, and arithmetic. They taught a little bit about history but, no Canadian history … It was all just what was happening in other countries, you speak of Europe, England, France, Iceland, you speak about every other country but our own."[42] If you didn't pay attention during these lessons, Keith mentioned that the "teacher would will remind you and a few times I got a pencil on top of the head."[43] The class would have a lunch break from 12:00 p.m. to 1:00 p.m., when he usually went home, followed by more lessons in the afternoon until 4:00 p.m., when the bell would ring and students could go home for the evening.

He reminisced about those walks home and the many different pathways students took through the village. He said, "that's when you could hear the birds singing through here, there were a lot of wild apples, and a lot of stuff you don't see anymore like Milkweed."[44] As this was the same time as the Second World War, Keith also remembers picking the milkweed in the fall so that the silk could be harvested and sent to make parachutes. While there were times the class learned about the natural environment, such as the names of the trees, "everything was in English only … you could not speak the language in the schoolyard there you would be probably strapped if you did that."[45] This was a challenge for Keith. While Anishinaabemowin was not spoken at home, he did learn it through other children and fluent community members. However, all students understood that speaking their language was forbidden at school or in the surrounding yard. Keith thought, "maybe that will fade in time, and they're almost succeeding. Because right now, how many within our community are fluent in the language? So, it's gradually going in that direction … and were more involved in their ways than our own ways. That's hard to believe, yet we call ourselves Indians."[46] It felt like for Keith that "after you left school, there's another school, you go to the school of life or school of learning, you pick up all this stuff in your lifetime."[47] Keith's reflection reveals the profound and lasting impact of the school's assimilationist policies on the erosion of language and cultural identity within the community. The punishment for speaking Anishinaabemowin created an environment where children were forced to choose between their culture and their physical safety, fostering a sense of alienation from their traditions. Over time, this contributed to the diminishing fluency in Anishinaabemowin that Keith observed, a loss that he recognized as part of a broader strategy to assimilate Indigenous Peoples into settler ways of life.

Despite the school's efforts to suppress Indigenous identity, Keith's notion of the "school of life" reveals the resilience of cultural learning beyond formal education. He acknowledged that knowledge was continually passed down through lived experiences and interactions with the community, emphasizing the importance of reclaiming and preserving these teachings. Keith's experiences highlight both the destructive legacy of colonial schooling and the enduring strength of Indigenous ways of knowing, even in the face of systemic erasure.

Before the 1947 academic school year began, a memo was sent to the day schools in the Peterborough area about the opportunity for "manual training." In partnership with the Ontario Ministry of Education, an expert in this type of education would provide opportunities for additional training within the day schools of the Peterborough area. The memo explained: "An annual course is put on in these schools and that the manual training teacher visits the school one day of each week and lays out work to be completed at his next call the following week. 60% of the instruction is in wood working; 20% of the time is taken up in instruction of sheet metal work, soldering, tinsmithing, and rope work; the remaining 20% is of miscellaneous work covering work in in leather, painting, glazing glass, and other appropriate work that be utilized by the Indians on the Reserve."[48]

Touted as a program that could help the Indigenous communities in this area, this type of "manual training" had, at this point, already been in use for over one hundred years in Ontario's residential schools. The closest residential school was Alderville, which had been developed by William Case and John Sunday in the 1830s and was called the "Industrial and Manual Training School."[49] After the Second World War, the provincial government began funding this manual training program on reserves to help increase the number of workers for the factories that continued to grow in the area (General Electric and Outboard Marine).

The cost of this additional manual training program was divided between the Department and the pupils who would be involved in the program. The logistics of this training were noted in the federal archives: "The instructor will be in charge of a small kit of wood working tools which he will leave at the school. A work bench and some tools have been purchased for the Mud Lake Indian Day School and these tools with the kit available from the manual training teacher would appear to be all the would be required in tools for the moment."[50]

The minimal costs of the program ($190 a year) centuated the fact that these opportunities were deliberately withheld from Indigenous children before 1947, despite the government's stated intentions of providing education. This low cost suggests that financial constraints were not the primary barrier to offering these programs earlier. Instead, it highlights the systemic neglect and lack of prioritization of Indigenous education, reinforcing how government policies were more focused on assimilation and control rather than ensuring equitable access to quality schooling. Furthermore, Eastwood explained to the government that in "Mud Lake [School] there is a large basement room originally intended for this work." While this type of "manual training" was not implemented in Curve Lake until 1947, it had been a government priority for nearly a decade, as an appropriate training room had been included when the school was built in 1939.[51]

OFF-RESERVE SCHOOLING

While students were forced to attend the day school on reserve if they lived within and were members of Curve Lake First Nation, some students received slightly different schooling as a result of the Indian Act and pressure from their Indigenous parents to attend high school. Some Indigenous students obtained education off reserve during the middle of the twentieth century; in doing so, this chapter demonstrates both the inadequacies of the Indian day school system and the control exerted by the federal and provincial governments. Even though students were outside of day school, the Department of Indian Affairs still controlled nearly every aspect of the education they received. It's important to highlight these stories as they illustrate students' experiences as they were slowly integrated into the public school system throughout the interwar period. This process unfolded through piecemeal agreements with parents who would pay for most of the costs relating to sending their child to a White school and were permitted by the government in rare instances when a student had progressed through the grades of an Indian day school.

By the end of the 1930s, several students from the Mud Lake reserve had been permitted to attend schools outside of the day school on reserve. The same policies of systemic racism that prevented qualified and educated teachers from teaching at Indian Day Schools on reserve also forced students who wanted a better or additional education into nearby White towns and communities. This removal of students from their reserves and into White and private boarding schools represents another form of assimilation into the dominant English-speaking society. Students who no longer lived on the reserve could not access the Indigenous languages that were still being spoken by Elders.

One student, Murray Whetung, attended the Peterborough Collegiate Institute at a cost of $17 per month, which included room and board and which the Department of Indian Affairs agreed to pay.[52] However, this payment would lead to questions concerning the costs and liabilities of sending students to nearby towns. A report submitted to the Department of Indian Affairs stated that, in a special meeting, "the township of Smith (nearby) do not assume liability for high school costs of pupils from Curve Lake Indian Reserve."[53] The tuition grants required to send graduates of the Indian day school elementary system to local high schools were, therefore, typically paid for by the community or by their families. This arrangement placed a significant financial burden on families and communities, limiting access to higher education for many Indigenous students. While the Department occasionally covered some of the costs, as in Murray Whetung's case, these instances were exceptions rather than the norm. Tuition grants were inconsistently provided and were often contingent on lengthy approvals, creating barriers for families already facing systemic inequities. To earn a grant that would cover only some of the cost, the parents of each student would have to apply for permission from the government, which would then make a decision dependent on additional funding, local school board politics, and whether they believed the student had the potential to succeed in other further educational grades. The reluctance of nearby municipalities, like the township of Smith, to assume responsibility for Indigenous students further highlighted the segregationist attitudes of the time, effectively excluding Indigenous youth from equitable participation in public education systems.

The lack of a consistent policy on tuition grants reflected the federal government's systemic neglect, which failed to provide a clear pathway for Indigenous students to continue their education beyond elementary school. This gap left families to navigate financial hardships or forgo further education altogether, perpetuating cycles of limited opportunity. For many communities, the question of who would pay for tuition became a source of frustration and contention, revealing the broader inequities within Canada's education system and its treatment of Indigenous learners.

Chief Daniel Whetung was notified of a policy change regarding the transfer of Indigenous students into White schools through a letter sent by the Department of Indian Affairs. This communication method was common during this period: the local school board would send private meeting minutes and decisions regarding Indigenous pupils to the federal government in Ottawa, which then relayed that information to the Chief and Council on reserve. This slow and cumbersome method of communication would cause difficulties and delays in transmitting crucial information to the community regarding their children's education. In response to the policy change, Chief Daniel Whetung wrote the Department on 11 May 1939: "I am writing to you as we know you better and you know us better than anyone in your department! We are unable to pay *Murray Whetung's High School* [emphasis in original] fee which are very high, $140.00 for this year. We paid last year $68.00 the Smith township paid the balance. But this year the township refuses to pay any of the costs; this winter was a hard long winter for us. And we find ourselves unable to pay this amount. Murray has worked hard in school, never missed a day and will graduate this year."[54]

As there would be no plan regarding the tuition payments of Indigenous children until changes were made to the Indian Act in the 1950s, Indigenous Peoples had no option but to petition the government to allow their children to further their education outside of the reserve. Chief Whetung's letter also requested that the official policy of the Smith township be forwarded to the community, as the federal government failed to explain the township's decision to no longer pay for Indigenous students' tuition. The following week, Superintendent of Welfare and Training R.A. Hoey wrote: "As you are aware the Department is allowing a grant of $200.00 a year toward the cost of the education of Murray Whetung. This is as much as we allow in any individual case. Under these circumstances it is felt that you should be sufficiently interested in your son's education to pay the cost of the tuition fees."[55]

The federal government's reluctance to provide the full cost of education beyond the day school on reserve continued throughout the Second World War period (1939–45). This reluctance was often justified by citing financial constraints imposed by the war effort, even though funding for other areas of public education in Canada was not similarly restricted. Indigenous families and communities were left to shoulder the financial burden of high school tuition, room, and board (as there were none in Curve Lake), which further limited opportunities for Indigenous students to pursue secondary education. In June 1942, parents from the Mud Lake reserve requested that their sixteen-year-old son, Raymond Taylor, be able to attend a Collegiate Institute in a nearby town, such as Peterborough, Lakefield, or Norwood. The student's father was in active service with the Prince of Wales Rangers in Niagara, Ontario, and was training to be deployed overseas.[56] His wife, Mrs Allan Taylor, wrote to the Department about her son: "You understand of course he has taken a general course in our school here in the village these last two years (41–42) he passed his entrance exams when he was 13 years of age and just kept on in our school. He is real anxious to continue we are also if it is at all possible. We were told other Indian children had received a grant from the Department to help out their expenses, so we thought if that was possible we would manage to pay the balance. I do not know exactly what it will be … it might be around $400.00."[57] The letter exemplifies the challenges Indigenous families faced in securing educational opportunities for their children. Mrs Taylor's willingness to cover part of the cost reflects the sacrifices families were prepared to make to ensure their children could access higher education. However, the dependency on departmental grants, which were inconsistently awarded, left families in a precarious position. The war effort added another layer of complexity as fathers, like Mr Taylor, served overseas while their families at home struggled to navigate the bureaucratic hurdles of securing funding for education. Despite the family's clear commitment to their son's education, the government's reluctance to fully support such requests highlighted its broader failure to invest meaningfully in the future of Indigenous youth. This neglect not only limited individual opportunities but also perpetuated systemic inequities within Canadian society.

The government agreed to pay $200 towards the cost of vocational school for the student.[58] After agreeing to pay for the education of this student, the Department began clarifying its position on this topic for other interested parents. R.A. Hoey wrote to one parent about the tuition grants, stating that there was "a very small amount for this purpose. The policy of the Department at the present time, however, is to confide these grants almost wholly to pupils who are proceeding with vocational or semi-vocational courses."[59] Only students who planned to pursue education in one of the manufacturing trades were able to receive additional support in furthering their studies.

Although Raymond Taylor was able to attend the Peterborough Collegiate and Vocational School, the federal government failed to inform the Peterborough Board of Education of this agreement. On 29 October 1942, the board stated: "We are not certain whether the costs of the tuition of this pupil should be charged to the County of Peterborough on our regular claim against them or whether costs should be paid by the pupil himself or by your department."[60] Clarity was also requested regarding another student who did not appear on any of the records of the federal Department of Indian Affairs.[61] In this case, the miscommunication between the parents, federal government, and provincial educational boards did not prove detrimental to the student.

The students graduating from the Curve Lake Indian Day School faced a further logistical and financial issue: they would be required to reside in Peterborough as the "Mud Lake Indian Reserve is 24 miles from Peterborough and the roads are not always open in the wintertime and regular attendance would be impossible."[62] The distance between the reserve and the closest public secondary school significantly impeded the older Indigenous students' ability to access higher levels of education.

It would be another five years before Curve Lake requested additional tuition grants to help students who had graduated from the day school attend the nearby high school in Peterborough. A pattern also emerged around the justification that the Indian agent provided to the Department when recommending that a student proceed to a higher level of education. The most crucial determinant was if the parents of the students could afford to pay the education costs themselves. The second determinant was whether the parents were involved in the military. These points were typically discussed when weighing the possibility of a student from the reserve attending a provincially operated elementary or secondary school.

Mable Taylor was one such student whose education was determined by the funding her parents could provide. In 1946, Taylor attended the Peterborough Collegiate and Vocational School without any assistance from the Department of Indian Affairs as her father was on active duty and, therefore, capable of paying the entire tuition.[63] Once he was discharged, he could not pay the costs of her tuition, and she was at risk of not furthering her education in a junior secretarial course. Indian Agent Eastwood stated that Taylor's father would "look after the cost of her boarding in Peterborough and arrangements can be made to have her reside at any older sisters' who works and resides in Peterborough."[64] In the same letter, Eastwood recommended that another student, Eric McCue, be granted "$200.00 and his father could possibly make up the balance of his costs or the boy could after school hours and help put himself through school."[65] Both of these students were granted tuition expenditures but were still required to pay for their transportation and boarding costs in the city.[66] Such expenses prevented numerous students from furthering their education; however, the provincial government was covering all education costs for White students.

Students tended to succeed when provided with an opportunity for additional schooling outside of the reserve. In the case of Eric McCue, the principal of the Peterborough Collegiate and Vocational School reported that he had been doing "very well" and had obtained an average grade of 70 per cent, which allowed him to proceed into grade 11.[67] The principal also noted that McCue had achieved first-class honours in English, geography, and physical education and health, so he warranted another tuition grant.

By the end of the 1940s, the Department of Indian Affairs had lost count of the Indigenous students who were attending a private or public school. In January 1949, the Department requested that Indian Agent Eastwood "ascertain the number of Indian children who are attending

Provincial or Private Schools."[68] It also requested a list of students who were not receiving tuition grants. In total twenty-four students from the Rice Lake Agency were not attending schools on reserve.[69] However, this list failed to include the names of ten of the students and did not indicate which reserve the Indigenous students were from. Vincent Eastwood admitted, "The last two entries on this list are not complete as I have not been as yet advised where the children were sent after the closing of the Chapleau Residential School and I do not know what grade they are in."[70] This statement indicates that the Indian agent's role on reserve was to act as an intermediary between the federal government and the community; they did not have the power to track students who attended institutions off reserve and, therefore, outside of the Indian agent's purview.

Helen Raptis and colleagues highlight another issue endemic to Indigenous education during this postwar period. They demonstrate that the government's integration of Indigenous students into White public school were unevenly implemented and thus caused a lot of confusion. Some day schools, such as the Port Essington Indian Day School, were quick to integrate into White public schools. Raptis argues that although postwar "human rights concerns shaped the integration discourse at the federal level, there is no evidence to suggest that such matters played a major role in developments at Port Essington."[71] However, Eve Chapple and Raptis demonstrate that the Telegraph Creek Public School began accepting Indigenous Tahltan children into provincial schools as early as 1906 because they lived too far from day schools.[72] These authors conclude: "The emphasis on the failings of federal policy has glossed over the role of provincial policy makers whose actions (or inactions) also contributed to an education system that, in the postwar era, never fully integrated Indigenous children into the public schools nor safeguarded them from the abuses the segregated system itself perpetuated."[73]

This historical research focuses on the civil servants who implemented policy in specific areas, such as at the Port Essington Indian Day School, observing that "they sometimes blurred the boundaries of policies and legislation that officially circumscribed students' lives in order to enhance youngsters' access to educational opportunities."[74] In the case of Curve Lake students who wanted to attend public schools, these boundaries were completely arbitrary and solely dependent on whether their parents could contribute financially to their education. Certain students who had the necessary funding were able to blur the boundaries of the segregated school system and attend nearby public schools without any specific changes to the Indian Act.

After the war, it became even more challenging to secure the services of a teacher due to the rising salary of teachers in public schools. In a letter to Indian Agent Eastwood, L.W. Copp, the principal of the Peterborough Normal School, clearly explained the reality for graduating teachers. One school in east Peterborough was short five teachers, so the province was setting minimum salaries at $1,200 to $1,600 a year.[75] Many of Copp's students were graduating with positions already secured, so the maximum $1,000 a year offered by the Department of Indian Affairs was not appealing. The Department was unwilling to pay more than $1,200 for a principal and, therefore, could not hire anyone for this position. Due to their wartime service, many veterans had been offered higher-paying jobs in local public schools, which diminished the number of applicants available for the lower-paying Indian day schools. As a result of this difficulty, Miss Hamilton withdrew her resignation; she would continue to teach at the Curve Lake Indian Day School until 1947, when she was married.[76]

After the war years, the task of securing teachers for the Curve Lake Indian Day School became the responsibility of the local school inspector rather than the church. Indian Agent Eastwood requested that both the principal of the normal school and the inspector of public schools find a suitable teacher. Since Miss Long was still the principal and made $110 a month after fifteen years of service, it was difficult to find a male teacher. Eastwood wrote: "In my opinion, it would be beneficial to have a male teacher on the staff of this school and this vacancy could be filled by a male teacher, but certain difficulties present themselves in that he could not be paid more than Miss Long and it is questionable that he would accept less."[77]

It was, therefore, nearly impossible to attract a male teacher as traditionally they would have served in the senior position while the female served as the "junior assistant." As a result, the Department, which was now under the direction of Superintendent of Welfare and Training Bernard F. Neary, agreed to raise the salary to $126 per month for a teacher with a first-class teacher's certificate.[78] With this more competitive rate, Indian Agent Eastwood secured an interested graduate from the Peterborough Normal School who was just completing her first-class teacher's certificate.

There was a significant systemic issue with hiring graduating teachers directly into day schools on reserves across the province. To earn a first-class certificate, the teacher was required to teach for a year after graduation in a provincial public school that received a grant from the Ontario government. As the federal government funded the day school system through grants, no graduating first-class teachers could get their required experience in a day school. Eastwood confirmed this problem with the Ontario Department of Education, which explained that the "Indian Day School is not regarded as the necessary qualifying experience."[79] As a result of this policy, the federal government could not hire graduating first-class teachers into the Indian day school system, as they would be ineligible to receive their certificate without first obtaining the required provincial teaching experience. Therefore, a first-class teacher who was interested in teaching at the day school and was one of the strongest students from the Peterborough Normal School was unable to take the position "in view of the existing regulations of the province."[80] This form of systemic racism created a situation where only uneducated and unqualified teachers were eligible to teach within the Indian day school system on reserve. Eastwood argued that the possibility of hiring any graduating teacher from the normal school was "very remote," as even lower certificates now required experience in a provincially funded school.[81] As a result, the Curve Lake school could not find a suitable teacher. Further, Miss Long could not teach seventy-six students in two separate classrooms by herself, so the school was forced to close from Easter through the summer of 1947.

Having run out of other options, the Department finally approved one of Chief Whetung's earlier recommendations. Indian Agent Eastwood wrote to the Department in the summer of 1947 to ask permission to "advertise locally for a teacher."[82] After decades of vetoing Chief Whetung's proposal, the Department finally agreed to pay a meagre $6.30 to advertise the position in the *Peterborough Examiner*. These efforts may have come too late, as it is unclear whether the school opened in 1948;

no new teaching hires records could be located for this year. The following year, the Department of Indian Affairs aggressively advertised the teaching position and offered a much higher salary. The Department also expanded its search area, posting an advertisement in the *Toronto Globe and Mail* in hopes of hiring a more experienced teacher.[83]

Securing a teacher during the first wave of the postwar baby boom was nearly impossible. The principal of the Peterborough Normal School, L.W. Copp, remarked, "Even our 'failure' students have been engaged for the past six weeks, and Boards coming to the school have not been able to secure even poor teachers."[84] The province-wide scarcity of teachers was so extreme that out of Copp's four hundred teacher candidates, everyone had secured a job before the summer break began.[85] He also said that the public inspectors were competing for any available teachers, and although he had a few volunteers who might be interested in the Curve Lake position, "under no circumstance will any of them do."[86] It was, therefore, impossible to secure a qualified teacher willing to take over the school, which was experiencing a surge in enrolment due to the reserve's own postwar baby boom. The search continued, and over the next few months, at least three different applications were submitted in response to the Department of Indian Affairs' advertisement.[87] The archival file for these documents ends with two letters from the Department inquiring whether Indian Agent Eastwood had "any success in securing a teacher for the vacant room at the Mud Lake School?"[88] The first letter was written by Superintendent of Welfare and Training Bernard F. Neary, and Philip Phelan, chief of the education division, wrote the follow-up letter.[89] As the Department of Indian Affairs has not released any records after 1951, the final part of this chapter relies on secondary sources, other forms of archival research, newspapers, and photographs to demonstrate the ongoing legacy of day schools within the community.

EDUCATION WITHIN BURLEIGH FALLS

Students who fell between racial identities had a markedly different educational experience, as evidenced by the experiences of a nearby Indigenous community. The swirling geological cascade of the Michi Saagiig

Territory, near Burleigh Falls, attracted Curve Lake members who were disconnected from their community. They came to the region to collect berries and harvest fish, including pickerel, bass, and muskellunge. Burleigh Falls is approximately thirty kilometres northeast of Curve Lake First Nation and is connected to the community through a series of waterways that include Lower and Upper Buckhorn Lake. This water route was also used to visit the petroglyphs and other gathering sites along the river. before the introduction of a dam at Burleigh Falls in the late 1800s, a small Indigenous community lived off the abundance of wild rice and fish.[90] The dam, which was not complete until 1910, disrupted traditional hunting and fishing activities but sparked an emerging cottage industry in guiding and logging. This community was further disrupted in 1912 when the Burleigh Falls dam was expanded to accommodate more industrial and tourist boats, leading to significant flooding and forcing the community to relocate. This Indigenous community grew to include Non-Status Indians and other members from nearby communities, such as Alderville First Nation, who had married into families living in the region.

During the interwar period (1919–39), this group of Indigenous Peoples were reported to be living on "desolate, barren and rocky" land near Burley (Burleigh) Falls.[91] A "concerned citizen" reported that among the group of alleged "Indians" were twenty-seven children who were not receiving an education and were unable to read and write. The citizen wrote to the Department to request assistance for the children, as she felt their parents were unconcerned with their education. The Department of Indian Affairs responded that they had investigated this group of "so-called Indians" on multiple occasions but determined only one of the individuals was "a bona fide Indian" of the Mud Lake Indian Band.[92] R.A. Hoey also noted: "It would appear that this group are really half-breed citizens, probably with a certain amount of Indian blood. As half-breeds, however, they are not the responsibility of the Dominion Government. They are citizens in a very absolute sense and as such are the responsibility of the Provincial Government insofar as their education and general welfare is concerned."[93]

The federal government absolved itself of its responsibility for the education and welfare of these people as they did not meet the government's rigid definition of "Indian." Moreover, as they were considered "half-breeds" whose families had married into "white" heritage, the government did not have an obligation to them under the Indian Act. This response did not satisfy Edith Maclaren, who informed the Department that multiple people living near Burleigh Falls had Indigenous blood. This concern was escalated in February 1941 to Indian Agent Eastwood to confirm the status of one of the "pure-blood Indians." R.A. Hoey also noted his issues with the provincial Department of Education: "I personally find it somewhat difficult to understand why the educational needs of this particular group has not been brought to the attention of the Provincial authorities. One would think that the people in the surrounding district would be sufficiently interested in these children to present their claims to the Department of Education, Toronto."[94]

Eastwood responded with a three-page typewritten letter that explained the complex legal issues that involved this group of Indigenous Peoples. He noted that one of the men was an "illegitimate son" of an Indigenous person and, since he was listed in the voter registry in the nearby town of Peterborough, he was "definitely not the responsibility of this Department."[95] This appeared correct; a "pure-blooded Indian" would not have been on a voter registry, as Indigenous Peoples were not allowed to vote in 1941. Eastwood also described the confusing situation whereby these people had "no legal status as Indians" but leased property on land belonging to both the federal and provincial governments. The question of who had the authority to provide education for this group was further complicated by the nearby township of Harvey, which also declined to take responsibility for these students. As result, for "a number of years" the children who lived in this area were without educational services and "nothing [was] being done" to help them. One of the only provincial schools was approximately three miles away, but it prevented children from this community from attending as they did not want to cover the transportation costs.[96] In Eastwood's perspective, "It would appear … that the whole set-up is to 'oust' these people and have somebody else look after this."[97] He also explained that the RCMP had been called to remove these people from government land but was met with opposition, as public opinion supported this group's intention to remain near Burleigh Falls.

The federal government and provincial authorities' dispute over the Indian Act's definition of Indigenous students began in the early 1930s and continued into the 1940s. Eastwood was adamant: "The provincial authorities have been well aware of the situation at Burleigh Falls for ten years or more but it would appear that the people in the surrounding district are more interested in getting these people out of the Township than looking after their interest."[98] Eastwood also commented that the main justification for providing few educational services was that "there are no taxes to support a school"; therefore, the provincial government was not obligated to provide these services. Instead, Eastwood recommended that correspondence courses for the high school students be sent to the community and that a nearby cottage be rented one day a week so students could have "study time."[99]

The federal government would only support the people who lived on the reserve and whose children attended the day school already in operation. As a result, the group of Indigenous Peoples who lived near Burleigh Falls but were not considered to be Curve Lake reserve members had few educational options. Any alternative suggestions resulted in a disagreement between the provincial and federal governments over who would pay for this type of schooling, and this directly impacted the quality of education these children received. In his final letter to Edith Maclaren, R.A. Hoey confirmed the racial status of the Burleigh Falls students. He wrote: "It is my earnest hope that some action will be taken by the provincial authorities to provide educational facilities for this nomadic group of children. You will, I feel sure, appreciate the fact that they are not Indians as defined by the Indian Act and consequently not the responsibility of this Department."[100] The welfare of the students and the quality of education they received was an afterthought, as clearly, the Department's priority was to determine who was responsible for paying for these students.

During the late 1970s, the Kawartha Branch of the Ontario Métis and Non-Status Indian Association published the first official history of this community. In this publication, authors Fay Tilden and Kathy Woodcock compile personal photographs, interviews, and recollections to provide some more insight into the Indigenous students' educational experience in this region. While the authors did not access the RG10 files for their research, they nonetheless reiterate what is evidenced in the archives: "Formal education at Burleigh Falls was slow in starting as the community was never recognized by government officials."[101] The federal, provincial, and municipal governments classified the residents as "squatters" who, therefore, did not pay the necessary taxes to send their children to school. After numerous complaints, such as those of Edith Maclaren, some of the residents were invited to the Provincial Department of Education in Toronto to petition for a new school in the region. As a result of this meeting, in 1941, the federal government, under the direction of R.A. Hoey, provided a room for classes that would be provided by a missionary. Tilden and Woodcock's historical overview describes the school and how it functioned. The initial teacher at this temporary school was Miss McClaren, a missionary adept at teaching all necessary academic subjects. For the first year, classes took place in a small lean-to near the shore. Subsequently, a small log building was constructed on the shore of Perry's Creek, where Miss McClaren also resided. Occasionally, a few younger students from Burleigh Falls would stay with her, assisting in keeping the school clean, stacking wood, and ensuring fires were ready for the next morning. A community member regarded Miss McClaren as a good person who effectively taught their children reading, writing, and arithmetic.[102]

In addition to not being paid, Miss McClaren also did not have the qualifications to be a teacher. Instead, for a number of years, she offered rudimentary classes and helped students complete correspondence courses that could be obtained through the provincial government. This agreement was in place until 1946–47, when the Ontario Department of Education finally built a school for the students of this community.

Over the next eighteen years, the school provided local education and "a centre for the community." Tilden and Woodcock explain that the community used the building as a dance and bingo hall and for important events that brought everyone together. One resident told the authors, "The learning atmosphere was much better than most of the larger schools today. The children knew each other, the teacher knew the parents and therefore the teachers took a better interest in the pupils."[103] During this period, it appeared that the school was an added benefit to the Burleigh Falls community and reflected their desire for a local education system.

During the 1960s, the provincial government decided, without the consent of community members, to integrate several small rural schools. The county school board believed that "an attempt to integrate the white and Indian children … would benefit everyone involved" and wanted to push forward with integration.[104] In 1964, the government decided to bus the students eighteen miles each way to a school in Apsley, Ontario. As a result, the community rallied together to protest this decision. Some members of the community argued that "the whole issue has been conducted in a very undemocratic way. When an important decision such as this one was made, we should have been consulted about it … If we can't fight for what's right or get the chance to express our opinion on matters that concern us, then we have no right to call ourselves citizens. We want to co-operate, but we have not been given the chance."[105]

As a result of this protest, the school board allowed the Burleigh Falls school to stay open another four years, but, in 1968, the board permanently closed the school, again without parental consent. Tilden and Woodcock argue that this protest was the community's first act of resistance and that it would spark further battles between the government and this group of Indigenous Peoples.

Over the next two decades, the community continued to face new challenges to their livelihoods. In the 1970s, the Kawartha Métis and Non-Status Indian Association (KMNSIA) was created; it provided the funding for Tilden and Woodcock's history book but was also intended to "relieve poverty and meet the social needs of the members."[106] This organization existed for over a decade in the community and provided an organized voice with which to speak to the provincial and federal governments. However, as a result of internal politics and a failed election, the organization became "inactive" in 1982 and closed their community hall and store.[107] By 1985, a new and permanent organization called the Kawartha Nishnawbe was established to help the "people of the Kawartha Métis who are preparing to apply for Indian Band status."[108] Following Bill C-31, *An Act to Amend the Indian Act*, a number of Non-Status Indians from Burleigh Falls who had unjustly lost their status organized to work together for three objectives: "A.) Achieve band status, B.) gain recognition of its land claims, C.) Establish a reserve at Burleigh Falls."[109] These goals, which were articulated almost sixty years after the founding of the community school in Burleigh Falls, represented decades of government inaction regarding Indigenous Peoples who were not considered "Indians" under the racist and gendered Indian Act.

In the late 1980s, the community at Burleigh Falls began its largest battle for status recognition, and Curve Lake First Nation supported their efforts. The first community members had broken away from Curve Lake over sixty years ago, and the kinship between the groups had diminished over the years. Marlene Brant Castellano, an Indigenous professor at Trent University, explains, "Ties of blood and friendship with Curve Lake have been weakened by the passage of time and the frequency of Indian-white marriages at Burleigh Falls."[110] Yet, in 1987, Curve Lake First Nation officially recognized the Kawartha Nishnawbe as their descendants. In a Chief and Council meeting, they resolved:

> And whereas, many members of the Kawartha Anishnabe are descendants of members of the Curve Lake Band and some of whom are entitled to be registered as members of the Curve Lake Band,
>
> And whereas, the Curve Lake Band has insufficient lands and resources to welcome back these people,
>
> And whereas, this council supports the desire for self-government of the Kawartha Anninsnabe Band for recognition of their ownership of the lands at Burleigh Falls.[111]

Curve Lake clarified that these people were indeed their descendants but stated that they lacked the resources to support them within the reserve, so they were in support of self-government at Burleigh Falls. This demonstrates that, despite the passage of time, the communities of Curve Lake First Nation and Burleigh Falls were still connected.

During the postwar period, Curve Lake First Nation would undergo significant changes to its governance, education, and finances as it adapted to the larger changes occurring elsewhere in the country. By the early 1950s, the day school had been operating on this reserve for over fifty years. It had undergone significant changes as the community members continued their fight for self-governance. The community of

Curve Lake constantly fought for more control over their education during this period and the disputes in this chapter were mostly between teachers' pedagogy and the government's approach to schooling. Earlier patterns of government underfunding and paternalism, coupled with a renewed focus on manual training education to produce capable workers, were the hallmarks of the Indian day school system between 1930 and 1951. These challenges were exacerbated for Indigenous students who were not defined as "Indians" under the Indian Act, especially at Burleigh Falls. The government was so focused on an educational system that would produce capable, assimilated workers that it would not support even the minor cost required to provide music instruction. Rather, the government's educational philosophy was one of social efficiency designed to quickly remove any Indigenous characteristics in favour of creating an assimilated working-class society. These changes forced Indigenous parents to look elsewhere for a better quality of education off the reserve – one that would hopefully provide their children with more and better opportunities.

CHAPTER 7

Experiencing Indian Day School: Education and Integration

On 29 June 1954, Curve Lake First Nation elected Elsie Knott, the first female Chief of a Band Council in Canada. This was only two years after Canada had changed the Indian Act to permit "Indian women to hold office in tribal affairs."[1] As a thirty-two-year-old mother of three, Knott's perspective regarding her community and the need for education played a significant role in the school on reserve. By the 1950s, the population of the community had risen to 445 people, 217 of whom were eligible to vote for Chief and Council but still did not have the right to vote in the provincial or federal elections. More than half of those 445 individuals were children who, when living on reserve, were still forced to attend the day school. According to Cora Voyageur, who chronicles Chief Knott in her book *Firekeepers of the Twenty-First Century: First Nations Women Chiefs*, "her tenure lasted for sixteen years, from 1952 to 1962 and then from 1970 to 1976. In the 1976 election, she was defeated by only twelve votes."[2] This book provides a valuable window into her experiences as a student of the day school and a community leader on reserve.

Chief Elsie Knott's experience in the day school on reserve was marked by difficulty. Because of a childhood illness, Knott did not attend school until the age of nine. When she arrived at school, she found that her language had been banned, and the names of students who were "'caught talking Indian' … were listed on the blackboard with big Xs beside them."[3] Her experience in the day school was isolating. Moreover, she was not expected to further her education as a woman. She remembered that "there was no mention of high school, we stopped at grade eight."[4] Her experience in the school was marked by a curriculum that did not value her identity as a person; this inspired her to seek new options once elected.

Knott decided to run for the Chief position at the age of thirty-two, which was a result of several issues that impacted her three children. For example, "she did not agree that the government should have total control over Indian people. She believed that the community should have more autonomy and control. She also wanted reserve children to be successful in school, believing education would help them out."[5] In the late 1950s, Knott began driving a group of five Curve Lake students to the Lakefield High School so they could extend their education beyond grade 8. She took this on after learning that some students had been forgotten about after school and were forced to walk home – fifteen miles away. Soon thereafter, when other students sought to attend the school, Knott applied for a bank loan for a larger vehicle. Unfortunately, the bank would not lend her the money, so "she convinced the Indian agent to cosign for two hundred dollars and bought an old hearse, converting it to school bus by placing bench seats on the floor."[6] Until 1993 – even during her tenure as Chief – she drove the school bus from Curve Lake to Lakefield High School. She created the Knott Bus Company, which expanded during this period to two twenty-eight-passenger school buses so that all interested students could attend high school.

Knott was concerned about the impacts of integration and realized that students were not always accepted in the nearby town. In an interview in 1995 with Cora Voyageur, Knott recalled "that the town children taunted the reserve children, calling them names and throwing rocks at the school bus."[7] As a result of Chief Knott's efforts, Indigenous students were now able to receive a full K–12 education, despite the nearby White communities not always accepting them. Chief Knott also continued to promote the community's culture and language through Ojibwa instruction classes for children and, in the evenings, for older community members.[8]

Figure 7.1
Indigenous students from Curve Lake First Nation board a school bus outside Lakefield District High School, mid-twentieth century. Elsie Knott, owner-operator of the school bus, collects her passengers at the Lakefield District High School for the drive back home to the Mud Lake Indian Reserve, September 1960.

A student named Valorie (Val) Whetung was born in 1948 and was one of five siblings who attended the day school in Curve Lake. Her schooling began when she was eight years old in 1956. On her first day, she was "terrified. I was a wimp. I was very terrified."[9] From her first class experience, she realized the quality of education was dismal. Val said, "We had this teacher in grade one, named Mrs. Bongarde … that's how I knew that we didn't get good teachers, because all she wanted to do was save the savages. And so, she spent most of the day telling us about heaven and hell."[10] This persisted throughout the first and second grades, and while the teacher taught Val how "to read and write" religious instruction was a key tenet of the schooling experience and required participation for the teacher to be in a good mood. The day would start with the Lord's

Prayer, and Val remembers the teacher "being all excited and cheery when we'd sing. So, she taught us all these hymns to sing and then she gets everybody to stand up, and we sing 'when we all get to heaven.' And she would get so emotional when all the little savage voices were praising the Lord. And she would be visibly moved."[11]

One moment from grade 1 that has stayed with Val was an interaction she had with Mrs Bongarde near the end of the school year. Val asked a question about heaven, a topic that had been the focus of much of her education. Val told me it was "assumed that the whole goal of living was to get into heaven. And so, I summoned up the courage. I remember specifically waiting until everyone was gone. And then I went up and I asked her if dogs go to heaven? And she just laughed at me and said, 'good heavens no child!' That's not the place for dogs."[12] This was devastating for Val as she loved animals and wanted them to come with her to the afterlife. Val said, "this is when I lost religion. I had no interest whatsoever in going to heaven. She made it very clear to me that was the most ridiculous thing anybody had ever asked her."[13] The rest of the class's content would focus on teaching students how to read through this religious lens. There were times they got to read books like *Dick and Jane*, but Val never saw herself in the curriculum. She said, "There was no question that we didn't live in those little dresses."[14] When large cities such as Toronto were talked about or shown in pictures, these places were completely foreign to her and her classmates.

Val's other memories of the school in this period are centred around the strict nature and punishments of the teachers. She explained, "We were like little robot kids. We would never step out of line. And they had straps. They all had straps."[15] Physical punishment through straps was common; however, Val also recalled other forms of punishment. On one occasion, after coming in after recess, Mrs Bongarde confronted a student at her desk. Val said, "she grabbed her two little skinny arms, and just banged them on the desk over and over again … and I can remember feeling so bad as I grew up in a home that was kind and wasn't violent. To see someone do that to a little kid was awful. Like it was horrible. How an adult could take those little tiny arms and beat them on the desk was unthinkable. I still can hear her screaming and seeing that."[16] On another occasion, she remembers her younger cousin being grabbed out of her seat and dragged up to the front, put over the teacher's knee, and spanked. "It was traumatic … and we all feared the violence."[17] These memories have stayed with Val all of her life, and reflecting back on the experiences she said, "You got to wonder, I couldn't think of anything that a kid could do that would warrant that level of violence."[18] Upon reflecting on these experiences in her kitchen one afternoon in April 2024, Val also mentioned how these fears manifested within her life. She said:

> I had terrible stomach problems. Like I just couldn't eat, and I would just double over, and I was really scrawny. My mother was a nurse, so she took me to the doctor to see if they could figure out why I was always lying somewhere curled up, crying with a stomach ache. They put me in the hospital and did all these kinds of tests. And I can remember my mom was really worried, but everything came back, and I was normal. I know from all my experiences in education that it was terror. I was paralyzed with anxiety and fear that spilled over into every day through my gut.[19]

These physical symptoms would continue to impact Val's quality of life long after she left the Curve Lake Indian Day School.

During Val's time at the day school, between 1956 and 1961, she relied on a network of friends to keep her going. One of her good friends, who she is still friends with today, named Florence, helped her get through the first grade. She said, "I certainly wasn't the smartest kid. The kid who sat behind me was way smarter than me because she would tell us what to do. And I wouldn't have a clue what we were supposed to do. I remember turning around and seeing what Florence was doing and then I'd do what Florence did. So, I only made it out of grade one because Florence was behind me. I would still be in grade one without her, and I am so thankful for her being there."[20] The reliance on friends was an essential method for students to manage the pressures of this different schooling system.

Val stayed in the day school until she was in fifth grade and then was sent to Lakefield for further schooling. She remembers that "she was the youngest of the first group and was the first generation that went on the school bus."[21] She loved the bus ride as her cousins and friends would spend the time singing songs and becoming closer friends. However, upon arriving in Lakefield at the newly created Ridpath Public School, it was a difficult experience. She said, "it was really a hit, to go from our school here, where we're with peers who are all the same age as kids in our grade, and then go to Lakefield where we were two years older than all the kids in our grade five class."[22] While being much older than other students and one of the first groups to be integrated into a White public school, other issues arose. Val explained that she "remembered menstruating and it's such a nightmare anyway. But it was a nightmare in that situation ... it was very awful."[23] She also dealt with a handful of bullies who she named the "bad boys" that would cause issues for her, including on one occasion when a snowball hit her in the back of the head.

Val managed to stay close with a group of Curve Lake students, who helped her eventual journey through the remaining grades at Ridpath, high school in Lakefield, and postsecondary degrees from Peterborough Teachers College and Trent University. However, her experiences in school continued to impact her long after she left. She told me, "I feel nauseous every time I go to school. So teaching was really hard. Or even going for my kids. Because you would get to the door, and you feel nauseous. You have to tell yourself, it's okay. You can go through the door, nothing bad is going to happen."[24] This was something Val kept hidden from the students in her class and later her own children when raising them.

As Val Whetung left the school in 1961, her cousin, Lorenzo Whetung, began grade 1. By the early 1960s, the day school in Curve Lake only went to the fifth grade; then students were transferred to Ridpath Public School for the rest of their elementary education. I interviewed Lorenzo Whetung during a walk at Kinoomaagewaabkong, or what he translated as "rocks that teach." When we began the walk, we looked for some petroglyphs that are outside of the building where the largest collection of these petroglyphs in Canada resides. The first thing he said was, "If I had this teaching (gesturing to the rocks) instead of getting *Dick and Jane*, I probably wouldn't be in the mess I'm in today. I don't know whether I'm Indian or white?"[25] Lorenzo explained, "I still wrestle with that because I prospered in the way of the white man."[26] He was able to graduate from school and attend postsecondary education, where he earned both an undergraduate degree and a teaching certificate. He had a successful career as a teacher in Curve Lake and outside his community, but he feels Western culture heavily influenced this teaching. Lorenzo was born in 1956 and was the middle child in a family of thirteen kids. His dad, Murray Whetung, had also attended the Day School in Curve Lake, and so would all his children. He remembers that his dad and other community members would constantly petition for a better quality of education on the reserve, but his experiences never gave him an opportunity to understand his Indigenous heritage.

Lorenzo also remembered the first day of his school and the early curriculum taught within the class. He told me, "I remember my first day. Kids were crying and screaming. Mothers were sniffling and leaving their kids there … I couldn't understand why they were crying. I don't think I ever saw any of my family cry before that."[27] Each class would start with the Lord's Prayer and be followed by God Save the Queen as soon as students arrived. The learning in class was focused on the "three R's" of "reading, writing, and arithmetic" but this was something Lorenzo excelled at and easily earned an 80–90 per cent average throughout his time in school. He also stressed that speaking his language at school was strictly forbidden, which frustrated him as some "kids knew how to speak" but he and other classmates could not.

We continued our walk up a small hill towards a sweat lodge overlooking a valley of flat granite. Lorenzo spent some time smoking his pipe and offered words to "respect the people who have been and the people who are going to return."[28] As soon as he was done smoking, he said, "I got the strap when I was in school. By the teacher, and in front of everyone."[29] He recalled an incident when he was caught "skiing" behind his Aunt's car by grabbing her bumper one day while leaving the school. He said they "saw me after lunch and they gave me the strap on the hand."[30] However, he explained that his punishment was less severe than other students. He once saw "a teacher beat a guy with a (wooden) ruler until the metal edge came out of it."[31] He watched countless interactions of physical violence that scared and made him reconsider the value of school in the first place.

Like Val, by this time, Lorenzo's school was integrated into Ridpath Public School by the fifth grade. He said, "I never had any siblings in the same class with me until I hit Lakefield. They failed my brother, and he had to stay back in grade five. I felt ashamed and bad for him. It would have been hard to be left behind by your peers and put in the same grade as your younger brother."[32] This caused a massive rift between Lorenzo and his brother, which the teachers in the school exacerbated. He said, "I was in a big fight in grade 5 over it ... One of the teachers took us into the basement of the school and made us fight each other."[33] This terrifying experience hurt their relationship in a way that took many years to repair. After this experience, Lorenzo's marks dropped into the 50 per cent range, where he continued to stay until graduating from high school in Lakefield in the early 1970s.

In 1960, the Department of Citizenship and Immigration took several photographs of the Curve Lake community to document their educational experiences. Figure 7.1 shows Chief Elsie Knott outside of Lakefield District High School, picking up a group of Curve Lake First Nation students. The photo was used to show how this reserve and the Chief were "taking an active part in the management of Band Affairs."[34]

Chief Knott was supported by members of the Curve Lake First Nation who were also prominent in the town of Lakefield. By 1967, Curve Lake First Nation was one of the first reserves in the country to take over their own administration from the Department of Indian Affairs. That year, the government allowed a "Band Administrator" to handle the finances of the community, which would still be governed by a Chief and Council system. While this was not full autonomy – the government could still set guidelines regarding how funds could be spent – this new governance structure was similar to the relationship between the province and individual municipalities. The first Band administrator, William Whetung, stayed in the position for fifteen years, significantly improving the community's economic, social, and educational quality, which could finally spend money where it was needed. During his tenure, the community created over one hundred homes, established a sewer system, paved roads, and enabled cable and telephone connections. These modern amenities were unavailable until Council took control of the community's funds. This revitalization of the essential infrastructure was not the only focus of William Whetung; he was also a strong proponent of education for the Curve Lake First Nation community. Whetung, who had earned a teacher's certificate in the late 1950s, started his career by serving as the chair of the Lakefield District School Board and had been involved with education ever since.

William Whetung was appointed Band administrator for Curve Lake First Nation and chairman of the board of governors for the newly established Sir Sandford Fleming College in nearby Peterborough. As an Indigenous person in a prominent postsecondary educational position, he facilitated the graduation of community members. In the late 1960s, he was asked by the province to serve on the Interim School Organization Committee, and he helped amalgamate and create the Peterborough Country Board of Education. Before his retirement, Premier of Ontario Bill Davis attended a testimonial dinner in his honour, and a newly renovated wing of the Lakefield District Secondary School was named the William F. Whetung Complex.[35] Finally, and perhaps most significantly, William Whetung "was instrumental in establishing a native studies program including native and Canadian art, to preserve Indian cultural heritage."[36] Whetung was concerned about the quality of education off the reserve and wanted to ensure that the community of Curve Lake First Nation had access to traditional education at the public school. In the late 1960s, he created "special programs in Ojibwa languages and heritage [that were] given to the students in Kindergarten and Grade 1 and 2 classes on the reserve."[37] After revisions to the Indian Act in 1951, Indigenous Peoples gained more power over the type of education provided, and so included their own traditional forms of teaching, language, and heritage in the curriculum.

In 1968, the *Globe and Mail* visited Curve Lake First Nation to see this new "Ojibwa" program that focused on art in action. The article "Indian Students End Up in Paint" contains three images of students using unconventional painting techniques. The article said: "They call it an art course and in one sense the art is true to Indian Tradition. Some of the dozen Ojibway children and four adults taking the eight-week course in the two-room junior school at the Curve Lake Reserve North of Peterborough finish their classes in what looks like full war paint."[38]

The parents of the students involved in the program were interested in extending the art classes for students in the community. The art teachers were impressed with the methods the students used, stating, "And they're doing some things I never thought of before. They'll spill paint all over the page and then blow it around. They paint their hands and slap their hands on the paper."[39] The leadership also promoted other classes that focused on Indigenous traditions, as Cora Voyageur observes: "Beginning in 1970, Elise [Knott] also taught weekly Ojibway language classes on the reserve with Glady Taylor. Ojibway language classes were included in the schools as part of the educational curriculum for children. Classes for Adults, which were open to Band members and other interested individuals, had about a dozen participants at any given time."[40]

In the 1960s, the Department of Indian Affairs – which had been renamed the Department of Citizenship and Immigration – learned of these promising educational initiatives and paid for a photographer to chronicle the school and its students. The images below show how the former day school was used after students returned home from public school classes in Lakefield.

These photographs were taken by the Department of Citizenship and Immigration and used to show how the "Indians of North America" were being educated. From the descriptions, it appears that the students wanted to learn more about Western studies in the nearby town of Lakefield, but the descriptions do not mention that these after-school classes provided students with options for learning their Ojibway language and traditions. It also appears that these photographs were staged and used as propaganda to promote the integration model of education to other Indigenous groups in the country. While these photographs show an idyllic educational experience during the integration period of day school in the province of Ontario, that was not always the case.

Stanford Taylor began his education in 1968, the same year the *Globe and Mail* wrote the "Indian Students End Up in Paint" article. By this time, day school in Curve Lake was from kindergarten to grade 5, and the rest of the education would take place in Lakefield, Ontario. Stanford remembered his whole first day of school and coming home saying "No, I'm not going back there. And my mom said, 'I got to go.' And shit

Figure 7.2
Two Indigenous students participate in a study period at Curve Lake Indian Day School, writing and cleaning the blackboard, mid-twentieth century. Girls at the blackboard are Pearl Johnson, age eleven, grade 5 (background) and Arlene Jacobs, age eleven, grade 4, Curve Lake Reserve, Ontario.

started from there. Right from that first day."[41] Stanford came from a large family with seventeen aunts and uncles, so he constantly attended school with his family, including at least five or six cousins and younger siblings. However, the size of the school was overwhelming as he had grown up with mostly extended family. He said, "I didn't know there was so many people in the world as there was as that school."[42] Due to the introduction of Kindergarten, there were a lot of issues with his younger brothers who also did not like going to school. Stanford remembers, "The teacher couldn't really handle them. So, I'd have to go in there and sit with them all day. I missed pretty much the whole first year of school."[43] This was a challenging experience as he felt that his one brother was in shock and "just cried and cried all day for a year, every time we went, and so I missed school again because I would have to go and look after him. So, I missed grade one and two!"[44] As a result of being so far behind other students and constantly having to look

Figure 7.3
Indigenous students engage in classroom activities at Curve Lake Indian Day School, with a teacher reading aloud, mid-twentieth century.

after his younger siblings, Stanford felt everything went "downhill from there. I didn't have any math, I couldn't read or write."[45] The teacher, who he recalled was Mrs Nancy Gillespie, began calling him "backwards Indian Boy" because he always wrote his words and letters in reverse. On one occasion, he said, "I put my hand up because I knew the answer to something she had put up on the board. And I turned away for a second and turned back. I guess she had called me or something when I wasn't looking, and she hit me right there [gesturing to forehead] with a blackboard brush and it bounced off my head. The classroom just went real quiet, and she says 'that's what happens to little Indians who don't listen.'"[46] He felt like the teachers didn't have the time or cared enough about students to help those who struggled to read or write at the same pace as others. Stanford noticed that "it took me longer to learn things like math and spelling and reading and all that kind of stuff. It took me longer than other kids. Well, there were a lot of us out

Figure 7.4
A teacher engages with Indigenous students at Curve Lake Indian Day School during a reading activity, mid-twentieth century. Boys in grades 3 and 4 get help from teacher Miss Irene Reesor.

here actually that were in that boat."[47] He felt that many families, including his own, were too busy trying to survive by working in various factories in Peterborough or hunting and fishing. As a result, they did not have much extra time for educational training. However, he fondly remembers his grandpa, who was a Second World War veteran and carried a lot of that horrific history with him but was "the most loving man I've ever met. You know, all my days, I'd never met a man who can love his grandkids like that."[48]

Stanford's parents and grandparents had attended versions of the day school in Curve Lake and had different ideas about education. He remembers his parents wanted him to attend and do well, while his grandparents "would keep me home any chance they got."[49] He often hid at his grandparents' house just down the street instead of going to school, which occurred frequently until his parents found out. His grandparents lived a traditional lifestyle, and he said, "I guess with me being the oldest

Figure 7.5
Boys of grades 8 and 10 find that the globe helps them with their studies of geography, Curve Lake Reserve, Ontario.

boy, going to school up there, they could see that starting to slip away. Even though we fished and hunted and trapped."[50] Stanford could feel that his grandparents were worried about losing their culture, and he also recognized that in the bush, "I did more learning up there than I ever had in school, you know. That is something you never forget, it becomes a part of you … while the [day] school became a part of me that I didn't like, almost like my enemy. Didn't matter what I did. I couldn't get it. I couldn't get that school."[51] This was a frustrating experience as he genuinely tried to learn in each grade but could not get caught up or understand how learning within a school worked. He said, "I never had one good day that was worth a pinch of shit. Going to school all my days … I couldn't learn how they did stuff. I just didn't get it. And there were a couple of students like me, but nobody worse off than I was."[52]

Throughout his education, both at the day school and when he moved into Lakefield for grade 5, the use of English was a priority. Stanford explained, "I lost my language as I wasn't used to talking English too much. And so, I tried and tried to talk English, but they took that Anishinaabeg out of me, that part anyway, the language." Stanford said that learning the language now is "really hard for me. I remember trying in high school because they had Indian language there. And I sort of made me nervous and embarrassed to say that. And I felt like I should know it, but it was gone. It was all gone."[53] Instead of his cultural teachings, Stanford recalled that "it did put a lot of stuff in my head and did change my ways of being I ended up in prison."[54]

By the time he was in grade 9, Stanford "didn't really give a shit anymore. The school bus was just a ride into Lakefield to do whatever. I didn't care then, I knew I wasn't going to amount anything as far as my education went, I knew this was it."[55] In high school, he kept close to other Curve Lake students; he said, "I did have good times with the kids from here, like we were pretty tight and we looked after each other."[56] In particular, Stanford recalled,

> The girls really looked after us. They could tell if we're going to get into trouble or something like that because they would put their foot down. I don't know why because they were the same age as us, but we listened to them when they spoke. Even though they were the same age as us. But they were our cousins and pretty much looked after us and others getting left behind … I don't think I would have gone as far as I did if it wasn't for my cousin, Pamela. And there was quite a few of them that really helped me out and looked after me as far as school.[57]

These students helped him keep moving into high school and were always there to talk or offer support.

Around the age of sixteen, Stanford had his first drink of alcohol and started partying. He said, "So I started quite a career, like drinking and partying, turned into a real bad actor there for a while."[58] The impact of the day school during this period was quite relevant. He felt that if nobody cared about him doing well, why would they care if he didn't follow the rules? He said the impacts "weren't good. It made me mean. I got mean. I went into prison while I was young on a big bid. I was actually 16, and went in for an eight-year term."[59] Right from that young age, he was in and out of prison. He explained, "I still drank and carried on and done prison bits here, out west, and here in Ontario. I just thought that's the way it went." However, he remembers that his people, especially his wife Lisa, were always there for him when he got out, and were ready to help him when he had enough of that lifestyle. He said, "my people really loved me, and they wanted the best for me. They didn't judge me."[60]

Historians, including George Cobb – who interviewed my great-great-grandfather, Moses Marsden, in the 1960s – asked questions about the language and education of Curve Lake First Nation. Working as an oral historian with Trent University, Cobb interviewed several Indigenous Peoples in the region including (Short) Tom Taylor, William Taylor III, and (Tall) Tom Taylor. The three relatives who were also connected with Stanford joined the project, and all commented on their experience and state of education and schooling in the community. In 1966, William Taylor III (dialogue in roman type) told Cobb (dialogue italicized) about his experiences:

> Yeah. Well, they make a good job at schools all right. But I tell ya, in my young days when I was at school, there was only … four books. First part, second part, third, fourth and that's, when you … we used to, up to read, read them two and three hundred times each book, see? When you get to fourth book …
>
> *What were they about? English books?*
>
> Yeah.
>
> *The Red Curricular [.] They were all in the one book?*
>
> Yeah. And ah, [*laughs*] and when they get through the fourth book two-three hundred times, well you were out of school.
>
> *That's it.*
>
> That's it, see? Now look at now … they get the bus here, they go out to high school; they get nurses and they get um … oh, salesmen and everything. And if they fund us, we were like that long ago; oh why we'd be something.
>
> *That's right.*
>
> And ah we were foolish, you know. I wouldn't say foolish but we help the country in the First World War. There was five brothers of

ours in it. And there was a heck of a lot of Indians from all over. And in the Second World War, just the same once it was over ... We lost our country.

Yes, you didn't have any choice, did you?

No ... we lost it.[61]

This interview reinforces the perspective that the education received on the reserve before the introduction of the Knott Bus Company was highly unsatisfactory. William Taylor felt that his community had lost so much and observed that its members were only now able to achieve higher-paying jobs such as nurses or salesmen. In addition, he thought the system could be improved "if they pay the Indians for all, all the land that they ... took off 'em."[62] This community member concluded that his community had "lost it" despite the significant sacrifices it made for Canada in the first half of the twentieth century.

Other members of his family also told Cobb about their inadequate experiences in the day school on reserve. On 27 May 1966, Cobb interviewed (Short) Tom Taylor, who was eighty-eight years old and had lived in the community since 1878. Taylor explained:

> There were no schools here in my time. Never bothered with schools. All hunting and camping out in them days. There was a little wee one. And the schoolteachers in them days would take you in the school and then they would go to sleep and you could do what you liked. That's how they teached in my time. The school was way down near the lake. By gosh, he'd ring his little bell and we'd go in and we'd all sit down and he'd lie over on his chair and he'd sleep there until about a quarter to twelve and tell us to go home and have our dinner. But now they have all the chance in the world to learn. Three teachers right here, and a bus takes them into Lakefield, what we hadn't. They've got all the chance in the world to go to school. Yes, it's a great thing for them. They can earn good money over it now days.[63]

Taylor also believed that the improved educational opportunities offered in the nearby town of Lakefield were an improvement over the previous decades of education provided by the Department of Indian

Affairs. Taylor reiterated the story of Mr Prosser, who, in 1911, regularly slept on the job at the day school on reserve, as evidenced in school inspection reports and internal Indian Affairs letters. This information provides a valuable window into the perspectives of Indigenous Peoples who had experienced the day school over several generations, as their children later attended the same school.

George Cobb also recorded information about the ongoing efforts to keep the "Ojibway" language in the community. William Taylor III said, "We always speak Ojibwa at home. Only an odd one of the children speak it. It's only the odd one that would understand you speaking Indian. (I ask a young lad of 10, who has been curled up on the bed where we were talking if he understood, and he said, 'just a little'). And I think it is a big mistake to forget your own language. (They don't teach them at school. They have to learn it at home). My mother, she never spoke any Indian and she was married to one. Funny, eh? She taught us English and my father used to speak to us in our own language. That's how we learned."[64]

Families on the reserve continued to practise their language and traditions at home, away from the government-operated day school on the reserve. The government could never eliminate the use of the language in Curve Lake, but this trend of English speaking still worried other community members. (Tall) Tom Taylor told Cobb on 12 June 1966:

> Well, anyway, the French and the English, when they discovered this country, this Indian country, they chased the Indians away and killed them and now the white man owns it all and the Indian hasn't got nothing. Just a little bit of land what he's got, and the white man is still going to crowd him out of that little village. Pretty soon there won't be no Indian. These children playing around here, if I go and talk Indian to them, they won't understand. They don't understand it. They talk English all the time. They might understand an odd word. They talk English before they go to school. As soon as they are able to talk, they talk English. In another 100 years there won't be no Indians around, I don't think. They might have the name "Indian," but that's all.[65]

Given the lack of proper support and the continual removal of land, (Tall) Tom Taylor was not optimistic about the next one hundred years on the reserve. He believed that English and the assimilation policies that followed would eventually lead to the erasure of his entire culture. He explained that within his lifetime, his livelihood had been destroyed: "There were times you could sell the fish them days, but the white man got so jealous of the Indian, that the white man took the fishing rights away from them (the Indians). And now, today, an Indian can't go out and catch even a frog. The game warden is right there at the tail of his boat, watching him."[66] The oral history that Cobb collected helps provide context about how the education system and the government's land policies impacted community members and influenced their perceptions of the present and future of the reserve.

In the 1960s and 1970s, two separate studies were conducted to determine the "success" of the Indigenous integration efforts in this area. In 1965, a doctoral student at the University of Toronto, John Harold Dilling, conducted a study called "Educational Achievement and Social Acceptance of Indian Pupils Integrated in the Non-Indian Schools of Southern Ontario."[67] He earned a PhD in education for the study, which included several interviews with principals and teachers who had been integrated into non-Indigenous schools. He primarily focused on obtaining sociometric data on Indigenous students – including intelligence and "degree of social acceptance among pupils" – which he compared with similar data on non-Indigenous individuals. He reported on twenty-four reserve communities that had been integrated in southern Ontario by 1965. He found: "In 1962, pupils from Grades I to IV went to the Curve Lake Indian Day School which had three classrooms. Integration had begun in September 1959, when 10 Indian pupils from Grade VIII attended Lakefield Public School. By 1962, there were 51 of these students from Grades V to VIII enrolled in Lakefield Public School (sixteen rooms – 510 pupils). However, the Indian people from the area had participated in sports and church activities in the surrounding non-Indian communities for many years, and although the trend is gradual, full mutual acceptance by both ethnic groups appears inevitable."[68]

This conclusion about integration efforts was reached without any interviews with students; instead, he relied on numerical information to compare various schools' attendance, grades, and geographical data. His report showed a five-fold increase of Curve Lake students attending

Lakefield Public School between 1959 and 1962, illustrating the impact of Chief Knott's efforts. Dilling would spend the rest of his career advising the provincial government on education-related matters.

One of the students who seemed to benefit from these new opportunities was Shelley Knott Fife. Shelley was born in 1960 and was the oldest of five children. She began attending the day school in 1966 at the age of five. She was brought up very close to home as her father, Keith Knott, remembered older siblings who had been taken to residential school, so they were quite protective of her. As a result, she said, "I couldn't wait to get to school because I think there's paper, I'm watching the box, the TV, and you hear all of these things."[69] Despite her excitement, it was like "going to the moon, the school itself we had never been into before I was five. So, it's clean, modern-looking and they had flush toilets. This was a big deal because we didn't have flush toilets."[70] It was overwhelming to first attend the school, as Shelley explained, "It was like, whoa, where did you guys come from? We didn't have a lot of social gatherings for kids as we do now."[71] For Shelley, the school was a place she came to love as she was a precocious learner. She said, "I don't have a lot of bad memories of the school. Because I loved school. So I got into it … And I couldn't wait to learn how to read."[72] She also has fond memories of her teacher, Miss Oliver, who taught at the school within a big cohort during the 1960s. She said, "It was the style of teaching at the time, where one of row of kids were struggling and at the end of the year they would say 'this row is staying behind.'"[73] Shelley also explained, "I was bullied quite a bit, because I enjoyed school."[74] However, Miss Oliver supported her through these challenges, and Shelley also credits her for pushing her towards university as she wrote on her grade one report card, "I can see you going to grade 13."[75]

As an academic just finishing her PhD at Trent University while we did our interview together, Shelley has also written about the quick development that occurred within her lifetime. She told me that in the same year she was born (1960), Indigenous Peoples got the right to vote, which quickly changed the social dynamics. She wrote, "In less than a decade, before I was a teenager, I saw our gravel roads become paved, our dark nights being lit by streetlights, and our tar-papered three-room house gain brick walls, four bedrooms, a bathtub with running water and a …

flush toilet."[76] Her chapter on the development of education in her lifetime is a powerful account of how Shelley made significant educational changes within Curve Lake. She also wrote, "A young me did not know about the missionary or any other influences on our reserve, which translated into the reality that I'd be accepted as long as I was speaking English and not Anishinaabe, learning settler protocols and wearing my 'indianness' in a non-threatening, reticent way."[77] Shelley told me, "Our way had been paved, though, right? Because the parents that are sending us up there … weren't encouraged to speak the language at all, to the point if you tried, they would say 'you weren't saying it right.' You just weren't encouraged."[78] For Shelley, the Anishinaabe language was just a secret language that her parents used when they didn't want the children to hear what they were speaking about. She asked her parents, "Why are you not teaching us? And they said, 'Well, we don't want you to be treated the way we were treated.' They were the way pavers."[79] She deeply respected her parents and said that "the way had already been paved. So do this. Sit at your desk, do what you're told, and you'll be fine. So that's what I did."[80]

Shelley followed that educational philosophy throughout the rest of her learning when she was sent to Lakefield from grades 4 through 13. She explained that students from Curve Lake "weren't talkers, we're pretty shy. But my mom's instruction was don't just hang around Curve Lake kids, go out there and make friends. So that's what I did."[81] Shelley remembers a specific occasion where students could make their own groups, and she picked a White student to work with, "it was like I just declared war or something."[82] That same year, Shelley won a Citizenship Award from the public school in Lakefield and felt like she stepped outside of the "rez box." It began a lifetime journey within education of walking between two worlds and trying to bridge the gaps between them. As she became older and had more interactions with students in town, she said, "I became more cognizant that there was a line … there are two experiences in Canada."[83]

By 1978, the federal government officially closed the day school on the reserve, as the community took ownership of the K–3 school and established their own provincially-funded daycare. In the mid-1970s, Curve Lake First Nation parents requested another study into the impacts of school integration. They were concerned that some "Indian students were not doing as well as other students in some subjects such as reading and mathematics."[84] Superintendent of Education J.D. McNabb conducted the study. He argued, "The study shows Indian students have reached the same level of academic achievement as other students."[85] The study compared eighty-nine elementary and high school students from Curve Lake First Nation with other students in the Peterborough region. Based on a formula that utilized IQ skills tests, average marks, and attendance, the board was confident that Indigenous students in the area were achieving the same results as other students in the country. McNabb also explained, "The study would not yield the same results as ones in Northern Ontario and Western Canada. They showed Indian students face a cultural bias and do not reach the same academic level as other students."[86] The results of this study were never released.

In 1985, a book was published that detailed the impact of this Indigenous education on the students of Curve Lake. Entitled *Giving Ojibwa Stories and Legends from the Children of Curve Lake*, the book was written and illustrated by students who attended the K–3 class at the former day school. The book provides a general history of the community and underscores the importance of stories being passed down to future generations: "Many older Anishinaabe were taught by the missionaries and white people that telling legends was not a good thing to do. This makes them shy and uncomfortable about telling them now. The young people need to seek out the old stories and tell their version of them so they are not lost for all time."[87]

The stories explained and illustrated by different students who have received teachings in the class range from "how the birds got their songs to how turtle set the animals free."[88] The children who participated in writing this book are the descendants of educational leaders from families such as Whetung, Taylor, Knott, and Jacobs. Images in the book show the old day school with smiling faces, Indigenous artwork on the walls, and students who were proud of their local heritage. The book explained that now, "children at Curve Lake go to school on the reserve up to grade 4. There is also a daycare centre for the very young and junior and senior kindergarten. Yellow school buses take older pupils in the village of Lakefield for grades 3 to 13. The Ojibwa language is taught in the

Curve Lake Day School ... Young people at Curve Lake get together regularly, once a week, after school to learn their native crafts, language, customs, legends, and music. They take part in the annual Pow-wow to which many visitors come."[89]

Despite the lack of a fully accessible education system on reserve, by the early 1980s, the community had taken control of their education and implemented their own system – one that protected their Indigenous language and heritage. Indigenous leadership significantly improved educational opportunities for Indigenous children at a time when the Indian day school system was rife with cultural suppression and inadequate teaching. Faced with these challenges, Elise Knott was relentless in her pursuit of better education for her community. She personally ensured that children could access high school by driving them to Lakefield High School and founding the Knott Bus Company, which grew to accommodate the increasing number of students. Her dedication extended beyond logistics as community members worked to preserve the community's cultural identity through language classes and cultural teachings.

Oral histories from students like Valorie Whetung and Lorenzo Whetung highlight the oppressive conditions they faced and the resilience they developed. Valorie's traumatic experiences with punishment and inadequate teaching, Lorenzo's struggle with cultural identity and systemic violence, and Stanford Taylor's testimony of physical and emotional abuse reflect the harsh realities of the education system at the time. Stanford's accounts of being punished and ridiculed in school underscore the deep-seated issues of discrimination and cultural erasure that Indigenous students faced. This was also complicated by the experiences of Shelley Knott Fife, who succeeded in the English-dominated schooling system despite these challenges.

CHAPTER 8

A Class in Resistance: Curve Lake First Nation's Fight for Education

In the summer of 2019, I travelled to Curve Lake First Nation to visit the Whetung Cultural Centre. I have travelled here several times as I lived just off the reserve, but this time was different and would radically alter the course of this book. I had arranged the trip as part of the conclusion for the Matariki Indigenous Student Mobility Program, which facilitated Indigenous students from around the world coming together to learn about Turtle Island. During this experience, Rachel Whetung arranged for an Elder named Freddy Taylor to speak to the group about his artwork. Taylor has lived on the reserve his entire life except for his years at a residential school. Before the age of six, Taylor was forcibly taken by a truant officer to the Mohawk Institute (residential school).[1] Taylor explained how his decade-long experience in the school traumatically impacted his later life. He also told us how he found Indigenous art and the growing community of artists at Curve Lake and how these significantly helped him deal with his abuse in the residential school. Knowing this result, I found it difficult, while researching this book, to read archival files that mentioned the truant officer's involvement in sending children of the Taylor family into residential schools.

This book was heavily impacted by the works of Elder Doug Williamsban and Mae Whetung-Derrick; both have written a history of the community, but neither of these histories focuses on the role of the day school. In particular, the authors demonstrate that resistance and resurgence have always been part of this Nation; evidence of this resistance can be found as far back as the nineteenth century in the community's response to early attempts at colonization by the government and the New England Company.

An early example of the Curve Lake community's resistance can be found in its fight to keep the school's operation in the hands of an Indigenous teacher, Alfred McCue. The community was ultimately successful, and McCue was reinstated as a teacher from 1901 to 1909. In one letter, Daniel Whetung wrote: "*The Indian Department must think that this Band of Indians are all fools and don't know how to carry on their own business. If they are? They are much mistaken. For there are Indians here who know as much about carrying on business as some of the membership of the Indian Department* [emphasis in original]."[2] Despite this early success, the community's dreams for the school were continually disrupted by the Department of Indian Affairs and the Methodist Missionary Society. This is evidenced by the firing of Mr McCue in 1909, which contravened the decision of Chief and Council. The events that followed McCue's firing demonstrate a correlation between a lack of Indigenous control over their education system and problems at the school. These problems – unqualified teachers, high teacher turnover, and inconsistent teaching methods – would cause serious disruptions to the way of life in Curve Lake. In 1910, following a period of high turnover of inexperienced teachers at the school, Daniel Whetung asked, "How is it that we cannot get a good teacher like you white people?"[3] As the community had no authority in selecting their teachers, significant disputes between community members erupted and caused the quality of education to suffer greatly. Continually resisting this inadequacy in education was the only option available to Chief and Council and concerned community members during this period.

In 1916, the federal government and Methodist Missionary Society's continual mismanagement of the hiring process would force the community to ask that they be given their own school board or be moved to new lands in the western province to start anew. In times of trouble, and only after they'd exhausted all options in finding a qualified teacher, the government and church would call on Alfred McCue to teach the rest of the term. The reliable McCue stepped in as the emergency supply teacher on five separate occasions, yet he was paid 50 per cent less than his White counterparts. In 1918, after McCue had worked for over a decade as a supply teacher, Indian Agent McCamus said: "I have been quite pleased with the way Mr. Alfred McCue is getting on and he is doing a much better than I expected."[4]

Despite the Indian agent's endorsement of McCue, the Department instead enlisted a cadre of White Methodist teachers that included circus trainers (Mr John Prosser), misogynists (Miss Zella May Hanes), and draft dodgers (Mr Arthur Buie); indeed, the Department sometimes found it preferable to provide no teacher at all. The church was also culpable; they failed to secure a qualified teacher and wasted nearly a decade of government and community funding on these failed attempts. In 1919–20, after the church had finally hired two promising teachers from Queen's University, the Spanish flu closed the school; consequently, these teachers taught for less than a full term. After the epidemic, the school experienced another period of high turnover, as the church unsuccessfully looked for a replacement teacher who would last more than one school year. This led Chief Daniel Whetung to write to the Department in 1923 to express his concern over the low quality of education on reserve: "I regret to say that not a single child has accomplished much as to pass the examination for high school in the last 50 or 70 years. I understand the government is spending money to advance Indians! Why not spend it in this section! We are willing to pay more for a qualified teacher and no other kind will do."[5]

Chief Whetung urged the government to hire someone from the nearby normal school or advertise the teaching position in the local newspaper. Finally, and of his own accord, Whetung secured a qualified teacher, Mr Arthur Smith, to teach the school. Even Indian Agent McCamus was impressed and said: "Mr. Smith is an excellent teacher and can handle the school with ease even with every child on the reserve in attendance." Under Smith's leadership, the average attendance at the school rose from only seventeen students in 1923 to over forty in 1925 (from a pool of about sixty registered students). Unfortunately, Smith was forced to resign a year later due to illness, but his successful tenure indicates a connection between Indigenous control over education and better results for the community. The events discussed in the fourth chapter of the book reveal the failure of the federal government and Methodist Missionary Society to provide adequate education but also demonstrate how Indigenous Peoples on the reserve petitioned for and were able to make changes to the operation of the institution in their community.

The fifth chapter in the book begins with the transition of the Methodist Missionary Society into the United Church of Canada; this transition marked a new period of organization for the school on the reserve. This period began with community members enlisting their local member of Parliament to pressure Deputy Superintendent Duncan Campbell Scott to secure a qualified teacher for the community. In addition, Chief Whetung remarked that the community was "willing to do anything reasonable" to secure a new school or additional classroom for the growing student population. As a result of this continued pressure from the community, a qualified teacher, Mr Lewis, was hired. He would later be joined by his first cousin, Mrs Lewis, and they would operate the school together for several years. Under their tutelage, and for the first time in the history of the day school on reserve, students qualified for high school education. But this success turned to failure when Mr Lewis left and was replaced by Miss Margaret Gardiner. Her hiring and later removal once again caused significant tension between members of the community, who disagreed over her teaching approach. These concerns were so serious that Superintendent of Indian Education Russell Ferrier conducted a full investigation into the concerns of community members. While the Department finally agreed that she should be released from her duties, she was still permitted to stay in the Indian day school system. While problems with the school building were first reported in 1919, Chief Whetung and other councillors would spend the next decade trying to get the Department to address their concerns. The Department's continued refusal to make significant repairs to the heating system, building, and interior led to problems that even closed the school on occasion (due to smoke in the classroom or a lack of heat). The events discussed in this book's fifth chapter demonstrate that the government prioritized micromanaging costs within the classroom over addressing serious and growing structural problems.

The sixth chapter of this book weaves together the many links between capitalism and education between the Great Depression and the postwar baby boom. The overlap of education and capitalism in Ontario's Indian day school was clearly visible within the archive. This period demonstrates both the government's focus on a manual training curriculum and the students' difficulty obtaining education outside the reserve. The day school adopted a "manual training" philosophy in its upper grades, funnelling students into nearby manufacturing industries to work for companies such as General Electric, Quaker Oats, and Outboard Marine. In addition, any Indigenous student who wanted to attend high school had to negotiate with the federal government for tuition waivers. This typically led to students dropping out instead of dealing with the government bureaucracy and ending up in industrial jobs in the city. These jobs required hard manual labour and solely benefitted the multinational companies that began operating in the area after the Second World War. This is evident in Library and Archives Canada's description of a 1965 photo from the Department of Citizenship and Immigration; the description reads,

> Wendell McCue, although a Mud Lake band member, lives in Peterborough. He has worked as a stores attendant at Outboard Marine for four years, plays on one of the plant's hockey teams and plays softball in the city's Industrial league. Ten members of the Mud Lake Band are steadily employed at Outboard Corporation of Canada Ltd. In Peterborough. Albert Watkins, a non-Indian foreman, says: "They work well – them – I don't separate Indians any more than I do Dutch, Hungarians or native-born Canadians." The Indians commute to work a distance of 25 miles from the reserve and like working at the plant. They have proved – through long service – that the myth of the Indian as an unsteady worker is completely false. Most work swing shifts and are able to make extra money in their spare time by guiding. "But it's only pin money," they say.[6]

The Department was happy to see Indigenous Peoples integrated into Canadian society, as they believed this was the goal of education and that

Figure 8.1
An assembly worker at an outboard motor production line, showcasing industrial labour practices in mid-twentieth-century manufacturing. Wendell McCue, although a Mud Lake band member, lives in Peterborough, Ontario.

it should be promoted to other communities. This chapter also introduces the story of Chief Keith Knott, whose voice and oral history fittingly serve as the first personal narrative we encounter in this book.

The next chapter also provides an overview of the educational experiences Curve Lake First Nation members received off the reserve in nearby Burleigh Falls and Lakefield, Ontario. Both the provincial and federal governments refused to provide education to Indigenous Peoples living in the area of Burleigh Falls because they were "half-breeds." Indigenous students were eventually permitted to enter local schools, but the government's continued refusal to recognize the status of these individuals led to increasing grievances. In addition, this community was at the mercy of the township school board, which discriminated against them and ultimately moved the school without their consent. These issues demonstrate the meagre alternatives available to Indigenous Peoples who did not want to send their students to the day school or residential schools. In the 1980s, Curve Lake First Nation officially recognized the people of Burleigh Falls as their descendants and supported their right to self-government.

Compounding the issue of manual training at the Curve Lake Indian Day School was the increasingly difficult task of securing a qualified teacher. The postwar baby boom exacerbated this issue, as not enough teachers were available for the expanding population. Even the "failure teachers" were hired long before graduating. The provincial government also had a significant role in denying quality education to Indigenous Peoples in Ontario; day schools were federally funded, but Ontario required that teachers seeking accreditation gain experience at a provincially funded school. The government and church officials' continual failure to obtain qualified teachers over nearly fifty years of constant operation of the Curve Lake Indian Day School forced the community to act in unprecedented ways over the next two decades. The vision, responsibility, and adaptability of leaders like Daniel Whetung and Elsie Knott and teachers like Albert McCue are remarkable, especially when considered against the catastrophic paternalism of the Department of Indian Affairs and the parade of underqualified teachers they employed.

The seventh chapter of this book highlights significant changes and challenges in the education system at Curve Lake First Nation through the experiences of community members like Val Whetung, Lorenzo Whetung, Shelley Knott Fife, Keith Knott, and Stanford Taylor. They teach us about resilience and the stark realities of the Indian day school system. Val Whetung highlighted the dismal quality of education, marked by religious indoctrination and traumatic punishment, which caused long-lasting emotional distress. Lorenzo Whetung discussed his struggles with cultural identity and systemic challenges, emphasizing the lack of Indigenous cultural education and the prevalence of physical punishment. Shelley Knott Fife recounted her experiences of integrating into a non-Indigenous school system, dealing with bullying, and the impact of having supportive teachers and friends who helped her navigate these challenges. Stanford Taylor shares his experiences of overwhelming school environments, language loss, and the harsh disciplinary actions that led to long-term negative consequences, including a strained relationship with education and subsequent encounters with the criminal justice system. These narratives collectively underscore the oppressive conditions faced by Indigenous students and their enduring resilience in the face of systemic discrimination and cultural erasure. By the late 1970s, Curve Lake First Nation took control of its education system, integrating traditional teachings and language instruction into the curriculum. The community's ongoing efforts to reclaim their educational sovereignty and preserve their cultural heritage underscore the resilience and determination of Curve Lake First Nation in the face of systemic adversity. This chapter highlights the power of community-led education and the importance of cultural preservation in fostering an inclusive learning environment.

Several limitations inherent to this type of book will impact the direction and conclusions of the research. One of the primary limitations is the nature of the evidence involved in this research. There are significant restrictions to accessing information concerning historical documents collected or maintained by the federal government or church organizations. While annual reports from the schools are available through national archives, there are some problems with unfiltered access without community consent. Moreover, records of the day-to-day operations of those schools that church organizations handled may be difficult to access, depending on the denomination of the organization; for example, the Roman Catholic Church continues to deny Indian residential school Survivors access to crucial documents.[7] Consequently, obtaining access to all day school documents is highly unlikely. Historians researching Indigenous topics often encounter this limitation; it is a direct result of the impacts of colonialism, as governments and organizations seek to protect themselves from litigation or criticism.

Indeed, I encountered exactly this type of challenge when I endeavoured to gain access to the full United Church of Canada's archives for this research project. Further, in 2022, I wrote an article for *Broadview Magazine* entitled "Day School Survivors Need Access to United Church Archives"; it detailed similar difficulties faced by day school Survivors who, as Murray Sinclair noted earlier in this book, were required to find their own documents to use as part of the 2019 Indian Day School Settlement Agreement.[8] I specifically wrote about my experience being offered an archival research position and being "tasked with examining 437 files that related directly to the United Church's Indian day school system. The goal was to produce a final comprehensive report, along with lists of staff and impacted Indigenous students and communities." Before accepting the role, there was a condition "not to disclose any such information to any person whatsoever except for employees, elected members, or other contractors of the United Church ... except with the advance written permission of the United Church." I finished the article with this idea: "Place yourself in the shoes of a survivor who may live thousands of kilometres from Toronto. How will they access this history about their life and people? I believe that the church must act quickly to digitize its archival holdings and make it easy to access this information anywhere. We need truth before reconciliation."[9]

Since that article's publication, the United Church of Canada Archives have posted a response to my article. Their "Response to Broadview Article" appears on their official archival website beside links to their residential and day school records collections. No author is listed, but it appears to be collectively written from the archive's perspective. The response reads, in part, "The information provided below provides context around some of the research and digitization work referred to in the Broadview article, 'Day school survivors need access to United Church Archives' and is specific to the work of The United Church of Canada Archives in Toronto, however the principles of supporting Indigenous access to records are reflected across all United Church of Canada's archives."[10]

Their 1,100-word response to the article is quite specific and details some digital archival work done to support the research into day schools. They wrote: "We are not waiting for all the digitization work to be complete before distributing copies. In 2016, the General Council Archivist travelled to Curve Lake First Nation's Cultural Centre to bring physical and digital copies of images related to the day schools in the area. As more digitized content is returned to us, we are providing hard drives to communities when they contact us. Within the last year we have sent out more than 27,000 pages and 728 images to communities."[11] This is not a clear policy as this information was not provided to any First Nation or the public before the article's publication. I tried to verify their visit to Curve Lake First Nation and the transfer of documents to the Curve Lake Cultural Centre with Jack Hoggarth, the cultural archivist at the time, but was unable to find these documents. He noted that the General Council Archivist did make a trip to the community, but since the publication of this article, repeated requests to gain access to these documents have gone unanswered. The United Church Archives notes that 27,000 pages were returned in 2022; however, they also admit that over 1,000,000 pages of files have yet to be digitized. From my calculations, based on what is available on the United Church Archives website, less than 2 per cent of all files were publicly shared during a time when thousands of Survivors required legal documentation to apply for full compensation under the Indian Day School Class Action Settlement.

Notably, it is unfair to blame the archivists themselves, as they are also frustrated with the institutional nature of archival holdings in this country. On the website, they explain, "United Church of Canada Archivists, like professional archivists in any repository, are passionate about preserving information and providing it to the public. We acknowledge, however, that archives institutions are inherently colonial operations and through their policies and practices can uphold and reinforce colonial power and privilege."[12] Clearly, the contemporary archivists working in these collections are aware of the recent international developments in the right to Indigenous archives and have been exposed to the trauma and frustration Survivors face when searching for missing records. They explained, "For many of us, it is a personal and professional frustration to be faced with gaps in records or witnessing the silence in existing records about the children and families dehumanized by these institutions knowing that settlement agreements ask for attendance documentation, continuing to unfairly put the burden of proof on survivors seeking reparations and justice."[13] I regret that my article appeared to target these people who have done nothing but try to preserve the archives of a system that has largely hidden these records from the public for decades. It's extremely frustrating for everyone who works within history not to have access to archival information that is crucial to the story that you are telling. Institutionally, the United Church and other denominations need to work together to share best practices regarding digital history and provide increased funding to ensure this work is completed before most day school Survivors pass away. Additionally, it is crucial to recognize that these gaps in archival records are not merely a historical inconvenience but an ongoing denial of justice for Survivors and their families. The inability to locate critical records perpetuates the harm caused by these institutions, leaving Survivors in a constant state of limbo as they seek recognition and reparations. Institutions must prioritize transparency and collaboration, actively working to decolonize archival practices and make records accessible to communities who have long been excluded from their own histories.

This work cannot be postponed any longer. With the aging population of Survivors, there is an urgent need to address these archival challenges now, before more knowledge and lived experiences are irretrievably lost. Establishing standardized protocols for digitization, enhancing collaboration across denominational and institutional lines, and allocating substantial funding to archival projects are steps toward historical accountability and acts of reconciliation and respect. Survivors and their families deserve access to the full truth, and archivists, while limited by institutional structures, remain essential allies in this vital process.

Since the publication of this response, the United Church Indian Day School Research Guide was removed from the United Church Archives website, which drastically impedes the ability to search their holdings. A previously saved copy from the site contains the list of 417 different fonds and 140 pages of archival information that will be relevant for other researchers, including files from the Methodist Missionary Church. It's unclear why this information was taken down from the website when some Survivors were using the material to apply for access to documents. The United Church of Canada Archives also noted in its response, "During the period of 2019–2022 we've responded to at least 169 remote requests from survivors and family members, communities and academics about records related to UCC Indian Residential Schools, day schools, missions, hospitals. When we locate physical records to respond to requests, we scan and provide digital copies. Since December 2020 for example, we've sent 1759 digital files out related to these requests."[14] This removal raises concerns about transparency and accessibility at a time when Survivors and their families urgently need these records to substantiate their claims, access reparations, and uncover the truth of their experiences. While the United Church Archives' response demonstrates their efforts to fulfill individual requests, removing a comprehensive resource like the research guide undermines the progress in facilitating broader access to archival materials. Survivors and researchers alike depend on tools that streamline the search process, particularly when dealing with complex and fragmented archival systems. The removal also highlights a broader issue of gatekeeping within archival institutions, where decisions about access can unintentionally replicate colonial power dynamics by limiting the ability of Indigenous communities to access their own histories. For those seeking justice, navigating an opaque system is emotionally and logistically taxing, reinforcing barriers rather than dismantling them. To address this, institutions must prioritize proactive transparency and Survivor-centred policies that acknowledge the unique challenges and importance of timely access to these records.

The United Church of Canada Archives continues this important work of digitizing their collections and has sought further funding to expedite this process. This stands in stark difference with the Catholic Church of Canada, which has withheld nearly all documents regarding the over 327 day schools they operated across the country. The federal government has an obligation to support the digitization of these documents, as they funded the churches to operate these schools and keep these records. The government also has a large role in implementing legislation to ensure that all these documents are quickly returned to their specific home communities rather than stored in the Library and Archives of Canada. First Nations in this country have the right to this knowledge as it enhances understanding of the ongoing challenges that impact them daily.

In late 2023, I could finally restart the oral history interviews that had been cancelled three years earlier. With the permission of the newly elected Chief and Council, I began finding former students of the Curve Lake Indian Day School who were willing to share their stories. With the support of Jack Hoggarth, now the chair of Anishinaabeg Knowledge at Trent University, I identified and interviewed five individuals. Each participant received a $500 honorarium and was given the opportunity to review early drafts of this work as it prepared for publication. Including oral histories adds a deeper layer of understanding to this book, and I am immensely grateful to those who shared their stories. What was particularly interesting about these interviews was the knowledge exchange between the archival documents and the oral histories recorded nearly fifty years after the day school closed. The approximately 10,000 documents contained information from a time before most interviewees were born, allowing me to share historical details they were unaware of. For instance, I shared the story of Mr Prosser, a teacher in 1910 who was investigated and dismissed for bringing a live bear into the classroom to train it for the circus. This anecdote provided moments of laughter during the often-difficult conversations and highlighted missing pieces of the school's history. In other cases, my analysis of the archival documents sparked important discussions during the interviews. For example, Val Whetung, a former statistician who worked for Stats Canada, was particularly interested in the statistical aspects of the school's history. I shared detailed funding reports showing how Indigenous teachers were paid 50 per cent less and how the Peterborough Normal School limited first-class teachers from working at day schools. Near the end of our interview, Val said, "the stuff that I just thought about. You've kind of put a finer point on it. Like why we had such bad teachers."[15] These interactions illustrate the value of combining archival research with oral histories, providing a richer, more comprehensive understanding of the historical context.

As part of these oral history interviews, I ended each conversation with a question on what former students would like to be remembered or commemorated about the day school in Curve Lake moving forward. For Shelley Knott Fife, she said, "I think we should make a push for language. I don't think we need to go back and celebrate anything. I think we need to say this is what was lost in that process, was that was our identity and our language and who we are wasn't even present."[16] For her father, Chief Keith Knott, he answered the question by explaining that there was no "ending to it" and there will never be a final chapter on the day school within his community. He said, "the day school is still being used, but under a different name. Learning is still taking place you know;

you have the day care there. So learning is still happening. You can't criticize the building itself because it's done its purpose … You're allowed to speak the language in the school now, when I was there, we couldn't speak the language. So, it's still a learning place as we move forward … we must remember in all of that. We have come a long, long, way."[17]

Stanford Taylor also considered this legacy and how the education system can evolve to better support children who don't conform to the traditional Western educational model. He expressed, "I just hope that they never slip into any kind of hole like that again and I hope that they learn that you can't treat people, you can't treat kids or even adults like that way."[18] In a joking tone, he also explained, "Some kids are just stupid. I was one of them … they got to get something going for those kids as there is no freaking way they can sit there and learn. It's all like, 'what am I doing here'? That's how I was, I was totally lost."[19] Stanford emphasized the crucial takeaway from this history is to acknowledge diverse learning styles and create varied educational environments, including outdoor learning spaces, alongside traditional classrooms. He underscored that schools should "make them into somebody that matters. Not somebody that feels shitty about themselves. That's the big thing … you spend so much of your life there. You got to come out of that place feeling good about yourself. Not like a piece of shit, you know? Not like you're just some fucking dummy. You can't do that; you can't do that to people."[20] Stanford felt on the land "like a real Anishinaabeg, where at school I felt like a dumb Indian."[21] Instilling confidence and recognizing diverse learning needs are essential for creating an education system that truly supports and values every child moving forward.

Val Whetung still feels nauseous when she attends any form of school over sixty years after leaving the day school. She said,

> I guess I'm concerned about all the lives that it damaged … The people who did Indian Day Schools had probably the best intentions, they came at it from what they thought was the right thing … I don't think they said "what can we do to totally fuck up and destroy society" … You got to understand where these people came from. They punished their kids horrible, and they deprived them. We should feel sorry for those people, and we should be com-

> passionate towards them, rather than condemning them for doing what they did with the school system. We should feel sorry for them because they suffered big time coming to Canada.[22]

This empathic response to the people who operated the system was not the answer I was expecting but she further explained her thinking by saying "I think we need to remember the day schools like that without anger, without judgement, because I think we need to understand where it came from and how it evolved. And yeah, there were some bad players, but there are some really good players too. There were some wonderful teachers who cared about kids and really wanted to see it through."[23] During the COVID-19 pandemic, Val's granddaughter stayed with her to attend online school and asked her to speak to the class on residential schools. The most important thing she told the students was that "you're not in any way responsible for what happened to those kids … so, where you come into your responsibility is to make sure that nothing like that ever happens again."[24] For Val, empathy and kindness are the solutions to prevent the harm of the day school from reoccurring.

Lorenzo Whetung has also reflected on what he wants to be remembered about the system moving forward, especially as he became a teacher and then a father. He began these reflections after entering teachers' college and being put in charge of the daycare in Curve Lake. He said, "I never realized the day school was such an evil tool until I went through the process [teacher's college] as both a teacher and as a human being."[25] He realized that his family had taught him "that if you're going to teach someone something, you had to bring it out of them and that's a difference between the education I had and the one I still deliver. I see it in the people, and I try and bring it out."[26] This was the most important lesson that Lorenzo would like remembered and has tried to apply to all aspects of his life, including his time as a councillor of Curve Lake and as a negotiator on the Williams Treaty settlement. However, he still feels robbed of his language and explained, "when you learn that English language, your tongue develops the muscles for it" which makes it harder to learn Anishinaabemowin. Finally, he also said, "I want them to consider the relationship that the governing bodies and that believed they could turn us into Zhaagenosh [White people]. It failed to an extent …

I'm winning. I'm winning this day just being here able to talk to you in this fashion."[27] By the time he was teaching daycare, he vividly remembers a staff member suggesting that they take the kids up to the petroglyphs or Kinomagewapkong, kicking off a wave of new cultural teachings that were integrated back into their education systems in the 1980s.

I thought all the responses to the question on remembrance were insightful and gave unique perspectives into how history can play an important role in talking about our collective pasts. The declining use of Indigenous languages, lower graduation rates, and missing and murdered Indigenous women and girls are all consequences of this elaborate system of education – a system that was funded by the federal government and supported by the provinces and religious organizations.[28] Including the voices of oral history in any narrative about the history of day schools is crucial. These voices are diverse, reflecting the varied experiences of students based on the time they attended, the teachers in charge, and the extent of cultural learning incorporated into the education system. The varied accounts of how the schools should be remembered are an excellent example of the narratives and perspectives that former students can share with researchers.

From my perspective, this research into the operation of the Curve Lake Indian Day School yielded two central lessons that I think should be remembered. The first lesson is that, through a coordinated effort that first began in 1899, if not earlier, Curve Lake First Nation has used resistance and creative means to fight the federal government for control over their own education. These efforts have included the proposal of a new separate school board, the creation of language programs, and the constant negotiation with federal officials for a better quality of education on reserve.

The use of Indigenous languages today demonstrates that Indigenous Peoples were protective and resilient in learning their traditional languages. This micro-focused research on one school out of the 699 that officially operated in the country reveals the constant and creative solutions Indigenous Peoples used to protect their language. In the 1920s, after two decades of education provided on the reserve by the Methodist Missionary Society and the federal government, Indian Agent McCamus still reported: "One of the chief holdbacks of Chemong is the determination of the parents to stick to their own language, with a few expectations. They are quite jealous of it and will not favour the use of English by the children when at play."[29] The parents of Curve Lake First Nation continued to provide learning opportunities for their children outside of the school hours on reserve. Importantly, this ensured that a generation of children who grew up on reserve had access to the traditional language and teachings that were never part of the school curriculum. This learning did not happen within the confines of the school but rather on the land surrounding the community; it was by far the greatest form of resistance against the educational initiatives of the federal government. As Leanne Betasamosake Simpson wrote: "It is because of the resistance and persistence of Indigenous Knowledge holders – men and women who have worked in opposition to these forces – that our dynamic, powerful, and beautiful knowledge systems have been passed on to our generation."[30] Perhaps this work by generations of people is why community members have become world-renowned scholars in Indigenous studies (Drew Hayden Taylor, Doug Williams). I consider my great-great-grandfather Moses Marsden to be one of the people who resisted attempts to change his way of life, identity, and education. Moses, his wife Nellie, and their thirteen children would grow up and attend the public and high schools in Lakefield, Ontario. My family's history and the history of education at Curve Lake are thus entangled, as my relatives were also educated in the primarily White high school of Lakefield. Recently, efforts have been made by the community to recognize Moses and Nellie as the first Indigenous family to live in the town.

The second central lesson is that these failures at the Curve Lake Indian Day School emerged from complex conditions and factors that included chronic underfunding, jurisdictional tensions, paternalism, systemic racism, and the personal failings of administrators and teachers. It wasn't just that the Department of Indian Affairs didn't put enough money into the school – which they did not – but that the bureaucratic structure devalued the decision-making of those best positioned to guide the school to success (namely, community members). It placed decision-making authority in the hands of others who were uninvested in the flourishing of the community (inspectors and representatives of the Methodist/United Church). Numerous examples throughout this book show the

Department's unwillingness to listen to the community and the larger issues this unwillingness caused down the road. These systemic conditions – conditions that were known to the Department and argued vociferously against by Curve Lake leadership – made it nearly impossible to keep teachers for sustained periods. Yet, the Department continued along this pathway and, in doing so, impeded student success for decades. While the Department wanted to assimilate Indigenous children into Canadian society, their incompetence in operating the school on reserve spurred Curve Lake First Nation members to seek better educational opportunities in the public system. Programs were established to protect their culture on the reserve, but the integration period introduced the enormous challenge of keeping the community's language protected outside of the reserve. Ironically, the federal government's underfunding of the school offered a benefit of sorts, as these funds were not enough to support the full assimilation of Indigenous children into Canadian society.

Despite the activism of numerous Indigenous leaders, the aims of settler colonialism were still facilitated by the introduction of the day school on reserve. During the period covered in this book, Curve Lake First Nation lost access and hunting and fishing rights to thousands of acres of wetlands, waterways, and lands. By the time the Williams Treaty was signed in 1923, the federal government had already spent two decades significantly underfunding the day school on the Curve Lake Reserve. As none of the students had passed grade 3 by this period, this ensured that the Indigenous Peoples who signed the treaty were not fully educated in the "Western" system of treaty negotiations. Instead, with no legal representation and only a handful of Western-educated Indigenous Peoples, they were forced to relinquish approximately 52,000 square kilometres of land, and for the first time in Canadian history, their traditional hunting and fishing rights.[31] This ensured that the growing population of southern Ontario could expand its industries into the region and create the growing summer tourist industry that exists to this day.

The transfer of Indigenous lands continued throughout the remainder of the twentieth century as hundreds of islands were taken by constant waves of settlers who moved into the region after the Second World War.

In the late 1950s, Curve Lake members reported that hundreds of islands throughout the Michi Saagiig Anishinaabeg territory had been sold without the knowledge of the community. The *Globe and Mail* reported in 1960 that the "islands were first given to the Indians as a reservation in return for 1,000,000 acres the Mississauga surrendered to the British in the Gunshot Treaty in the 1800s."[32] These islands had been protected in the Williams Treaty of 1923, but in 1958, the Department of Indian Affairs allowed the communities of Curve Lake, Hiawatha, and Scugog Lake to keep only seventy islands and auctioned "about 640 Kawartha Lakes Islands."[33] Curve Lake Councillor Clifford Whetung said, "Ottawa officials repeatedly failed to reply to the tribe's request for information as to which islands they would get, and for information of past sales to establish who now legally owns them."[34] White resort owners in the region had also been working with legal offices to try to obtain the proper paperwork for the lands on which they were already operating their businesses. This dispute was not settled until 2018, when both the provincial and federal governments gave $1.1 billion to Williams Treaty First Nations as compensation for stolen lands and the removal of hunting and fishing rights. Both governments also apologized for the removal of these lands, yet the day schools they deployed and maintained helped to facilitate the removal of Indigenous Peoples on their lands. This land dispossession was at the heart of the government's efforts when providing education only on reserve. By forcing students to attend the strictly regimented school on reserve, the government ensured that parents would also live on the reserve, thereby removing them from the land, which could then be settled. And when families did not want to live on the reserve and moved to nearby Burleigh Falls, the government claimed they were no longer "Indians," as the federal or provincial government now owned the land. Even after the Williams Treaty was signed in 1923, the government still refused to fund a new school in Curve Lake. A new school would not be built until 1939, after repeated efforts by Chief and Council to secure the use of their own funds, which were controlled by the federal government. The link between the history of land dispossession and education is crucial in understanding the long-term impacts of settler colonialism. This book aims to help increase the granular understandings of Indigenous education in Canada by moving beyond the study of residential schooling and portraying the complex system of settler-colonial power and Indigenous resistance that sustained itself over several decades in Michi Saagiig Anishinaabeg territory.

By failing to provide treaty rights, the government also did not fulfill its fiduciary duty towards Curve Lake First Nation regarding education. Monies that were held in trust for the community per the terms of several treaties with the federal government were repeatedly withheld by the government, which refused to support critical infrastructure development. This pattern of mismanagement of Indigenous Peoples' lives is still impacting them today. In February 2021, *The Tyee* interviewed former Chief Emily Whetung (Lorenzo's daughter) about the issue of securing clean water on Curve Lake First Nation. This issue has been ongoing since colonization, highlighting another problematic area of government policy. Whetung stated that she learned her family had been infected by E. coli bacteria in the drinking water on the reserve and had become violently ill as a result. When health officials tested the water, "they were terrified about the E. coli levels."[35] Whetung expanded on the problematic long-term effects of the community's lack of clean water: "For far too long our community has gone without access to clean drinking water. Not having access to clean water has impacted our community in so many ways ... Moreover, many of our families suffer serious health consequences, whether it is rashes, stomach illness, or concerns for little ones and elderly resulting from lack of water, lack of clean water, high sodium or magnesium levels or other related causes."[36] As a result of this experience, Whetung has seriously considered leaving the community and "is often questioned about why she does not just move to a city. 'When you choose to leave the reserve, there's social consequences, there's cultural consequences, there's absolutely language and knowledge consequences that are far more significant than someone who decides that living outside of a city is better for them.'"[37] Frustrated by decades of inaction and failed promises from the federal government, Curve Lake and 120 other First Nations entered into a class action lawsuit. Whetung wrote, "We have seen time and time again with lawsuits, like the Indian Day School and the Residential School Class Actions that when we stand together, our voices are heard!"[38] The parallels between the lack of clean water and the inequities in the education system are striking. Both reflect a broader disregard for the treaty obligations and fiduciary responsibilities that were meant to uphold Indigenous rights and well-being. Just as day schools failed to provide adequate education while simultaneously eroding cultural and linguistic heritage, the water crisis demonstrates how the federal government's chronic neglect of infrastructure continues to harm the health, safety, and sovereignty of Indigenous communities. Whetung's advocacy, both for water rights and within the context of the class action lawsuits, underscores the ongoing necessity of collective action to hold the government accountable and to seek justice for generations of neglect and harm.

On 30 July 2021, Chief Emily Whetung, representing Curve Lake along with 120 other First Nations, announced the settlement of an $8 billion lawsuit against the federal government over the inability to access clean water. In total, 142,000 individuals across the country will be compensated. The government has agreed to address fifty-one long-term water advisories that have impacted thirty-two First Nations, including Curve Lake. Whetung told CBC News, "I feel like we're really embarking on the journey that will take our communities to meaningful access to clean water."[39] After decades of failing to provide access to clean drinking water – this issue was first raised when the government began infrastructure development at the day schools – the courts forced the government to settle these claims. I am thankful that both Chief Whetung and Curve Lake First Nation supported my own research during this incredibly busy time.

Western education provided through the day school in Curve Lake First Nation failed to assimilate the language, customs, traditions, and laws that are now being reclaimed through the descendants of these former students. The impact of this form of education still has severe consequences that are being felt today. During the Matariki trip to Curve Lake, which I referenced at the beginning of this chapter, we also travelled to Kinomagewapkong or Petroglyphs Provincial Park. We toured the site with D.J. Fife, a Curve Lake First Nation member and park warden (and the son of Shelley Knott Fife) who explained the region's history. His focus was on sharing his Anishinaabemowin language and stories about the caretakers of this place, Curve Lake First Nation. He recently wrote down some of these stories in a blog post for Ontario Parks and *The Lindsay Advocate*, where he also explained the importance of protecting the language. In a May 2021 interview, Fife said,

> The language is seriously endangered at Curve Lake. I would say there are perhaps fewer than 20 proficient Anishinaabemowin speakers left in our community … Most of the people born after 1960 in Curve Lake don't speak Anishinaabemowin fluently. Most knew some words but didn't know the language. My mom's generation forward could understand the language to an extent, but they could not speak it.'[40]

This book demonstrates that the Indian day school system in Curve Lake contributed to the loss of Indigenous language, as teaching English was a primary focus of this schooling system. Fife explained that the language was forged from this land or Aki in Anishinaabemowin, and without it, we may no longer have the ideas to relate to and understand some of the most important Anishinaabeg cultural sites.[41] As a result of the longer history of settler colonialism, the language has become a difficult topic to broach with some people. Fife argued, "Anishinaabemowin can be a bit of a sensitive subject for some Anishinaabeg. Some feel shame for not knowing it, or frustration with the challenges of learning and using it. Others still may associate a serious concern with the dire situation of the language."[42] These contemporary consequences of colonial education that forbade Indigenous languages from being nourished have created serious and long-standing problems with which the descendants of these students are still grappling. Without this language, the keys to understanding the significance of Canada's largest collection of Indigenous petroglyphs are also at risk. This book employs archival records and oral history to demonstrate that learning at the Curve Lake Indian Day School was most effectively fostered when Indigenous teachers were involved in pedagogy, when the community was involved in the selection of teachers and vested with the authority to make decisions about the school, and when Anishinaabe language and culture were not expressly and violently forbidden.

This book does not capture the full story or experience of attending day school in Ontario, but it offers something else: a new path – "Miikan" in Anishinaabemowin. By rereading these documents and layering in oral histories, I translated hundreds of handwritten or difficult-to-read letters into a searchable document that links directly back to the original source files. This process has intrinsic value for Indigenous communities interested in data sovereignty; this new path facilitates searching for information about a particular person, time, or place within archives that have been largely inaccessible over the last century. Moreover, it brings former students' voices into conversation with this historical record, which in many ways produced the experiences they felt in the Curve Lake Indian Day School.

These physical files, kept and stored by the government, have now been digitized to provide accessible representations of the Indian day school system and the government's attempts to assimilate Indigenous children through education. The paper itself was likely created in one of the hundred paper mills that emerged in southern Ontario during the same period when the government expanded the Indian day school system to every reserve in the country to gain access to more land, more trees, and more resources for its economic pursuits. Eventually, these original files – even the digitized versions – will decay back into the earth. This process will happen over an unknown amount of time; indeed, some of the examined files have already decayed beyond recognition or understanding in less than one hundred years.

So, at this precise moment – when the files are readable but also hold significance for the living Survivors, their immediate descendants, and a class action lawsuit – we must seriously consider the files' meaning on a wider scale. While most of the people who wrote letters in the archive have now passed away, their insights about our society are still accessible; they can be found hidden within the papers on which Indigenous Peoples and non-Indigenous people regularly wrote their hopes, dreams, and beliefs about education. Historians rarely acknowledge that their work will ultimately also decay like the files they study, but we should admit that the only thing we share with the people we research is the present.

Thus, the continual now is irrevocably linked with the choices of those who have come before and the forms of learning and education they received from their ancestors. Yesterday, today, and tomorrow are connected in a circle where the past constructs the present, which leads to the future. If these files are provided to the right person or family – at the right time – I believe they can be used to help remember what was experienced individually or collectively and can inspire change in the present, which will impact the future of Indigenous education. By combining archival research with the oral histories of individuals like Val Whetung, Lorenzo Whetung, Stanford Taylor, and Shelley Knott Fife, we gain a richer, more comprehensive understanding of this history and its ongoing influence on Indigenous communities.

AFTERWORD

Boozhoo Nindinawenmaaganaadok. Ma'iingan ndizhnakoz. Waabizheshii ndodem. Ma'iingan n'dewe maa. O'shkiigmong ge Jimsokweidjiwan ndoonjibaa. Miswendaan nwii midewiyaan.

Geget a'aw Anishinaabe gii-pi-nigaa'igoon inow wayaabishkiiwen. Ishke a'aw zhaagenosh gii-aanawenimaan inow bemaadizinijin inow bakaan enaanzozhenijin biinish go gaye ngiw bakaan nendaagozinijin da-ni-zhi-bimaadiziwaad. Mii imaa gaa-onjikaamagadinig a'aw Anishinaabe gii-aanooji'igod inow wayaabishkiiwen da-ni-debweyendanzig da-ni-zhi-bimiwidoosig i'iw akeyaa inow Manidoog gaa-nenimigod da-ni-zhi-bimaadizid biinish gaye da-ni-kowebinang i'iw gaa-miinigod inow Manidoog da-ni-inwed.

My name is Jack Hoggarth, and I am from Kawartha Nishnawbe First Nation, Curve Lake First Nation, Teetł'it Zheh, and Old Crow First Nation. I would usually translate what has been said in Anishinaabemowin (i.e., the Ojibwe language), but due to the resurgence within our ceremonial practices, language, and culture, I want to leave a message for my Anishinaabeg family to view and reflect upon.

Dr Jackson Pind's research within the Mud Lake Day School is only the beginning chapter of the colonial legacy left behind within Curve Lake First Nation and the surrounding territories. As one of my Elders has noted, Mishkogaabowe, the Canadian government now refers to the events of the colonial past as a part of Truth and Reconciliation, but this saying now retains little meaning. Truth and Reconciliation must be viewed as Truth and Assimilation and the Truth about Extermination.[1]

We are seeing a resurgence within our cultural traditions within Curve Lake First Nation. Our people are beginning to look for their true identities, as the ones imposed upon us do not reflect our true spirits. Slowly, we are starting to free ourselves from the chains of assimilation, but there are still mechanisms in place to control our people. We are one of the only ethnic groups in the world that has a number that is assigned to us by an external government, to which we are also told which First Nation we belong. Curve Lake First Nation still operates within the Indian Act, which dictates who is a member of our Nation, how we are to govern ourselves, and how Indigenous Services Canada (ISC) funding is to be spent. Through initiatives such as the Gchi-Naaknigewin, which our current Gimaa (Chief) Keith Knott helped co-develop, we are trying to break free from the colonial grips of our oppressors.[2]

As you have read this book, you have been exposed to the inner workings of Curve Lake First Nation and our continued resistance to assimilative and colonial tactics imposed upon us. In most cases, we used the system that was to oppress us and turned it around to benefit our people. I will caution, however, that if we stay within this system for too long, we will grow complacent, and the system will not work for us.

The Indian Act system has already divided our Nation, communities, families, and people, yet we still rely on this system for structural and monetary purposes. Have we grown so complacent within this system that we are slowly assimilating ourselves right before our very eyes? How many of our people speak the original language that the spirits and Creator have given us? How many of our people travel the land freely and continue to build upon our relations with the animals, grasses, waters, trees, and medicines? Do we still honour the treaties our ancestors made with one another before contact or shortly thereafter (e.g., Haudenosaunee Friendship Belt, Dish with One Spoon/Many Ladles, Yellowhead Belt, etc.)? Are we familiar with our fundamental teachings, such as how the Seven Grandfather Teachings came to our people?

Currently, I propose that only a small portion of our community would be able to list the Seven Grandfather Teachings, let alone recount how the teaching was brought to our people. We are so heavily entrenched in Western ways of living and obsess over differentiating ourselves from our own people that we are slowly forgetting who we are as Anishinaabeg.

There is a prophecy among our people, which some call the crossroads prophecy. As humankind, we will come to a fork in the road of life, in which one path leads to technological advances, leading us to our ultimate demise. The other fork in the road, though, leads to the original ways of life that we have lived since time immemorial, leading to the prosperity and longevity of humankind.

I will leave you with this one question… which path will you choose?

Aambe maajtaadaa. Jibwaa biidaaban. Ke-ni-megomin, ganaak nigen go baa.[3]

APPENDIX

Letter of Support from Curve Lake First Nation

Government Services Building
22 Winookeedaa Road
Curve Lake, Ontario K0L1R0

CURVE LAKE FIRST NATION

Phone: 705.657.8045
Fax: 705.657.8708
www.curvelakefirstnation.ca

October 28, 2020

Jackson Pind (Principal Investigator}
Jackson.pind@queensu.ca

RE: Letter of Support for Indian Day School Research (Curve Lake First Nation)

Dear Jackson Pind,

As the Chief of Curve Lake First Nation, I am pleased to express our enthusiastic support for your research study: "An Oral and Written History of Indian Day Schools in Ontario." We are willing to work with you in meeting our shared researching the history of the Curve Lake Indian Day School.

Your planned project that focuses on documenting the written and oral history of this school is clearly aligned with our interests in understanding the impacts of this institution run by the Federal government on our territory. Your exploration of this topic is particularly timely given the Indian Day School Settlement Agreement that is currently ongoing until 2022. In particular, Curve Lake First Nation, consents to the search of the Federal and provincial archives for information regarding the Indian Day Schools and the sharing of information in the form of a final report on this subject. In addition, Curve Lake First Nation consents for the promotion of this study to the community for oral history interview's which will follow the protocols outlined in Jackson's presentation on August 31st, 2020. No community members will be directly contacted without the permission of Chief Emily Whetung.

As part of your project, we plan to work on the research advisory team. Specifically, we will be serving as research liaisons between the researcher and the community making sure the research is shared with Curve Lake First Nation members and forwarding interested oral history participants.

Our organization looks forward to contributing to this important research endeavour and hope that our strong support reflects positively on your application.

Sincerely,

Chief Emily Whetung
Curve Lake First Nation

NOTES

CHAPTER ONE

1 Georg G. Iggers, *Historiography in the Twentieth Century: From Scientific Objectivity to the Postmodern Challenge* (Middletown, CT: Wesleyan University Press, 2005), 145.

2 Shawn Wilson, *Research Is Ceremony: Indigenous Research Methods* (Winnipeg: Fernwood Publishing, 2008), 32.

3 Elwood H. Jones, and Bruce Dyer, *Peterborough, the Electric City: An Illustrated History* (Windsor Publications, 1987).

4 James Thomas Angus, *Respectable Ditch: A History of the Trent-Severn Waterway, 1833–1920* (Montreal: McGill-Queen's University Press, 1988).

5 Ibid.

6 Truth and Reconciliation Commission Canada, *Canada's Residential Schools: The History, Part 1 Origins to 1939* (Montreal: McGill-Queen's University Press, 2015), 71–8.

7 Rebecca Chartrand, "Anishinaabe Pedagogy," *Canadian Journal of Native Education* 35, no. 1 (2012): 149.

8 Sheila Cote-Meek, *Colonized Classrooms: Racism, Trauma and Resistance in Post-Secondary Education* (Halifax: Fernwood Publishing, 2014), 184; Tweeted by @nick_ngafook on 8 April 2021.

9 Maurice Switzer, "After 100 Years, Ruby Still Remembers the Important Things," *Anishinabek News*, 31 May 2019, https://anishinabeknews.ca/2019/05/31/after-100-years-ruby-still-remembers-the-important-thin.

10 Drew Hayden Taylor, *Cottagers and Indians* (Vancouver: Talonbooks, 2019).

11 RG10, Library and Archives of Canada, Letter from Indian Agent J. Thackery to the Department of Indian Affairs, Alnwick Agency – Correspondence, Reports And Memoranda Regarding The Dispute Between The Indians Of Rice And Mud Lakes And The Alnwick And Alderville Bands Relating To The Wild Rice On Rice Lake, 1897–1933, p. 16. Volume: 2898, Microfilm: C-11294, File number: 183,727. http://central.bac-lac.gc.ca/.redirect?app=fonandcol&id=2068968&lang=eng.

12 "Top Court Rejects Appeal on Frog Hunt," *The Globe and Mail*, 23 December 1981.

13 Madeline Whetung, "(En)gendering Shoreline Law: Nishnaabeg Relational Politics Along the Trent Severn Waterway," *Global Environmental Politics* 19, no. 3 (2019): 16–32.

14 Ibid., 30. In her thesis, Whetung also argued, "It is clear from the nearly decade long historical correspondence that regardless of whether the Department of Railways and Canals believed the Mississauga claim or not, they would go to great lengths to avoid legal culpability. The purpose of tracing the specifics of this historical correspondence over a seemingly simple property dispute is to highlight how it is the very bracketing out of the different branches, issues, and categories intended to simplify that renders the issue too complicated for resolution. These documents demonstrate who held the power and when, but also, makes visible the colonial constellation that these historical relations overlaid on the land and continue to structure our embodied encounters in and with the colonial scape today." Madeline Whetung, "Nishnaabeg Encounters: Living Indigenous Landscapes" (PhD diss., University of Toronto, 2016), 73.

15 Ian Getty, *As Long as the Sun Shines and Water Flows: A Reader in Canadian Native Studies* (Vancouver: University of British Columbia Press, 1983).

16 Trent University Library and Archives, George Cobb Tapes, Tape #9 transcription, Accession 82-006, https://archives.trentu.ca/uploads/r/trent-university-archives/5/c/f/5cf3cb45931300b3428c84c9cebde16b17bab07ceed231f9e57e7b519c6857ce/82-006_cobb_tape_9_transcript.pdf.

17 Ibid., 17.

18 Angela Sterritt, "'A Punch in the Gut': Mother Slams B.C. High School Exercise Connecting Indigenous Women to 'Squaw,'" CBC News, 18 September 2017, https://www.cbc.ca/news/canada/british-columbia/susanna-moodie-roughing-it-in-the-bush-racists-language-vancouver-school-board-1.4294224.

19 Ken Montgomery, "Banal Race–Thinking: Ties of Blood, Canadian History Textbooks and Ethnic Nationalism," *Paedagogica Historica* 41, no. 3 (2005): 313–36.

20 Anishinaabe traditions acknowledge that the language holds the key to understanding mino-bimaadiziwin (the good life), which "is a unifying and transcendent concept that, when activated, contains the past, present, and future of Good and respectful approaches in daily life, which includes Indigenous research." Related to this concept is pimadaziwin, which is central to the Anishinaabe cultural system. This term loosely translates as "life in the fullest sense, life in the sense of health, longevity, and well-being, not only for oneself but for one's family. The goal of living was a good life and the Good Life involved pimadaziwin." This knowledge was passed down through the language and ceremonies but was interrupted by colonialism. Brent Debassige, "Re-conceptualizing Anishinaabe mino-bimaadiziwin (The Good Life) As Research Methodology: A Spirit-Centered Way in Anishinaabe Research," *Canadian Journal of Native Education* 33, no. 1 (2010): 11.

21 Andrew M. Stuart, "Water and Land," in *Before Ontario: The Archaeology of a Province*, ed. Susan M. Jamieson and Marit K. Munson (Montreal: McGill-Queen's University Press, 2013), 24.

22 Dagmara Zawadzka, "The Peterborough Petroglyphs/Kinoomaagewaabkong: Confining the Spirit of Place," paper presented at 16th ICOMOS General Assembly and International Symposium: "Finding the Spirit of Place – Between the Tangible and the Intangible," September/October 2008, Quebec, Canada.

23 Ibid.

24 William Augustus Ritchie, *An Archaeological Survey of the Trent Waterway in Ontario, Canada: And Its Significance for New York State Prehistory. No. 9* (Rochester: Rochester Museum of Arts and Sciences, 1949); R.B. Johnston, "The Archaeology of the Serpent Mounds site. Art and Archaeology Occasional Paper, 10" (Toronto: Royal Ontario Museum, 1968), 76–9.

25 Stuart, "Water and Land," 24–34.

26 According to Anishinaabe traditions, the suffix "ban" is applied to a person's name when they pass onto the spirit world. Doug Williams sadly passed away on 13 July 2022.

27 Doug Williams, *Michi Saagiig Nishnaabeg: This Is Our Territory* (Winnipeg: ARP Books, 2018), 30.

28 Ibid., 29.

29 Whetung, "(En)gendering Shoreline Law," 16–32.

30 Ibid., 21.

31 Williams, *Michi Saagiig Nishnaabeg*, 59.

32 Ibid., 68.

33 Mae Whetung-Derrick, *Oshkigmong: The Curve in the Lake: A History of the Mississauga Community of Curve Lake: Origins of the Curve Lake Anishinabek* (Peterborough, ON: Peterborough Historical Society, 2015), 6–7.

34 Ibid., 9.

35 Williams, *Michi Saagiig Nishnaabeg*, 71.

36 Ibid., 10.

37 Ibid., 86.

38 Ibid., 9.

39 This information was classified and does not recognize the New England Company efforts discussed earlier. This was the time when the federal government was specifically engaged with the operation of the school and thus liable to the members of the class action. Please see Schedule K, List of Federal Day Schools, https://indiandayschools.com/en/wp-content/uploads/schedule-k.pdf.

40 Whetung-Derrick, *Oshkigmong: The Curve in the Lake*, 10.

CHAPTER TWO

1 "Government Reaches Agreement with Former Indian Day School Students," CPAC video, 6 December 2018, https://www.cpac.ca/episode?id=409ebaf1-5daa-412e-87e5-8e3f552bc20f. Minister Bennett notes 1920, as that is the year for which the current class action suit is seeking compensation.

2 Ka'nhehsí:io Deer, "Federal Court Approves Indian Day Schools Class-Action Settlement," CBC News, 19 August 2019, https://www.cbc.ca/news/indigenous/indian-day-school-settlement-court-approves-1.5252211.

3 Karen Pauls, "'Just Get It Done': Indian Day School Survivors Divided Over Proposed Settlement," CBC News, 14 May 2019, https://www.cbc.ca/news/canada/manitoba/just-get-it-done-indian-day-school-survivors-divided-over-proposed-settlement-1.5132262.

4 "'Champion' of Indian Day School Survivors Dead at 67," CBC News, 20 February 2019, https://www.cbc.ca/news/canada/manitoba/garry-mclean-dies-1.5025517.

5 "Government Reaches Agreement," CPAC.

6 Pauls, "'Just Get It Done.'"

7 Truth and Reconciliation Commission Canada, *Canada's Residential Schools: The Legacy* (Montreal: McGill-Queen's University Press, 2015), 71–8.

8 Ibid.

9 Ibid.

10 Thomas Fleming, Lisa Smith, and Helen Raptis, "An Accidental Teacher: Anthony Walsh and the Aboriginal Day Schools at Six Mile Creek and Inkameep, British Columbia, 1929–1942," *Historical Studies in Education / Revue d'histoire de l'éducation* 19, no. 1 (2007): 4; Willis David Hamilton, *The Federal Indian Day Schools of the Maritimes* (Fredericton, NB: Micmac-Maliseet Institute, 1986), 50; Susan Elaine Gray, "Methodist Indian Day Schools and Indian Communities in Northern Manitoba, 1896–1925," *Manitoba History* 30 (1995).

11 John S. Milloy, *"Suffer the Little Children": A History of the Residential School System, 1830–1992* (submitted to the Royal Commission on Aboriginal Peoples, Ottawa, 1996), 323.

12 Ibid.

13 Brittany Luby and Kathryn Labelle, "'The New Generation': Cooperative Education at the Day School on Dalles 38C Indian Reserve, 1890–1910," *Ontario History* 107, no. 1 (2015): 90.

14 David J. Rowe, "'The Only Thing Native in the Schools Were the Children,' Former Indian Day School Students Reflect on Traumatic Legacy," CTV News, 9 June 2021, https://montreal.ctvnews.ca/the-only-thing-native-in-the-schools-were-the-children-former-indian-day-school-students-reflect-on-traumatic-legacy-1.5460999

15 Luby and Labelle, "'The New Generation,'" 105.

16 Ibid., 103.

17 Ibid., 104.

18 Ibid., 90.

19 Fleming, Smith, and Raptis, "An Accidental Teacher," 1.

20 Ibid., 154.

21 Ibid., 4.

22 Ibid., 16.

23 Ibid., 12.

24 Ibid., 19.

25 Helen Raptis, *What We Learned: Two Generations Reflect on Tsimshian Education and the Day Schools* (Vancouver: University of British Columbia Press, 2016), 152–3.

26 Ibid., 152.

27 Ibid., 149.

28 Sean Carleton, *Lessons in Legitimacy: Colonialism, Capitalism, and the Rise of State Schooling in British Columbia* (Vancouver: University of British Columbia Press, 2022), 207.

29 Ibid., 209.

30 Ibid., 210.

31 Ibid., 211.

32 Curve Lake First Nation to Jackson Pind, letter of support (Appendix 1).

33 Sandra D. Styres, *Pathways for Remembering and Recognizing Indigenous Thought in Education: Philosophies of Iethi'nihsténha Ohwentsia'kékha (Land)* (Toronto: University of Toronto Press, 2017), 7.

34 Pauls, "'Just Get It Done.'"

35 "Why the Former Chair of the TRC Is Worried About the Indian Day School Settlement," CBC News, 14 May 2019, https://www.cbc.ca/radio/thecurrent/the-current-for-may-14-2019-1.5134138/why-the-former-chair-of-the-trc-is-worried-about-the-indian-day-school-settlement-1.5134211.

36 Federal Indian Day School Class Action Settlement, Claims Form, 10–11, https://indiandayschools.com/en/wp-content/uploads/indian-day-schools-claim-form-en.pdf.

37 Jo-Ann Archibald, *Indigenous Storywork: Educating the Heart, Mind, Body, and Spirit* (Vancouver: University of British Columbia Press, 2008).

38 Ibid.

39 Ibid., 12.

40 Cheryl Bartlett, Murdena Marshall, and Albert Marshall, "Two-Eyed Seeing and Other Lessons Learned within a Co-Learning Journey of Bringing Together Indigenous and Mainstream Knowledges and Ways of Knowing," *Journal of Environmental Studies and Sciences* 2, no. 4 (2012): 340.

41 Maggie Walter and Michele Suina, "Indigenous Data, Indigenous Methodologies and Indigenous Data Sovereignty," *International Journal of Social Research Methodology* 22, no. 3 (2019): 237.

42 Tahu Kukutai and John Taylor, *Indigenous Data Sovereignty: Toward an Agenda* (Canberra, Australia: Anu Press, 2016), 2.

43 To understand the difficult nature of navigating the current digital database for specific files, please see Library and Archives Canada, RG10, School Files Series – 1879–1953, https://www.bac-lac.gc.ca/eng/discover/mass-digitized-archives/school-files-1879-1953/Pages/school-files-1879-1953.aspx.

44 James Frideres, "Aboriginal Identity in the Canadian Context," *The Canadian Journal of Native Studies* 28, no. 2 (2008): 322.

CHAPTER THREE

1 C. Pelham Mulvany, *History of the County of Peterborough* (Toronto: C. Blackett Robinson, 1884), 366.

2 Ibid., 370.

3 Ibid.

4 Report for 1875–76, 129.

5 Henry William Busk, *A Sketch of the Origin and the Recent History of the New England Company* (London: Spottiswoode, 1884), 45.

6 Whetung-Derrick, *Oshkigmong: The Curve in the Lake*, 13.

7 "Six Years' Summary of the Proceedings of the New England Company," 127.

8 Busk, *Origin of the New England Company*, 46.

9 Ibid., 135.

10 Mulvany, *History of the County of Peterborough*, 371.

11 RG10, Letter from Inspector Brown to the Minster of Education for the Province of Ontario, Volume number: 2291, Microfilm reel number: C-11196, File number: 58,155: 2. http://central.bac-lac.gc.ca/.redirect?app=FonAndCol&id=2078000&lang=eng.

12 Williamm Marshall Venning, "Origin of the New England Company, London With an Account of its Labours on Behalf of the North-American Indians," *Transactions of the Royal Historical Society* 2, no. 3 (1885): 299.

13 Ibid., 297.

14 Whetung-Derrick, *Oshkigmong: The Curve in the Lake*, 13.

15 Ibid.

16 RG10 School Files Series, C-8207, Letter from J.D. McLean to Indian Agent McFarlane, 9 February 1899: 1296; due to McFarlane being an extremely popular name in this time period, it was not possible to find additional details about his life.

17 Ibid.

18 RG10 School Files Series, C-8207, Mud Lake Chief and Council Resolution, 6 February 1899: 1298. Gidney and Millar explain the complicated nature of teacher certification from 1900 to 1940: "From the time Canadian public-school systems were first organized, anyone wishing to teach in the system required a license issued under the authority of a provincial education act." This provincial licence was linked directly to a teacher's level of academic education and professional experience. Gidney and Millar write, "But during the first half of the century, only high school teachers were likely to have a university degree; elementary school teachers were required to have only a

high school education (and not a university education). An adequate general education was conventionally identified as the completion of 'junior' or 'senior matriculation.' Junior matriculation indicated the completion of that standard of high school education that allowed a student to enter first-year university. In the early twentieth century this normally required three years of high school study everywhere except in Ontario, where it was set at four years. Senior matriculation required an additional high school grade and usually admitted the student to the second year of an undergraduate program. By the turn of the century there was quite often a parallel 'teacher's course' in the high school program, in which students might not be required to have Latin, advanced math, or the same number of foreign languages required of the university matriculation course; but both required the same number of years of study in high school ... Next in order was the first-class certificate, which would usually require senior matriculation and a full year of professional training. This was the highest elementary school certificate, but it might qualify an individual to teach at the secondary level as well. The second-class certificate commonly required junior matriculation plus a full year or some lesser amount of professional training. The third-class certificate, usually the lowest category, required something less than junior matriculation and a short period of professional training or none at all." This professional ranking system would largely stay the same in Ontario until after the Second World War when additional Faculty of Education programs were introduced. Robert D. Gidney and Wyn P.J. Millar, *How Schools Worked, 1900–1940* (Montreal: McGill-Queen's University Press, 2012), 125–6.

19 RG10 School Files Series, C-8207, Letter from J.D. McLean to Indian Agent McFarlane, 8 February 1899: 1299.

20 RG10 School Files Series, C-8207, Letter from J.D. McLean to Indian Agent McFarlane, 9 February 1899: 1300.

21 RG10 School Files Series, C-8207, Memorandum of Agreement between Indian Agent McFarlane and Lily Middleton, 16 February 1899: 1303.

22 RG10 School Files Series, C-8207, Letter from J.D. McLean to Indian Agent McFarlane, 1 April 1899: 1308.

23 RG10 School Files Series, C-8207, Resolution from Mud Lake Chief and Council, 31 March 1899: 1309.

24 RG10 School Files Series, C-8207, Letter from J.D. McLean to Indian Agent McFarlane, 5 July 1900: 1312.

25 RG10 School Files Series, C-8207, Letter from Indian Agent McFarlane to Department of Indian Affairs, 23 August 1900:1315.

26 RG10 School Files Series, C-8207, Letter from J.D. McLean to Indian Agent McFarlane, 6 September 1900: 1318.

27 RG10 School Files Series, C-8207, Resolution from Mud Lake Chief and Council, 5 February 1901: 2132.

28 RG10 School Files Series, C-8207, Letter from Indian Agent McFarlane to Department of Indian Affairs, 12 February 1901: 2133.

29 RG10 School Files Series, C-8207, Letter from Chief Irons to the Department of Indian Affairs, 9 March 1901: 2135.

30 RG10 School Files Series, Letter from J.D. Mclean to Indian Agent McFarlane, 24 April 1901: 2144.

31 RG10 School Files Series, C-8207, Report of the Committee of the Honourable Privy Council, 15 August 1901: 2204.

32 RG10 School Files Series, C-8207, Letter from Architect Blackwell to the Department of Indian Affairs, 3 December 1901: 2256.

33 RG10 School Files Series, C-8207, Resolution from Mud Lake Chief and Council the Department of Indian Affairs, 16 December 1901: 2261.

34 RG10 School Files Series, C-8207, Letter from Chief Irons and Secretary Daniel Whetung to the Department of Indian Affairs, 26 December 1901: 2271.

35 RG10 School Files Series, C-8207, Letter from Indian Agent McFarlane to the Department of Indian Affairs, 1 February 1902: 2282.

36 RG10 School Files Series, Resolutions of Mud Lake Chief and Council, 12 June 1903: 2305.

37 RG10 School Files Series, C-8207, Extract from Indian Agent McFarlane, 27 May 1901: 1325.

38 RG10 School Files Series, C-8207, Letter from Indian Agent McFarlane to Department of Indian Affairs, 5 October 1901: 1332

39 RG10 School Files Series, C-8207, Letter from Assistant Secretary S. Steward to Indian Agent McFarlane, 8 October 1901: 1333.

40 I could not confirm if this Alfred McCue was the same Alfred McCue who taught at the New England Company Indian Day School in 1878, but it is possible. In addition, I could not verify his involvement as the grand secretary of the Indian Council of Ontario in 1926. Although it would have been possible to encompass all these roles, there is a clear need for more Indigenous biographies of prominent educators and political leaders. To read more about the Indian Council of Ontario and this Alfred McCue, see Norman D. Shields, "Anishinabek Political Alliance in the Post-Confederation Period: The Grand General Indian Council of Ontario" (master's thesis, Queen's University, 2002), 130–41.

41 RG10 School Files Series, C-8207, Memo from Curve Lake Chief and Council, 11 April 1905: 1337.

42 RG10 School Files Series, C-8207, Letter from Daniel Whetung Sr to the Department of Indian Affairs, 27 January 1901: 2325.

43 RG10 School Files Series, C-8207, Resolution from Chemong Lake Chief Joesph Whetung and Council, 17 November 1900: 2326.

44 RG10 School Files Series, C-8207, Letter from J.D. Mclean to Indian Agent McFarlane, 18 February 1909: 2327.

45 RG10 School Files Series, C-8207, Letter from Daniel Whetung to Department of Indian Affairs, 15 February 1909: 2328–30.

46 Ibid., 2330.

47 RG10 School Files Series, C-8207, Letter from Daniel Whetung to Department of Indian Affairs, 1 March 1909: 2337–8.

48 RG10 School Files Series, C-8207, Letter from Chief Accountant to Mr Pedley, n.d.: 2339.

49 RG10 School Files Series, C-8207, Report on Chemong Lake Indian Reserve, architect John E. Belcher to Indian Agent McFarlane, 27 March 1909: 2343.

50 Ibid.

51 RG10 School Files Series, C-8207, Extract from School Inspector Ramsden to Deputy Superintendent General, Department of Indian Affairs, Re: Mud Lake School, 8 April 1905: 1340.

52 Ibid.

53 RG10 School Files Series, C-8207, Letter from J.D. McLean to Indian Agent McFarlane, 31 May 1909: 1345.

54 RG10 School Files Series, C-8207, Letter from Indian Agent McFarlane to Department of Indian Affairs, 21 May 1909: 1346.

55 RG10 School Files Series, C-8207, Resolution from Curve Lake Chief and Council, 28 June 1909: 1348.

56 RG10 School Files Series, C-8207, Letter from J.D. McLean to Indian Agent McFarlane, 31 July 1909: 1354.

57 Martha Elizabeth Walls, "'The Teacher That Cannot Understand Their Language Should Not Be Allowed': Colonialism, Resistance, and Female Mi'kmaw Teachers in New Brunswick Day Schools, 1900–1923," *Journal of the Canadian Historical Association/Revue de la société historique du Canada* 22, no. 1 (2011): 37. For more information on this topic please see Martha Elizabeth Walls, *No Need of a Chief for This Band: The Maritime Mi'kmaq and Federal Electoral Legislation, 1899–1951* (Vancouver: University of British Columbia Press, 2011).

58 Ibid., 57.

CHAPTER FOUR

1 George William Henderson was a Methodist minister from London, Ontario, who was born in 1852. He received his education in theological studies at McGill University and progressed into a trusted leadership system within the church. His report was sent to Alexander Sutherland, the general secretary of the Wesleyan Methodist Church and a staunch advocate of moral Christian education and the Sunday school movement. Please see George Krassoc, William Henderson – Methodist Minister, 9 September 2012, https://krassoc.wordpress.com/2012/09/09/george-william-henderson-methodist-minister/; for a biography of Alexander Sutherland, please see *Dictionary of Canadian Biography*, vol. 13, s.v. "Alexander Sutherland" by David B. Marshall (University of Toronto/Université Laval, 2003), http://www.biographi.ca/en/bio/sutherland_alexander_13E.html.

2 RG10 School Files Series, C-8207, Report from Rev. George W. Henderson to Rev. Sutherland and Department of Indian Affairs, 9 July 1909: 1350.

3 Ibid.

4 Ibid.

5 RG10 School Files Series, C-8207, Methodist Teacher's Application, George Cork, 23 August 1909: 1365.

6 RG10 School Files Series, C-8207, Letter from J.D. McLean to Rev.

Sutherland, General Secretary, Methodist Missionary Society, 26 August 1909: 1368.

7 RG10 School Files Series, Mud Lake First Nation Resolution, C-8207, 4 September 1909: 1372.

8 Ibid.

9 RG10 School Files Series, C-8207, Letter from George Cork to the Department of Indian Affairs, 4 September 1909: 1377.

10 Ibid.

11 RG10 School Files Series, C-8207, Letter from George Cork to the Department of Indian Affairs, 1 March 1910: 1380–1.

12 RG10 School Files Series, C-8207, Letter from Chief Joesph Whetung to the Department of Indian Affairs, 12 March 1910: 1385.

13 Ibid.

14 RG10 School Files Series, C-8207, Letter from J.D. McLean to Chief Joesph Whetung, 16 March 1910: 1386. John Milloy showed that the Chief of Georgina Island had accused John Prosser of "stealing and swearing at students" while also not listening to the concerns of the Council. He also argued that under the direction of Alexander Sutherland, the Methodist Church only responded to complaints from the federal government and not the Indigenous Peoples on reserve. See J.R. Miller, *Shingwauk's Vision: A History of Native Residential Schools* (Toronto: University of Toronto Press, 1996), 475.

15 While employed by the provincial government, public school inspectors were regularly asked to inspect the Indian day schools within their school boundaries. In the 1930s, the federal government paid the provincial government fifteen dollars per classroom to conduct these inspections.

16 RG10 School Files Series, C-8207, Letter from Chief Daniel Whetung to the Department of Indian Affairs, 29 October 1910: 1391.

17 RG10 School Files Series, C-8207, Letter from J.D. McLean to Deputy Minister of Education A.G.U. Colquhoun, 16 November 1910: 1394.

18 RG10 School Files Series, C-8207, Letter from John Prosser to the Department of Indian Affairs, 8 December 1910: 2383–4.

19 RG10 School Files Series, C-8207, Letter from School Inspector Ramsden to J.D. McLean, Department of Indian Affairs, 31 December 1910: 1397.

20 Ibid.

21 Ibid.

22 Ibid.

23 Ibid., 1398.

24 RG10 School Files Series, C-8207, Letter from J.D. McLean to John Prosser, 13 January 1911: 1399.

25 RG10 School Files Series, C-8207, Letter from John Prosser to the Department of Indian Affairs, 13 January 1911: 1400.

26 RG10 School Files Series, C-8207, Letter from Mud Lake Indian Day School students to the Department of Indian Affairs, 5 September 1910: 1408.

27 RG10 School Files Series, C-8207, Letter from School Inspector Ramsden to J.D. McLean, Department of Indian Affairs, 23 February 1911: 1409.

28 Ibid., 1410.

29 Ibid., 1411.

30 RG10 School Files Series, C-8207, Letter from J.D. McLean to John Prosser, 6 March 1911: 1416.

31 RG10 School Files Series, C-8207, Letter from John Prosser to the Department of Indian Affairs, 13 May 1911: 1420.

32 Ibid., 1418.

33 RG10 School Files Series, C-8207, Letter from John Prosser to the Department of Indian Affairs, 27 May 1911: 1415.

34 RG10 School Files Series, C-8207, Letter from the Methodist Missionary Society to John Prosser, 13 May 1911: 1422.

35 RG10 School Files Series, C-8207, Letter from Chief Daniel Whetung to the Minister of Education Ontario, 16 June 1911: 1426.

36 Ibid.

37 RG10 School Files Series, C-8207, Letter from J.D. McLean to Deputy Minister of Education A.H.U. Colquhoun: 1429.

38 RG10 School Files Series, C-8207, Letter from John Prosser to the Department of Indian Affairs, 12 October 1911: 1431.

39 RG10 School Files Series, C-8207, Letter from J.D. McLean to John Prosser, 7 December 1911: 1437.

40 RG10 School Files Series, C-8207, Letter from John Prosser to the Department of Indian Affairs, 5 February 1912: 1440–1.

41 RG10 School Files Series, C-8207, Letter from J.D. McLean to John Prosser, 29 May 1912: 1448.

42 RG10 School Files Series, C-8207, Letter from George Gordon to the Department of Indian Affairs, 12 June 1912: 1449.

43 RG10 School files Series, C-8207, Letter from Daniel Whetung Sr, to the Department of Indian Affairs, 9 July 1912: 1456.

44 RG10 School Files Series, C-8207, Letter from Jane Armour to Egerton Shore, General Secretary Methodist Missionary Society, 18 August 1911: 1463. The Ryerson Indian Day School was located in Parry Sound and was likely the school referenced in this letter.

45 RG10 School Files Series, C-8207, Letter from the Methodist Missionary Society to Jane Armour, 21 August 1912: 1464; Marta Danylewycz and Alison Prentice have argued that women teachers were heavily undervalued in this period in Ontario and Quebec and had limited options for higher education. They write, "Turn-of-the-century women teachers in Ontario and Quebec were increasingly aware of their special problems and some were already aware of the ambiguity of their position. Many also knew that a major source of their difficulties was the fact that they were women in school systems largely designed for and controlled by men." Marta Danylewycz and Alison Prentice, "Teachers' Work: Changing Patterns and Perceptions in the Emerging School Systems of Nineteenth-and Early Twentieth-Century Central Canada," *Labour/le travail* 17 (1986): 80.

46 RG10 School Files Series, C-8207, Letter from Jane Armour to General Secretary Egerton Shore, Methodist Missionary Society, 26 August 1912: 1466.

47 RG10 School Files Series, C-8207, Letter from J.D. McLean to Methodist Missionary Society, 5 September 1912: 1470.

48 RG10 School Files Series, C-8207, Letter from General Secretary Egerton Shore, Methodist Missionary Society to J.D. McLean, Department of Indian Affairs, 17 September 1912: 1472.

49 Ibid.

50 RG10 School Files Series, C-8207, Letter from J.D. McLean, Department of Indian Affairs to General Secretary Egerton Shore, Methodist Missionary Society, 24 September 1912.

51 RG10 School Files Series, C-8207, Letter from J.D. McLean, Depart-

ment of Indian Affairs to General Secretary Egerton Shore, Methodist Missionary Society, 30 September 1912: 1474.

52 RG10 School Files Series, C-8207, Letter from J.D. McLean, Department of Indian Affairs to General Secretary Egerton Shore, Methodist Missionary Society, 12 November 1912: 1487.

53 RG10 School Files Series, C-8207, Mud Lake Council Resolution, 31 October 1912: 1488.

54 RG10 School Files Series, C-8207, Letter from Indian Agent McFarlane to Department of Indian Affairs, 1 November 1912: 1489.

55 RG10 School Files Series, C-8207, Letter from J.D. McLean to Indian Agent McFarlane, 18 November 1912: 1494.

56 RG10 School Files Series, C-8207, Letter from J.D. McLean to H.C. Buffam, 23 September 1913: 1500; 1502.

57 Ibid.

58 RG10 School Files Series, C-8207, Extract from Report of School Inspector G.E. Broderick, 8 November 1913: 2412.

59 Ibid.

60 RG10 School Files Series, C-8207, Memo for Dr Scott, 19 November 1913: 2413.

61 RG10 School Files Series, C-8207, Letter from H.C. Buffam to Department of Indian Affairs, 17 March 1914: 1506.

62 RG10 School Files Series, C-8207, Letter from H.C. Buffam to Department of Indian Affairs, 8 June 1914: 1510.

63 Ibid.

64 RG10 School Files Series, C-8207, Resolution of Chemong Council, Signed by Chief Whetung and Secretary Alfred McCue, n.d.: 2430.

65 RG10 School Files Series, C-8207, Letter from Indian Agent R.J. McCamus to Department of Indian Affairs, 3 April 1915: 1521. It was difficult to find personal information about Agent McCamus due to the common nature of his name in twentieth-century Canada. McCamus was involved in a precedent-setting case about the voting of Chief and Council members on reserve. In the 1980s, the Department of Indian and Northern Affairs wrote, "When Parliament enacted the election provisions of the Indian Act and the Indian Advancement Act it had not specified in either piece of legislation any particular procedure with regard to voting. The Department lacking any specific instruc-

tions had adopted the method of open voting. It was not long, however, before the question of the secret ballot arose." In 1915, McCamus asked the department if they would allow Curve Lake to return to "open voting" of the Council and Chief positions without any form of secret ballot. Assistant Deputy and Secretary S. Stewart wrote, "With reference to the subject of the 'secret vote'; referred to by Whetung, it is presumed that by that term he means voting by ballot. If so, the Department sincerely hopes that the majority of the Indians would be wise enough to oppose such retrograde movement as to return to the method of open voting, and no such change should be made without the sanction of the Department." As a result, the government started using only secret ballots for voting of Councils and Chiefs throughout Canada but no "conscious effort was ever made to implement the procedure as part of its electoral policy." Wayne Daugherty and Dennis Madill, "Indian Government under Indian Act Legislation, 1868–1951" (Ottawa: Department of Indian and Northern Affairs, 1980), 60–2, http://publications.gc.ca/collections/collection_2017/aanc-inac/R5-183-1980-eng.pdf.

66 RG10 School Files Series, C-8207, Letter from Department of Indian Affairs to Indian Agent R.J. McCamus, 16 April 1915: 1522.

67 Truant officers were ultimately the federal government's last resort for enforcing the attendance of Indigenous students in schools. The TRC report found: "In 1894, the *Indian Act* was amended to authorize the government 'to secure the compulsory attendance of children at school.' Government officials had already noted the necessity for family ties to be 'severed during the school term.' The *Regulations Relating to the Education of Indian Children* granted Indian agents and justices of the peace the power to authorize the apprehension and placement of Aboriginal children in industrial or boarding schools, if they were satisfied that their parents or guardians were 'unfit or unwilling to provide for the child's education.' Indian agents were authorized to appoint truant officers with 'police powers.' A year later, the acting superintendent general of Indian Affairs asked the Department of Justice to develop a standard warrant for the removal of Aboriginal children from their families where 'adequate provision is not being and will not be made for the care, or education or the education and

care of the said [child].'" Truth and Reconciliation Commission Canada, *Canada's Residential Schools: The Legacy*, 13.

68 RG10 School Files Series, C-8207, Letter from Department of Indian Affairs to Agent R.J. McCamus, 4 May 1915: 1523.

69 RG10 School Files Series, C-8207, Letter from H.C. Buffam to the Department of Indian Affairs, 28 June 1915: 1524.

70 Ibid.

71 RG10 School Files Series, C-8207, Letter from Buffam to the Department of Indian Affairs, 9 August 1915: 1526.

72 RG10 School Files Series, C-8207, Letter from Agent McCamus to Department of Indian Affairs, 27 August 1915: 1533.

73 Ibid.

74 RG10 School Files Series, C-8207, Letter from J.D. McLean to Rev. James Endicott, General Secretary, Methodist Missionary Society, 8 September 1915: 1534.

75 RG10 School Files Series, C-8207, Letter from J.D. McLean to Indian Agent R.J. McCamus, 5 September 1915: 1535.

76 In 1905, the Conservative government, led by James Whitney, consolidated teacher training into four new normal schools developed to train elementary teachers. This new system would respond to the fact that most students only attended elementary school before joining the workforce; therefore requiring an industrialized education. Susan Gelman explains, "The decision to place the new normal schools in Stratford, Hamilton, Peterborough, and North Bay was based on population density, railway connections, local conditions, and proximity to existing schools in Toronto, Ottawa, and London." The Peterborough Normal School existed until the late 1960s when it was closed in favour of teacher-education programs developed through universities. Susan Gelman, "Stratford (Normal School) Teachers' College, 1908–1973," *Historical Studies in Education/Revue d'histoire de l'éducation* (2002): 115.

77 RG10 School Files Series, C-8207, Letter from Rev. James Endicott to Department of Indian Affairs, 17 September 1915: 1541.

78 RG10 School Files Series, C-8207, Letter from Indian Agent R.J. McCamus to the Department of Indian Affairs, n.d.: 1551.

79 RG10 School Files Series, C-8207, School Fair Report from R.H. Abra-

ham, October 1916: 1556. R.H. Abraham was originally a teacher at the Guelph Ontario Agricultural College and, beginning in 1916, was one of the regular school inspectors in Curve Lake. Abraham was invited to visit the day schools around Ontario to promote agricultural education. Research by Allison Norman in Six Nations demonstrates that "in the years following the war, Abraham worked for the Department of Indian Affairs, and found the School Fair, and exhibition held at the No.2 School in Ohswkeen, meant to parallel the 'big fair' held by the Six Nations Agricultural society." Norman also argues, "Clearly it was not just the DIA using agricultural education as a 'civilizing' influence on the children." Alison Elizabeth Norman, "Race, Gender and Colonialism: Public Life Among the Six Nations of Grand River, 1899–1939" (PhD diss., University of Toronto, 2010), 130–1.

80 RG10 School Files Series, C-8207, Letter from Joseph Whetung to the Department of Indian Affairs, 23 October 1916: 1558.

81 RG10 School Files Series, C-8207, Letter from Arthur Whetung to the Department of Indian Affairs, 2 November 1916: 1560.

82 Ibid.

83 RG10 School Files Series, C-8207, Report on the Mud Lake Reserve, R.H. Abraham, 11 July 1916: 2470.

84 Ibid.

85 Ibid.

86 RG10 School Files Series, C-8207, Memorandum Indian Affairs, 9 November 1916: 1561.

87 RG10 School Files Series, C-8207, Letter from J.D. McLean to Indian Agent McCamus, 21 November 1916: 1563.

88 RG10 School Files Series, C-8207, Letter from Chief Daniel Whetung to Mr Benson, School Inspector, 8 December 1916: 1564.

89 Ibid.

90 Ibid.

91 Ibid., 1565.

92 Ibid.

93 Library and Archives of Canada, RG10, Volume 3194, File 486,661, "Removal to West – more land." Letter from Indian Agent McCamus to the Department of Indian Affairs, 4 October 1916: 3, http://central.bac-lac.gc.ca/.redirect?app=fonandcol&id=2076354&lang=eng.

94 Ibid.

95 RG10, Volume 3194, File 489,661, Memorandum to Mr Scott, 5 December 1916: 4, http://central.bac-lac.gc.ca/.redirect?app=fonandcol&id=2076354&lang=eng.

96 Ibid., 5.

97 RG10 School Files Series, C-8207, Letter from Chief Daniel Whetung to the Department of Indian Affairs, 6 December 1916: 1567.

98 Library and Archives of Canada, RG10, Volume 3194, File 489,602, "Mud Lake School Board." Resolution sent from Mud Lake Chief and Council to the Department of Indian Affairs, 5 December 1916: 3, http://central.bac-lac.gc.ca/.redirect?app=fonandcol&id=2076375&lang=eng.

99 RG10 School Files Series, C-8207, Letter from Chief Daniel Whetung to Mr Benson, School Inspector, 8 December 1916: 1564–5.

100 RG10 School Files Series, C-8207, Letter from Chief Daniel Whetung to the Department of Indian Affairs, 6 December 1916, 1566–7.

101 RG10 School Files Series, 3194, File 489,602, Letter from Indian Agent McCamus to the Department of Indian Affairs, 11 December 1916: 3, http://central.bac-lac.gc.ca/.redirect?app=fonandcol&id=2076375&lang=eng.

102 RG10 School Files Series, 3194, File 489,602, Letter from J.D. Mclean to Indian Agent McCamus, 5 January 1917: 5, http://central.bac-lac.gc.ca/.redirect?app=fonandcol&id=2076375&lang=eng.

103 RG10 School Files Series, C-8207, Letter from Methodist Society of Canada to the Department of Indian Affairs, 8 December 1916: 1568.

104 Ibid.

105 Ibid.

106 RG10 School Files Series, C-8207, Letter from Indian Agent Robert McCamus to the Department of Indian Affairs, 7 December 1916: 1571–3.

107 RG10 School Files Series, C-8207, Letter from Zella May Hanes to the Methodist Missionary Society, 11 December 1916: 1575.

108 RG10 School Files Series, C-8207, Letter from Methodist Missionary Society to the Department of Indian Affairs, 19 December 1916: 1576–7.

109 RG10 School Files Series, C-8207, Letter from Zella May Hanes to the Department of Indian Affairs, 22 December 1916: 1579–83.

110 Ibid. The mission house was used primarily as a teacher's residence on reserve, as the facility no longer housed missionaries. This residence was maintained through Curve Lake's funds to attract teachers to the community who wanted to have their own place to live. The ensuing debate was over equipment ownership within the facility and whether the government, teacher, or community should pay for upkeep.

111 RG10 School Files Series, C-8207, Letter from Chief Daniel Whetung to the Department of Indian Affairs, 2 January 1917: 1582.

112 RG10 School Files Series, C-8207, Letter from Constable John Jacobs to the Department of Indian Affairs: 1585–6.

113 RG10 School Files Series, C-8207, Letter from School Inspector Parker to the Deputy Superintendent of Indian Affairs, Duncan Campbell Scott, 19 January 1917: 1606–7.

114 Ibid., 1607.

115 RG10 School Files Series, C-8207, Letter from Methodist Missionary Society to the Department of Indian Affairs, 15 February 1917: 1610.

116 RG10 School Files Series, C-8207, Letter from the Department of Indian Affairs to Chief Daniel Whetung, 20 February 1917: 1613.

117 Ibid.

118 Chief Whetung mentioned that Zella May Hanes specifically targeted his daughter, Daisey Whetung, with those comments.

119 RG10 School Files Series, C-8207, Letter from Chief Daniel Whetung to the Department of Indian Affairs, 26 February 1917: 1616.

120 Ibid.

121 It is difficult, and I feel inappropriate, to find information about other community members who weren't directly referenced within the archive; however, Joseph and Arthur Whetung were cousins to Chief Daniel Whetung. William Knott was another prominent community member, and his descendants appear later in this book.

122 RG10 School Files Series, C-8207, Letter from Arthur Whetung to Deputy Superintendent Duncan Campbell Scott, 23 May 1917: 1640.

123 RG10 School Files Series, C-8207, Letter from Methodist Missionary Society to the Department of Indian Affairs, 26 March 1917: 1620.

124 Ibid.

125 RG10 School Files Series, C-8207, "Case Tried at Chemong Village," *Peterborough Examiner*, 17 May 1917.

126 Ibid.

127 RG10 School Files Series, C-8207, Letter from Joseph Whetung, William Knott, 22 May 1917: 1637–8.

128 Ibid. These communications indicate that Indigenous community members were acutely aware of the political relationship that had developed between the Chief and the department. Any grievances with the Chief would lead other members to contact the department about their concerns, as the department ultimately had the power to decide on key educational issues such as funding, the hiring of teachers, and other administrative problems.

129 RG10 School Files Series, C-8207, Letter from the J.D. McLean to Indian Agent McCamus.

130 Ibid.

131 RG10 School Files Series, C-8207, Letter from Chief Daniel Whetung to the Department of Indian Affairs, 7 June 1917: 1645.

132 Ibid., 1646.

133 Ibid.

134 RG10 School Files Series, C-8207, Letter from Deputy Superintendent Duncan Campbell Scott to Chief Whetung, 9 June 1917: 1647.

135 RG10 School Files Series, C-8207, Report on the Mud Lake Reserve by R.H. Abraham, May 1917: 1632.

136 RG10 School Files Series, C-8207, Letter from J.D. McLean to Rev. J.H. Arnup, Methodist Missionary Society, 12 July 1917: 1648.

137 RG10 School Files Series, C-8207, Letter from A. Buie to Indian Agent McCamus, 9 July 1917: 1650.

138 According to conscription records, an Arthur H. Buie, with a place of birth in Hamilton, Ontario, was conscripted to the Canadian Expeditionary Force on 24 October 1917. As Buie was also a student in Hamilton at McMaster University, and his signature is similar to the Indian Affairs archive, it appears that he did serve in the First World War. He was conscripted from a hotel in Dauphin, Manitoba, that served as his primary residence. He also indicated that he fled Curve Lake after the first day of school. Particulars of Recruit, Drafted Under the Military Service Act, 1917. "Arthur H. Buie." King's Hotel, Dauphin, Manitoba, 24 October 1917, http://central.bac-lac.gc.ca/.item/?op=img&app=CEF&id=270561a.

139 RG10 School Files Series, C-8207, Telegram from R.H. Abraham to Duncan Campbell Scott, 6 September 1917.

140 RG10, School Files Series, C-8207, Letter from J.D. McLean to Indian Agent McCamus, 7 September 1917: 1656.

141 Ibid.

142 RG10 School Files Series, C-8207, Letter from Indian Agent McCamus to the Department of Indian Affairs, 4 January 1918: 1659.

143 RG10 School Files Series, C-8207, Report from Inspector R.H. Abraham, 29 June 1918: 1661.

144 RG10 School Files Series, C-8207, Report from Inspector Broderick, 3 May 1918: 1662.

145 RG10 School Files Series, C-8207, Letter from J.D. McLean to Indian Agent McCamus, 6 August 1919: 1675.

146 RG10 School Files Series, C-8207, Report from Inspector Broderick, 3 May 1918: 1662.

147 RG10 School Files Series, C-8207, Letter from J.D. McLean to [missing], 13 September 1918: 1918.

148 Ibid.

149 RG10 School Files Series, C-8207, Report from Inspector Broderick, 3 May 1918: 2488.

150 Ibid.

151 RG10 School Files Series, C-8207, Report from Inspector Broderick, 14 February 1919: 1668.

152 RG10 School Files Series, C-8207, Report from Inspector Broderick, 4 February 1918: 2490.

153 RG10 School Files Series, C-8207, Letter from Indian Agent R.J. McCamus to the Department of Indian Affairs, 2 August 1919: 1674.

154 RG10 School Files Series, C-8207, Letter from Methodist Missionary Society to J.D. McLean, 30 August 1919: 1680.

155 Robert Gidney and Wyn P.J. Millar found that "male teachers in Ontario and British Columbia were relatively well paid compared to other male occupations, standing ninth out of sixty-five [in total earnings]." In the period between 1910 and 1929, the salary for white male elementary teachers in the public school system rose nearly 40 per cent to an average of $1,685 in 1921. Robert Gidney and Wyn P.J. Millar, "The Salaries of Teachers in English Canada, 1900–1940: A Reappraisal,"

Historical Studies in Education/Revue d'histoire de l'éducation (2010): 8–9, 25.

156 RG10 School Files Series, C-8207, Letter from Indian Agent R.J. McCamus to the Department of Indian Affairs, 25 November 1919: 1687.

157 Ibid.

158 RG10 School Files Series, C-8207, Letter from Wesley Watson to Duncan Campbell Scott, 22 November 1919: 1688.

159 Ibid., 1699.

160 RG10 School Files Series, C-8207, Letter from Harold J. Bell to the Department of Indian Affairs, 9 February 1920: 1699.

161 RG10 School Files Series Letter, C-8207, from Indian Agent McCamus to the Department of Indian Affairs, 13 March 1920: 1706.

162 Ibid., 1707.

163 RG10 School Files Series, C-8207, Letter from Indian Agent McCamus to the Department of Indian Affairs, 21 April 1920: 1709.

164 This was still nearly $700 cheaper than the average white male teacher's salary in public schools in 1921. Gidney and Millar, "The Salaries of Teachers in English Canada," 25.

165 RG10 School Files Series, C-8207, Letter from Methodist Missionary Society to J.D. McLean, 19 February 1920: 1700.

166 RG10 School Files Series, C-8207, Letter from Indian Agent McCamus to the Department of Indian Affairs, 19 October 1920: 1711.

167 RG10 School Files Series, C-8207, Letter from Indian Agent McCamus to the Department of Indian Affairs, 17 June 1921: 1712.

168 Ibid.

169 The average salary of a white female teacher was $974, or nearly double what was being paid to Miss Jessup in the yearly reports. Specifically, "in 1920, women teachers in the one-room schools of these inspectorates made 88% of the salaries earned by male teachers in similar schools. In 1925, women earned 94% of male salaries; by 1930, they had near-parity, at 98%." Gidney and Millar, "The Salaries of Teachers in English Canada," 14, 25; Compared with other available positions at the time, white women teachers had strong wages and respected social standing within their communities. Eric W. Sager, "Women Teachers in Canada, 1881–1901: Revisiting the 'Feminization' of an Occupation," *Canadian Historical Review* 88, no. 2 (2007): 201–36.

170 RG10 School Files Series, C-8207, Letter to from [missing] to Superintendent of Indian Education Ferrier, 26 July 1921: 1714. This letter came directly after Miss Jessup's resignation, and the handwriting matches her earlier correspondence with the department, but the letter's signature is cut off in the archive. For a full review of female teaching opportunities in this period, please see Alison L. Prentice and Marjorie R. Theobald, eds, *Women Who Taught: Perspectives on the History of Women and Teaching* (Toronto: University of Toronto Press, 1991). The last chapter by Allison Prentice, "Scholarly Passion: Two Persons Who Caught It," describes the ability of two Ontario teachers to progress into higher education or training.

171 Ibid.

172 Ibid.

173 RG10 School Files Series, C-8207, Letter from Superintendent of Indian Education Russell T. Ferrier to Indian Agent McCamus, 27 December 1921: 1718.

174 RG10 School Files Series, C-8207, Letter from Indian Agent R.J. McCamus to the Department of Indian Affairs, 6 July 1922: 1731.

175 Ibid.

176 RG10 School Files Series, C-8207, Letter from Ethel Browne to The Department of Indian Affairs, 5 November 1922: 1739.

177 Ibid.

178 RG10 School Files Series, C-8207, Letter from Indian Agent R.J. McCamus to the Department of Indian Affairs, 2 April 1923: 1742.

179 RG10 School Files Series, C-8207, Letter from Indian Agent R.J. McCamus to the Department of Indian Affairs, 30 June 1923: 1744.

180 RG10 School Files Series, C-8207, Letter from Acting Assistant Deputy A.F. MacKenzie to Rev. A Lloyd Smith, Methodist Missionary Society, 8 September 1923: 1747.

181 RG10 School Files Series, C-8207, Letter from Rev. A Lloyd Smith, Methodist Missionary Society to the Department of Indian Affairs, 14 September 1923: 1748.

182 Ibid.

183 RG10 School Files Series, C-8207, Letter from Acting Assistant Deputy A.F. MacKenzie, to Rev. A Lloyd Smith, Methodist Missionary Society, 18 September 1923: 1749.

184 RG10 School Files Series, C-8207, Letter from Chief Daniel Whetung to the Department of Indian Affairs, 18 September 1923: 1750–1.

185 Ibid.

186 Ibid., 1751.

187 RG10 School Files Series, C-8207, Letter from Acting Assistant Deputy A.F. MacKenzie, to Chief Daniel Whetung Jr, 22 September 1923: 1752.

188 A teaching collegiate was a specialized high-school program created to help train larger numbers of students for specific roles. Gidney and Millar state, "Ontario had its 'collegiate institutes' and its 'high schools,' the former almost all located in the cities and large towns, the latter in a variety of settings, including many of the province's more populous villages … The collegiate institutes, high schools, and vocational schools or departments in Canada's larger towns and cities represented the modern face of secondary education – large, well-equipped facilities, many of them new and many still in use today. Though different in some important respects, these were institutions that any adult educated in the second half of the last century, indeed any modern teenager, would instantly recognize as schools providing a secondary education." These schools also provided a matriculation certificate that could be used to earn employment in various fields, from business to education. Gidney and Millar, "How Schools Worked," 109, 111.

189 RG10 School Files Series, C-8207, Letter from Methodist Missionary Society to the Department of Indian Affairs, 26 September 1923: 1753.

190 RG10 School Files Series, C-8207, Letter from A.F. MacKenzie to the Methodist Missionary Society, 29 September 1923: 1755.

191 RG10 School Files Series, C-8207, Letter from Rev. Arthur Barner to the Methodist Missionary Society, 17 November 1923: 1759.

192 RG10 School Files Series, C-8207, Extract from Report – 3 December 1923: 1762.

193 RG10 School Files Series, C-8207, Memo for File, 12 December 1923: 1763.

194 RG10 School Files Series, C-8207, Letter from J.D. McLean to the Methodist Missionary Society, 28 December 1923.

195 RG10 School Files Series, C-8207, Letter from the Methodist Missionary Society to the Department of Indian Affairs, 22 January 1924: 1766.

196 RG10 School Files Series, C-8207, Letter from J.D. McLean to the Methodist Missionary Society, 25 January 1923: 1767.
197 RG10 School Files Series, C-8207, Letter from Indian Agent McCamus to the Department of Indian Affairs, 3 April 1924: 1768,
198 RG10 School Files Series, C-8207, Extract of Report for Chemong Indian Day School, Edna Harris, Teacher, 31 March 1924: 2515.
199 RG10 School Files Series, C-8207, Letter from J.D. McLean to Indian Agent McCamus, 10 April 1924: 1769.
200 RG10 School Files Series, C-8207, Telegram from Chief Whetung to J.D. McLean, 29 April 1924: 1772.
201 Gidney and Millar, "The Salaries of Teachers in English Canada," 25.
202 RG10 School Files Series, C-8207, Letter from J.D. McLean to Indian Agent McCamus, 30 April 1924: 1774.
203 RG10 School Files Series, C-8207, Letter from J.D. McLean to Methodist Missionary Society, 11 July 1924: 1783.
204 RG10 School Files Series, C-8207, Letter from Indian Agent McCamus to the Department of Indian Affairs, 9 July 1924: 1784.
205 RG10 School Files Series, C-8207, Letter from Chief Daniel Whetung to the Department of Indian Affairs, 19 July 1914: 1790.
206 RG10 School Files Series, C-8207 Letter from Indian Agent McCamus to the Department of Indian Affairs, 4 April 1925: 1793.
207 RG10 School Files Series, C-8207, Letter from Indian Agent McCamus to the Department of Indian Affairs, 20 June 1925: 1794.
208 RG10 School Files Series, C-8207, Letter from Indian Agent McCamus to the Department of Indian Affairs, 28 July 1925: 1798.
209 RG10 School Files Series, C-8207, Memo to Duncan Campbell Scott, from Superintendent of Indian Education Russell T. Ferrier, 9 April 1926: 1799.

CHAPTER FIVE

1 RG10 School Files Series, C-8207, Letter from J.D. McLean to Indian Agent McCamus, 30 June 1926: 1804.
2 RG10 School Files Series, C-8207, Letter from Chief Daniel Whetung to the Department of Indian Affairs, 13 July 1926: 1808.
3 RG10 School Files Series, C-8207, Letter from J.D. McLean to Chief Daniel Whetung, 16 July 1926: 1809.

4 RG10 School Files Series, C-8207, Letter from Russell T. Ferrier to James Shannon, Missionary Society accountant, 17 July 1926: 1812
5 RG10 School Files Series, C-8207, Letter from Member of Parliament E.A. Peck to Duncan Campbell Scott, 24 July 1926: 1813.
6 RG10 School Files Series, C-8207, Letter from J.D. Mclean to Member of Parliament E.A. Peck, 27 July 1926: 1814.
7 RG10 School Files Series, C-8207, Letter from the United Church of Canada to Department of Indian Affairs, 16 August 1926: 1815.
8 RG10 School Files Series, C-8207, Letter from Chief Daniel Whetung to the Department of Indian Affairs, 25 October 1926: 1817.
9 Ibid., 1818.
10 Ibid.
11 RG10 School Files Series, C-8207, Extract of Report from R.F. Downey, 22 October 1926: 2560. As the city school inspector for the Peterborough region, R.F. Downey still has a K–6 public school named in his honour. The school website notes: "R.F. Downey Public School officially opened its doors on May 8th during the Centennial year of 1967. The school is named after Roscoe Frederick Downey who served the area of Peterborough as teacher, principal, inspector, and educational counsellor." "School History" (n.d.), https://rfdowney.kprdsb.ca.
12 RG10 School Files Series, C-8207, Letter Indian Agent R.J. McCamus to the Department of Indian Affairs, 13 November 1926: 1821.
13 Ibid.
14 RG10 School Files Series, C-8207, Letter from the United Church of Canada to Russell T. Ferrier, Department of Indian Affairs, 20 December 1926: 1824.
15 RG10 School Files Series, C-8207, Letter from Jean Scott to the Department of Indian Affairs, 30 December: 1926.
16 RG10 School Files Series, C-8207, Letter from the United Church of Canada to the Russell T. Ferrier, Department of Indian Affairs, 28 December 1926: 1828.
17 RG10 School Files Series, C-8207, Letter from Bert McCue to the Department of Indian Affairs, 1 June 1928: 1833.
18 RG10 School Files Series, C-8207, Letter from Bert McCue to the Department of Indian Affairs, 17 April 1928: 1834.
19 RG10 School Files Series, C-8207, Letter from Indian Agent Eastwood to the Department of Indian Affairs, 30 June 1928. Lt Vincent

McCarter Eastwood was a well-known First World War veteran who was awarded the Military Cross for his service by King George V at Buckingham Palace. It was reported that he had "conspicuous gallantry and devotion to duty when in command of a raiding party. He carried out several valuable reconnaissances previous to the raid. During the operations, he, with a few men, entered the enemy's trenches, personally shot two of the enemy, and bombed his way along their front line, inflicting several casualties before withdrawing." After he earned this medal, he was seriously injured with a broken back and right scapula during the battle of Passchendaele in 1917, which led to over two years in hospital before being released. Eastwood wrote extensively about his wartime experience in the trenches; this has been preserved by the 18th Battalion, in which he enlisted at the age of nineteen in Peterborough. "Vincent McCarter Eastwood: Lieutenant (Military Cross)," War Diaries of the 18th Battalion CEF, accessed 31 May 2021, https://18thbattalioncef.blog/soldiers-listed-in-diary/eastwood-vincent-mccarter-lieutenant/. Indian Agent Vincent Eastwood would be the local representative of the federal government from 1927 until his retirement in 1950. He would also serve in the Second World War in 1942.

20 RG10 School Files Series, C-8207, Letter from Morgan Lewis to the Department of Indian Affairs, 28 June 1928: 1837–9.

21 RG10 School Files Series, C-8207, Letter from Acting Assistant Deputy A.F. MacKenzie to Morgan Lewis, Teacher, 2 July 1929: 1840

22 RG10 School Files Series, C-8207, Letter from Indian Agent Eastwood to the Department of Indian Affairs, Department 20, 1929: 1843.

23 RG10 School Files Series, C-8207, Letter from Acting Assistant Deputy A.F. MacKenzie to Indian Agent Eastwood, 4 December 1929: 1848.

24 RG10 School Files Series, C-8207, Letter from A.F. MacKenzie to the United Church of Canada, 10 December 1929: 1851.

25 RG10 School Files Series, C-8207, Letter from Indian Agent Eastwood to the Department of Indian, 26 April 1930: 1852.

26 See the comments by Chief Daniel Whetung earlier in this chapter regarding the struggle of getting students into high school.

27 RG10 School Files Series, C-8207, Letter from A.F. MacKenzie to Indian Agent Eastwood, 16 June 1930: 1853.

28 RG10 School Files Series, C-8207, Letter from Indian Agent Eastwood to the Department of Indian Affairs, 14 July 1930: 1856.

29 RG10 School Files Series, C-8207, Letter from Themla Carveth to Indian Agent Eastwood, 3 July 1930: 1858.

30 RG10 School Files Series, C-8207, Telegram from A.F. MacKenzie to Indian Agent Eastwood, 2 July 1930: 1862.

31 RG10 School Files Series, C-8207, Extract from School Inspection by R.F. Downey, 23 October 1930: 1866.

32 Information about this teacher and why or when she was hired is missing from the archival record.

33 RG10 School Files Series, C-8207, Letter from Thelma Carveth to Indian Agent Eastwood, 7 July 1931: 1874.

34 RG10 School Files Series, C-8207, Letter from Scott Wildman to the Department of Indian Affairs, 25 July 1931: 1883–4.

35 Both Miss Browne and Mr Lewis noted the significant issues with the mission house and looked for other opportunities where the teachers' residence was part of the school, such as in Rama First Nation.

36 Ibid. See also chalk payments in RG-10 School Files Series, C-8208, Letter from Indian Agent, V.M. Eastwood to the Secretary, Department of Indian Affairs, n.d.: 19.

37 RG10 School Files Series, C-8208, Extract from Report of Inspector Downey on the Mud Lake Indian Day School, 30 May 1927: 10.

38 Ibid.

39 RG10 School Files Series, C-8208, Extract from Report of Inspector Downey on the Mud Lake Indian Day School, 26 September 1927: 15. The number of inspections varied by year, economic conditions, and the ability of inspectors to travel to the community in the winter months. Typically, fall and spring reports were submitted to the department that provided updates about the school year.

40 RG10 School Files Series, C-8208, Letter from Assistant Deputy and Secretary of Indian Affairs J.D. McLean, to Indian Agent V.M. Eastwood, 20 October 1927: 16.

41 RG10 School Files Series, C-8208, Letter from Assistant Deputy and Secretary of Indian Affairs J.D. McLean to Indian Agent V.M. Eastwood, 20 October 1928: 38.

42 RG10 School Files Series, C-8208, Extract from Report of Inspector Downey on the Mud Lake Indian Day School, 28 May 1929: 56.

43 RG10 School Files Series, C-8208, Letter from Assistant Deputy and Secretary of Indian Affairs A.F. MacKenzie to Indian Agent V.M. Eastwood, 28 June 1929: 57.

44 RG10 School Files Series, C-8208, Letter from Assistant Deputy and Secretary of Indian Affairs A.F. MacKenzie to Indian Agent, V.M. Eastwood, 17 January 1928: 26.

45 RG10 School Files Series, C-8208, Letter from Assistant Deputy and Secretary of Indian Affairs J.D. McLean to Indian Agent V.M. Eastwood, 23 October 1928: 36.

46 RG10 School Files Series, C-8208, Letter from Indian Agent V.M. Eastwood to Assistant Deputy and Secretary of Indian Affairs J.D. McLean, 27 October 1928: 39.

47 RG10 School Files Series, C-8208, Letter from Assistant Deputy and Secretary of Indian Affairs J.D. McLean to Indian Agent V.M. Eastwood, 30 October 1928: 40.

48 Ibid.

49 RG10 School Files Series, C-8208, Letter from Indian Agent V.M. Eastwood to Assistant Deputy and Secretary of Indian Affairs J.D. McLean, 27 October 1928: 43.

50 RG10 School Files Series, C-8208, Letter from Indian Agent V.M. Eastwood to Assistant Deputy and Secretary of Indian Affairs J.D. McLean, 2 February 1929: 49.

51 RG10 School Files Series, C-8208, Letter from Indian Agent V.M. Eastwood to Assistant Deputy and Secretary of Indian Affairs J.D. McLean, 22 February 1929: 50.

52 RG10 School Files Series, C-8208, Letter from Assistant Deputy and Secretary of Indian Affairs J.D. McLean to Indian Agent V.M. Eastwood, 30 October 1928: 51.

53 RG10 School Files Series, C-8208, Letter from Indian Agent V.M. Eastwood to Assistant Deputy and Secretary of Indian Affairs A.F. MacKenzie, 8 August 1929: 58.

54 Ibid.

55 RG10 School Files Series, C-8208, Letter from Indian Agent V.M.

Eastwood to Assistant Deputy and Secretary of Indian Affairs A.F. MacKenzie, 27 August 1929: 60.

56 The federal government had a fiduciary duty to protect the interests of Indigenous Peoples under its control through the Indian Act and was, therefore, responsible for this type of maintenance.

57 RG10 School Files Series, C-8208, Letter from Assistant Deputy and Secretary J.D. Mclean, Department of Indian Affairs, 29 August 1929: 61.

58 RG10 School Files Series, C-8208, Letter from Chief Daniel Whetung to Department of Indian Affairs, May 1929: 62.

59 RG10 School Files Series, C-8208, Letter from Indian Agent V.M. Eastwood to the Department of Indian Affairs, 4 September 1929: 63–4.

60 RG10 School Files Series, C-8208, Letter from Acting Assistant Deputy and Secretary A.F. MacKenzie, 12 September 1929: 65.

61 As a majority of the community attended services at the United Church and this community also controlled the mission, Band funds were sometimes used to support these initiatives with or without the consent of Chief and Council. Rev. George Henderson reported that over a hundred community members attended church services at the Methodist – now United – Church. He said, "These Methodist church, common consent, has the right of way. Winter evenings they have a congregation of about 100 to 120. About 55 are members of our church. They hold class and prayer meetings. Last year, they paid a minister's salary $50, and contributed to the missionary society $53. They have an active Ladies' Aid Society which raised about $50 last year the most of which was spent caring for the sick." RG10 School Files Series, C-8207, Report from Rev. George W. Henderson to Rev. Sutherland and Department of Indian Affairs, 9 July 1909, 1350.

62 RG10 School Files Series, C-8208, Letter from Acting Assistant Deputy and Secretary A.F. MacKenzie, 12 September 1929: 65.

63 RG10 School Files Series, C-8208, Letter from Indian Agent V.M. Eastwood to Assistant Deputy and Secretary of Indian Affairs A.F. MacKenzie, 13 September 1929: 72.

64 RG10 School Files Series, C-8208, Letter from Indian Agent V.M. Eastwood to Assistant Deputy and Secretary of Indian Affairs A.F. MacKenzie, 14 September 1929: 68.

65 RG10 School Files Series, C-8208, Telegram from Indian Agent V.M. Eastwood to the Department of Indian Affairs, 5 October 1929: 84.

66 RG10 School Files Series, C-8208, Letter from Assistant Deputy and Secretary of Indian Affairs J.D. McLean to Indian Agent V.M. Eastwood, 30 October 1928: 85.

67 RG10 School Files Series, C-8208, School Inspection Report, Inspector McGookin, 29 October 1929: 89.

68 Ibid.

69 RG10 School Files Series, C-8208, W.R. Turner Furnance Receipt, payable by V. Eastwood, 23 November 1929: 115.

70 RG10 School Files Series, C-8208, Letter from Indian Agent V.M. Eastwood to Assistant Deputy and Secretary of Indian Affairs A .F. MacKenzie, 10 December 1929: 116.

71 RG10 School Files Series, C-8207, Letter from Margaret Gardiner to the Department of Indian Affairs, 5 August 1931: 1890.

72 RG10 School Files Series, C-8207, Letter from A.F. MacKenzie to Margaret Gardiner, 15 August 1931: 1898. During this period, it was socially acceptable for women to work as nurses or secretaries but not as teachers. Women were paid less than their male counterparts in all these positions and had limited opportunities to advance to higher positions within these institutions. As Gidney and Millar note, "In the 1920s elementary school teaching increasingly required something like three years of high school education. Although there were considerable variations for entry into nursing, the Canadian median in 1930 was two years of high school, and the larger, prestigious training schools required more than that." Gidney and Millar, *How Schools Work*, 67.

73 RG10 School Files Series, C-8207, Letter from Indian Agent Eastwood to the Department of Indian, 3 October 1931: 1900.

74 Ibid.

75 Success in the school was defined as progressing through the Indian Day School to write the high school entrance examinations, leading to more profitable positions within Canadian society. At this point in the school's history, this system was woefully unfunded and unable to keep regular teachers, which suggests that the government systematically prevented Indigenous children from reaching high school. This

process may have been unintentionally influenced by Indian agents, Chiefs, or other community members, but it relied entirely on the funding provided by the government to help students succeed. This funding was not comparable to the salaries and funding provided to the Ontario public schools, as evidenced in a number of preceding endnotes.

76 RG10 School Files Series, C-8207, Letter from Chief Daniel Whetung to Superintendent of Education Russell Ferrier, 16 December 1931: 1901.

77 RG10 School Files Series, C-8207, Letter from Indian Agent Eastwood to the Department of Indian Affairs, 19 December 1931: 1904.

78 Ibid.

79 RG10 School Files Series, C-8207, Letter from Superintendent of Education Russell Ferrier to Indian Agent Eastwood, 18 January 1932, 1906.

80 RG10 School Files Series, C-8207, Letter from Margaret Gardiner to the Department of Indian Affairs, 7 January 1932: 1912.

81 Ibid., 1913.

82 Ibid., 1914.

83 Ibid., 1917.

84 Ibid., 1916.

85 RG10 School Files Series, C-8207, Letter from Margaret Gardiner to the Superintendent of Education, Department of Indian Affairs, 11 January 1932: 1919.

86 Ibid., 1922.

87 Ibid., 1922.

88 Ibid., 1924–5.

89 Ibid., 1925.

90 RG10 School Files Series, C-8207, Letter from Indian Agent Eastwood to the Department of Indian Affairs, 21 January 1932: 1928.

91 RG10 School Files Series, C-8207, Letter from Russell Ferrier, Superintendent of Education to Margaret Gardiner, 21 January 1932.

92 RG10 School Files Series, C-8207, Letter from Margaret Gardiner to Russell Ferrier, Superintendent of Education, 20 January 1932: 1929.

93 Ibid., 1932.

94 RG10 School Files Series, C-8207, Petition from Mud Lake Band Members to Department of Indian Affairs, 22 January 1932: 1934–5.

95 Ibid.

96 RG10 School Files Series, C-8207, Letter from Alex Knott to Superintendent of Education Russell Ferrier, C-8207, 25 January 1932: 1936–7.

97 RG10 School Files Series, C-8207, Memo for File, R.F., 29 January 1932: 1938.

98 Ibid.

99 The superintendent of Indian education was responsible for all the Indian day schools and residential schools, which numbered well over six hundred institutions across Canada by that time. Due to these logistics, it was rare for the superintendent to visit a school. Please see www.indiandayschools.org.

100 Ibid.

101 The connection between physical education and assimilation was well documented in the TRC report. It was used as a method of bringing Indigenous students into the Canadian identity by creating "truly Anglo-saxon vigor" and to ensure students were physically fit in case of war. The TRC report stated, "Choirs, brass bands, and organized sports were common at many Residential Schools. Authorities believed that these activities, in addition to whatever pleasure they might give to students, would contribute to their cultural assimilation. This flowed from the confused belief that one could not be 'Indian' and play the trumpet or ice hockey; a belief that ignored the fact that cultural and recreational activities had long had a central role in the lives of Aboriginal people. This belief also failed to recognize that, for centuries, Aboriginal people had managed to incorporate a variety of Euro-Canadian technologies and activities into their lives, including arts and sports, while remaining Aboriginal." Truth and Reconciliation Commission Canada, *Canada's Residential Schools: The History*, 353, 360, 367.

102 RG10 School Files Series, C-8208, Letter from Indian Agent Eastwood to the Department of Indian Affairs, 4 August 1933: 653.

103 RG10 School Files Series, C-8208, Memo on file from Russell Ferrier, 5 February 1930: 129.

104 RG10 School Files Series, C-8208, Special Resolution Mud Lake Council, 4 May 1930: 140.

105 RG10 School Files Series, C-8208, Letter from Chief Whetung to Indian Agent Eastwood, May and September 1930: 140, 158.

106 RG10 School Files Series, C-8208, Extract from School Inspection Report, Inspector McGookin, 17 September 1930: 151.

107 RG10 School Files Series, C-8208, Letter from Assistant Deputy A.F. MacKenzie to Indian Agent V.M. Eastwood, 26 September 1930: 152.

108 Ibid.

109 RG10 School Files Series, C-8208, Memo for File, Mud Lake Day School, 12 January 1931: 181.

110 Ibid.

111 RG10 School Files Series, C-8208, Letter from Indian Agent V.M. Eastwood to A.F. MacKenzie, Assistant Deputy and Secretary of Indian Affairs, 22 April 1931: 191.

112 RG10 School Files Series, C-8208, Extract from School Inspection Report, Inspector McGookin, 29 January 1934: 238.

113 RG10 School Files Series, C-8208, Letter from Indian Agent V.M. Eastwood to Department of Indian Affairs, 26 May 1934: 239.

114 RG10 School Files Series, C-8208, Letter from the Mississauga of Mud Lake Band Council to Indian Agent Eastwood, 17 December 1934, Curve Lake, Ontario: 249.

115 RG10 School Files Series, C-8208, Letter from Indian Agent V.M. Eastwood to Department of Indian Affairs, 17 January 1935: 250.

116 Ibid.

117 Ibid.

118 Ibid.

119 RG10 School Files Series, C-8208, Letter from Indian Agent V.M. Eastwood to Department of Indian Affairs, 17 January 1935: 252.

120 RG10 School Files Series, C-8208, Letter from Assistant Deputy A.F. MacKenzie to Indian Agent V.M. Eastwood, 22 January 1935: 253.

121 Ibid.

122 RG10 School Files Series, C-8208, Letter from Assistant Deputy A.F. MacKenzie to Indian Agent V.M. Eastwood, 1 May 1935: 257.

123 Ibid.

124 RG10 School Files Series, C-8208, Letter from Mud Lake Council to Indian Agent V.M. Eastwood, 13 May 1935: 261.

125 RG10 School Files Series, C-8208, Letter from Acting Secretary T.R.L. MacInnes to Indian Agent V.M. Eastwood, 21 May 1935: 264.

126 RG10 School Files Series, C-8208, Letter from Indian Agent V.M. Eastwood: 266.

127 RG10 School Files Series, C-8208, Letter from Assistant Deputy A.F. MacKenzie to Indian Agent V.M. Eastwood, 26 June: 267.

128 RG10 School Files Series, C-8208, Letter from Indian Agent V.M. Eastwood to the Department of Indian Affairs, 15 September 1937: 304.

129 Ibid.

130 RG10 School Files Series, C-8208, Letter from Philip Phelan, Chief Training Division to Indian Agent V.M. Eastwood, 11 June 1938: 310. This quote also demonstrates that one of the primary reasons for keeping these detailed records was to ensure accountability for monies being spent in the Indian day school system. This form of paper record was routinely used to question the intentions of the community or Indian agent in requesting items.

131 RG10 School Files Series, C-8208, Letter from Indian Agent V.M. Eastwood to Philip Phelan, Chief Training Division, 13 June 1938: 312.

132 RG10 School Files Series, C-8208, Extract from School Inspection of Mud Lake Indian Day School, 11 October 1938: 319.

133 These provisions were made before the outbreak of the Second World War, but there is no clear reason why the funding increased during these years.

134 RG10 School Files Series, C-8208, Letter from Superintendent of Welfare and Training R.A. Hoey to Indian Agent V.M. Eastwood, 16 December 1938: 324.

135 RG10 School Files Series, C-8208, Proposed Building Data, Mud Lake Indian Day School, December 1938: 330–1.

136 RG10 School Files Series, C-8208, Letter from Indian Agent V.M. Eastwood to the Department of Indian Affairs, Mud Lake Indian Day School, 21 December 1938: 328.

137 RG10 School Files Series, C-8208, Memorandum, Director Harold McGill, New day school, Mud Lake Indian Reserve, Ontario, 9 February 1939: 338. This occurred a few months after the official go-ahead; it was decided not to include electricity to the school as the nearest hydro line was 3.5 miles away. RG10 School Files Series, C-8208, Proposed Building Data from Indian Agent V.M. Eastwood, 16 December 1938: 325–6.

138 Ibid. Curve Lake First Nation still does not fully have clean water on the reserve. Please see the conclusion of this book for further discussion.

139 RG10 School Files Series, C-8208, Extract from 30 September 1939, Indian Agent V.M. Eastwood Report: 351.

140 RG10 School Files Series, C-8208, Letter from Indian Agent V.M. Eastwood to Department of Indian Affairs, 15 December 1939: 367.

141 RG10 School Files Series, C-8208, Memo from Dr McGill re: Mud Lake Indian Day School: 376.

142 RG10 School Files Series, C-8208, Letter from Indian Agent V.M. Eastwood to Department of Indian Affairs, 5 January 1940: 393.

143 Ibid.

144 RG10 School Files Series, C-8208, Letter from Indian Agent V.M. Eastwood to Department of Indian Affairs, 5 January 1940: 394.

145 RG10 School Files Series, C-8208, Memorandum, Director Harold McGill, Indian Day School, Mud Lake Indian Reserve, 20 January 1940: 407.

146 RG10 School Files Series, C-8208, Letter from Indian Agent V.M. Eastwood to Department of Indian Affairs, 15 February 1940: 410.

147 RG10 School Files Series, C-8208, Memo, Chief Engineer J.W. Wardle, re: Indian Day School, Mud Lake Reserve, Ontario, 27 February 1940: 418. The federal government used the residential schools to experiment on Indigenous children for nutrition research. Ian Mosby, "Administering Colonial Science: Nutrition Research and Human Biomedical Experimentation in Aboriginal Communities and Residential Schools, 1942–1952," *Histoire sociale/Social History* 46, no. 1 (2013): 145–72.

148 RG10 School Files Series, C-8208, Memo, Dr McGill, 2 March 1940: 419.

149 RG10 School Files Series, C-8208, Letter from Indian Agent V.M. Eastwood to Department of Indian Affairs, 12 June 1940: 434.

150 RG10 School Files Series, C-8208, Letter from Indian Agent Eastwood to Department of Indian Affairs, 22 May 1940: 424.

151 Ibid.

CHAPTER SIX

1 Carleton, *Lessons in Legitimacy*, 10.

2 Ibid.

3 Ibid.

4 Ibid., 181.

5 Ibid., 208.

6 RG10 School Files Series, C-8207, Letter from Cyril Rice to Indian Agent Eastwood, 25 March 1936: 1941.

7 RG10 School Files Series, C-8207, Letter from Indian Agent Eastwood the Department of Indian Affairs, 11 April 1936: 1943.

8 RG10 School Files Series, C-8207, Letter from A.F. MacKenzie to Indian Agent Eastwood, 15 April 1936: 1944.

9 RG10 School Files Series, C-8207, Mud Lake Chief and Council Resolution sent to Indian Agent Eastwood, 1 June 1936: 1945.

10 RG10 School Files Series, C-8207, Letter from A.F. MacKenzie to Indian Agent Eastwood, 5 June 1936: 1947.

11 RG10 School Files Series, C-8207, Report from Indian Agent Eastwood, 5 January 1937: 1948.

12 Patrice Milewski summarizes the changes to this new curriculum, which is often referred to as the "Little Gray Book" or "The Programme": "One of the most striking aspects of the new curriculum and pedagogy was the way in which it sought to normalize the way in which children learned. In many respects The Programme enunciated an epistemology that positioned the child as the initiator and source of learning. This represented a shift from a transmission model that placed the teacher at the center (dispenser of knowledge) to one that suggested that 'a child develops by virtue of his own activity.'" Patrice Milewski, "'The Little Gray Book': Pedagogy, Discourse and Rupture in 1937," *History of Education* 37, no. 1 (2008): 104.

13 Thornton Mustard was the principal of the Toronto Normal School and was one of the key individuals who pushed for this educational reform in Ontario. Patrice Milewski describes his "pivotal role in teaching and conveying the new curriculum and pedagogy to prospective teachers." Stuart Mackey was one of those teachers who provided this new form of education in an Indian day school. Mustard believed the teacher's role was to help rather than be "a driver and taskmaster." Instead, they should promote "the hope that the new courses of studies would enable the next generation to grow up with 'greater initiative, more interests, and better attitudes' especially in relation to work – not as something that has be to be done, but something worth doing for very joy of it.'" It was thought that the students would see

the benefits of work if they had a guiding teacher who could instruct them in the latest production methods. Patrice Milewski, "'The Little Gray Book,'" 103, 106–7.

14 RG10 School Files Series, C-8207, Letter from. Stuart Mackey to the Department of Indian Affairs, 19 August 1938: 1952–3.

15 RG10 School Files Series, C-8207, Letter from R.A. Hoey to Stuart Mackey, 27 August 1949: 1957.

16 RG10 School Files Series, C-8207, Quarterly Report from Indian Agent Eastwood, September 1948: 1963.

17 RG10 School Files Series, C-8207, Letter from Stuart Mackey to Indian Agent Eastwood, 13 October 1938: 1964–7

18 Ibid. This quote is a criticism of the residential school system from an Indian day school teacher – the first that appears in this archive.

19 Ibid.

20 Ibid.

21 Ibid.

22 Ibid.

23 Ibid., 1965.

24 Ibid.

25 Ibid., 1966.

26 Ibid.

27 Ibid.

28 Ibid., 1967. Theodore Christou wrote about the rise of efficiency concepts in Ontario during the Depression: "These views informed the goal of relating the school and the home, the notion of school planning for increased efficiency in light of budget cuts and increasing numbers of students, the emphasis on testing and examination, and the curricular attention to vocational education and guidance. These themes were in line with the movement towards 'social efficiency', which engulfed the ethos of educational reforms in Canada and in the United States during the interwar period." Theodore Michael Christou, "'Schools Are No Longer Merely Educational Institutions': The Rhetoric of Social Efficiency in Ontario Education, 1931–1935," *History of Education* 42, no. 5 (2013): 568.

29 RG10 School Files Series, C-8207, Letter from R.A. Hoey to Indian Agent Eastwood, 14 November 1938: 1969.

30 RG10 School Files Series, C-8207, Letter from Indian Agent Eastwood to the Department of Indian Affairs, 22 April 1940: 1972.

31 RG10 School Files Series, C-8207, Extract of Report from Indian Agent Eastwood to the Department of Indian Affairs, 30 June 1940: 1973.

32 RG10 School Files Series, C-8207, Extract of Report from Indian Agent Eastwood to the Department of Indian Affairs, 12 August 1940: 1975.

33 RG10 School Files Series, C-8207, Report from Indian Agent Eastwood to the Department of Indian Affairs, 29 November 1940: 1976.

34 Ibid.

35 RG10 School Files Series, C-8207, Letter from R.A. Hoey to Miss Long, 3 May 1941: 1977. Robert Alexander Hoey was a politician who was elected to the Manitoba Legislature until 1936, when he took the position of "Superintendent of Welfare and Training, Indian Affairs Branch, Department of Mines and Resources at Ottawa (December 1936 to March 1945), Director of the Indian Affairs Branch (March 1945 to September 1948)." He was also a strong supporter of human eugenics, as he introduced legislation to sterilize individuals with intellectual disabilities under the Mental Deficiency Act. Gordon Goldsborough, "Memorable Manitoban: Robert Alexander Hoey (1883–1965)," Manitoba Historical Society, January 23, 2021, http://www.mhs.mb.ca/docs/people/hoey_ra.shtml.

36 RG10 School Files Series, C-8207, Letter from W.S. Arneil, Inspector Indian Agencies to Dr. McGill, Department of Indian Affairs, 19 May 1941: 1980. W.S. Arneil would later become the first Indian commissioner for British Columbia; please see Eve Chapple and Helen Raptis, "From Integration to Segregation: Government Education Policy and the School at Telegraph Creek, British Columbia, 1906–1951," *Journal of the Canadian Historical Association* (2013): 149.

37 RG10 School Files Series, C-8207, Letter from Chief Training Division, Philip Phelan to Indian Agent Eastwood, 28 August 1941: 1981.

38 RG10 School Files Series, C-8207, Letter from Indian Agent Eastwood to the Department of Indian Affairs, 11 October 1941: 1990.

39 RG10 School Files Series, C-8207, Memo to Representative of the Treasury, Chief Training Division, Philip Phelan, 17 December 1943: 1991.

40 RG10 School Files Series, C-8207, Letter from Miss Shirley Hamilton to the Department of Indian Affairs, 26 July 1945: 2002.

41 Interview with Chief Keith Knott, April 2024, 6:39.

42 Ibid, 4:55.

43 Ibid., 24:21.

44 Ibid., 26:55.

45 Ibid., 28:24.

46 Ibid., 39:38.

47 Ibid., 42:57.

48 RG10 School Files Series, C-8798, Letter from V.M. Eastwood to Department of Indian Affairs, 3 September 1947: 785.

49 The TRC found that this form of manual-training education was a core part of nearly all residential schools: "Manual training included tailoring, farming, carpentry, painting, printing, and shoe repair. Working in the laundry, one of the least desirable jobs, was reserved from the newly arrived or those being punished." Truth and Reconciliation Commission Canada, *Canada's Residential Schools: The History*, 146.

50 RG10 School Files Series, C-8798, Letter from V.M. Eastwood to Department of Indian Affairs, 3 September 1947: 785.

51 RG10 School Files Series, C-8798, Letter from V.M. Eastwood to Department of Indian Affairs, 3 September 1947: 786.

52 RG10 School Files Series C-8798, Rice and Mud Lake Agency, Tuition Agreements 27 March, 27 April 1939: 584.

53 RG10 School Files Series, C-8798, Rice and Mud Lake Agency, Memo to Department of Indian Affairs, 4 May 1939: 585.

54 RG10 School Files Series, C-8798, Letter from Chief Daniel Whetung to Inspector McGookin, Department of Indian Affairs, 11 May 1939: 587–8. This letter was originally sent to Inspector McGookin and then forwarded to the Department of Indian Affairs. From the first sentence, it appears that Chief Whetung knew this inspector well and was trying to use this personal relationship to gain more clarity regarding school payments.

55 RG10 School Files Series, C-8798, Letter from R.A. Hoey to Chief Daniel Whetung, 13 May 1939: 589. Tuition fees were paid to the provincial government to support the education of these additional students within their secondary system.

56 RG10 School Files Series, C-8798, Letter from V.M. Eastwood to R.A

Hoey, Superintendent of Welfare and Training, Department of Indian Affairs, 17 June 1942: 650.

57 RG10 School Files Series, C-8798, Letter from Mrs Allan Taylor to Indian Agent V.M. Eastwood, 4 August 1942: 654.

58 RG10 School Files Series, C-8798, Letter from Superintendent of Welfare and Training R.A. Hoey, Department of Indian Affairs to V.M. Eastwood, 3 September 1942: 658.

59 RG10 School Files Series, C-8798, Letter from Superintendent of Welfare and Training R.A. Hoey, Department of Indian Affairs to Minnie Beaver, 11 September 1942: 661.

60 RG10 School Files Series, C-8798, Letter from Peterborough Board of Education to Department of Indian Affairs, 29 October 1942: 664.

61 RG10 School Files Series, C-8798, Letter from Superintendent of Welfare and Training R.A. Hoey, Department of Indian Affairs to V.M. Eastwood, 11 December 1942: 668.

62 RG10 School Files Series, C-8798, Letter from Indian Agent, V.M. Eastwood to Department of Indian Affairs, 21 August 1947: 771.

63 Ibid.

64 Ibid. The price of this course was $175, with an additional $18 for books.

65 Ibid.

66 RG10 School Files Series, C-8798, Letter from Superintendent of Welfare and Training Bernard F. Neary to Indian Agent, V.M. Eastwood, 26 August 1947: 773.

67 RG10 School Files Series, C-8798, Peterborough Collegiate and Vocational School Report, Eric McCue, January 1949: 1046.

68 RG 10 School Files Series, C-8798, Letter from Superintendent of Welfare and Training Bernard F. Neary to Indian Agent, V.M. Eastwood, 20 January 1949: 989.

69 RG 10 School Files Series, C-8798, Indian children attending provincial or private schools, Rice Lake Agency: 991–2.

70 RG10 School Files Series, C-8798, Letter from Indian Agent V.M. Eastwood to Department of Indian Affairs, 28 January 1949: 995.

71 Helen Raptis, "Exploring The Factors Prompting British Columbia's First Integration Initiative: The Case of Port Essington Indian Day School," *History of Education Quarterly* (2011): 520.

72 Chapple and Raptis, "From Integration to Segregation," 138.
73 Ibid., 155.
74 Helen Raptis, "Blurring the Boundaries of Policy and Legislation in the Schooling of Indigenous Children in British Columbia, 1901–1951," *Historical Studies in Education* (2015): 73.
75 RG10 School Files Series, C-8207, Letter from L.W. Copp to Indian Agent Eastwood, 18 August 1945: 2006.
76 RG10 School Files Series, C-8207, Letter from Shirley Hamilton to Indian Agent Eastwood, 17 February 1947: 2014.
77 RG10 School Files Series, C-8207, Letter from Indian Agent Eastwood to the Department of Indian Affairs, 14 March 1947: 2019.
78 RG10 School Files Series, C-8207, Letter from Superintendent of Welfare and Training Bernard F. Neary to Indian Agent Eastwood, 20 March 1947: 2020.
79 RG10 School Files Series, C-8207, Letter from Indian Agent Eastwood to the Department of Indian Affairs, 28 April 1947: 2025.
80 RG10 School Files Series, C-8207, Letter from Indian Agent Eastwood to the Department of Indian Affairs, 22 May 1947: 2027.
81 Ibid.
82 RG10 School Files Series, C-8207, Letter from Indian Agent Eastwood to the Department of Indian Affairs, 7 July 1947: 2028.
83 RG10 School Files Series, C-8207, A Receipt for the *Peterborough Examiner* and *Toronto Globe and Mail* advertisements, 30 May 1949: 2040.
84 RG10 School Files Series, C-8207, Letter from L.W. Copp to Indian Agent Eastwood, 15 June 1949: 2042.
85 RG10 School Files Series, C-8207, Letter from L.W. Copp to Indian Agent Eastwood, 14 July 1949: 2043.
86 Ibid.
87 RG10 School Files Series, C-8207, Letter from John [missing] to Department of Indian Affairs, 5 September 1949: 2051.
88 RG10 School Files Series, C-8207, letter from Superintendent of Welfare and Training Bernard F. Neary to Indian Agent Eastwood, 18 October 1949: 2056.
89 RG10 School Files Series, C-8207, Letter from Philip Phelan, Chief Education Division to Indian Agent Eastwood, 24 October 1949: 2057.
90 Fay Tilden and Kathy Woodcock, *A History of the Burleigh Falls Settle-*

ment, sponsored by the Kawartha Branch of the Ontario Metis and Non-Status Indian Association (Tweed, ON: Quinte Web-Press, 1978), 1.

91 RG10 School Files Series, C-8798, Letter from Edith D. Maclaren to Philip Phelan, Chief of Training Division, Department of Indian Affairs, 10 January 1941: 613.

92 RG10 School Files Series, C-8798, Letter from to Superintendent of Welfare and Training R.A. Hoey, Department of Indian Affairs to Edith D. Maclaren, 29 January 1941: 617.

93 Ibid.

94 RG10 School Files Series, C-8798, Letter from to Superintendent of Welfare and Training R.A. Hoey, Department of Indian Affairs to Indian Agent, V.M. Eastwood, 8 February 1941: 622.

95 RG10 School Files Series, C-8798, Letter from V.C. Eastwood to R.A. Hoey, Department of Indian Affairs, 17 February 1941: 623.

96 Ibid.

97 Ibid.

98 Ibid.

99 Ibid.

100 RG10 School Files Series, C-8798, Letter from Superintendent of Welfare and Training R.A. Hoey, Department of Indian Affairs to Edith B. Maclaren, 21 February 1941: 628.

101 Fay Tilden and Kathy Woodcock, *A History of the Burleigh Falls Settlement*, 25.

102 Ibid., 26.

103 Ibid., 26.

104 Ibid., 26–7.

105 Ibid., 27.

106 Please see "Metis of Burleigh Falls Final Report" (Ottawa: Public History Inc., 2000), 51, www.docplayer.net/37988812-Metis-of-burleigh-falls-final-report.html.

107 Ibid., 54.

108 Ibid., 56.

109 Ibid., 57.

110 Ibid., 33.

111 Ibid., 33.

CHAPTER SEVEN

1 "Curve Lake Elects Woman Indian Chief," *The Globe and Mail* (1936–2016), 30 June 1954.
2 Cora Voyageur, *Firekeepers of the Twenty-First Century*, 25.
3 Ibid., 28.
4 Ibid.
5 Ibid., 30.
6 Ibid., 30.
7 Ibid., 31.
8 Ibid., 37.
9 Interview with Val Whetung, April 2024, 48:12.
10 Ibid., 48:44.
11 Ibid., 52:10.
12 Ibid., 53:51.
13 Ibid., 54:31.
14 Ibid., 1:11:24.
15 Ibid., 1:04:04.
16 Ibid., 1:05:37.
17 Ibid., 1:06:43.
18 Ibid., 1:07:21.
19 Interview with Val Whetung #2, April 2024, 8:33.
20 Interview with Val Whetung, April 2024, 1:08:49.
21 Ibid., 58:51.
22 Ibid., 59:56.
23 Ibid., 1:00:33.
24 Interview with Val Whetung #2, April 2024, 9:16.
25 Interview with Lorenzo Whetung, April 2024, 1:18.
26 Ibid., 1:31.
27 Ibid., 7:55.
28 Ibid., 12:43.
29 Ibid., 13:11.
30 Ibid., 13:52.
31 Ibid., 14:06.
32 Ibid., 17:46.
33 Ibid., 18:11.
34 RG10, Elsie Knott, owner-operator of the School Bus, collects her pas-

sengers at the Lakefield District High School for the drive back home to the Mud Lake Indian Reserve September 1960. Library and Archives Canada/Department of Indian Affairs and Northern Development fonds/e011308220, http://central.bac-lac.gc.ca/.redirect?app=fonand col&id=5320370&lang=eng.

35 *The Leader*, "Thank-you Dinner for Bill," Facebook, 30 October 1980, from Vintage Lakefield Facebook post: https://www.facebook.com/photo?fbid=10156610751497140&set=oa.1937831209602038.

36 Ibid.

37 *Peterborough Examiner*, "Curve Lake Administrator Dies," Facebook, 22 March 1982, from Vintage Lakefield Facebook post: https://www.facebook.com/photo?fbid=10156610751497140&set=oa.1937831209602038.

38 "Indian Students End Up in Paint," *The Globe and Mail* (1936–2017), 20 March 1968.

39 Ibid.

40 Cora Voyageur, *Firekeepers of the Twenty-First Century*, 38.

41 Interview with Stanford Taylor, April 2024, 0:49. After reviewing the transcripts of my interview with Stanford, he expressed concern about the profanity he used throughout the section. Upon reading the text, he was surprised by how frequently he used swear words when discussing his Indian day school experience. After several discussions with his partner, Lisa, we decided to keep the profanity in the text, as it authentically conveys his emotions while speaking about the school.

42 Ibid., 3:00.

43 Ibid., 3:48.

44 Ibid., 4:08.

45 Ibid., 4:49.

46 Ibid., 5:1.

47 Ibid., 18:26.

48 Ibid., 20:48.

49 Ibid., 14:57.

50 Ibid., 17:26.

51 Ibid., 18:42.

52 Ibid., 33;14.

53 Ibid., 11:47.

54 Ibid., 12:30.

55 Ibid., 21:41.

56 Ibid., 23:14.

57 Ibid., 25:53.

58 Ibid., 25:38.

59 Ibid., 46:00.

60 Ibid., 27:05.

61 Trent University Library and Archives, George Cobb Tapes, Accession 82-006, Tape #45 transcription, p. 7–8, https://archives.trentu.ca/uploads/r/trent-university-archives/4/8/2/482c66bc15a6e58efefbe07ea10128ea1541172526af1c4cc5eeabe8f1e77368/82-006_cobb_tape_45_transcript.pdf.

62 Ibid., 8.

63 Trent University Library and Archives, George Cobb Tapes, Accession 82-006, Tape #47 transcription, p. 2, https://archives.trentu.ca/uploads/r/trent-university-archives/7/9/8/798c5304ee9d5fffbd412daff3b9b7d0f050b83fc32f90fc1c3b36eb21d1d045/82-006_cobb_tape_47_transcript.pdf.

64 Ibid.

65 Trent University Library and Archives, George Cobb Tapes, Accession 82-006, Box #1 Tall Tom Taylor, p. 2, https://archives.trentu.ca/uploads/r/trent-university-archives/1/5/c/15c22e0430deb844961e0f18e458eb46e2d092a3524c49efc190c770e9cd436c/82-006_cobb_transcript_-_Tall_Tom_Taylor.pdf.

66 Ibid., 1.

67 John Harold Dilling, "Educational Achievement and Social Acceptance of Indian Pupils Integrated in the Non-Indian Schools of Southern Ontario" (PhD diss., University of Toronto, 1965).

68 Ibid., 353.

69 Interview with Shelley Knott Fife, April 2024, 2:47.

70 Ibid., 4:00. Shelley writes more about these stories in her chapter: Shelley Knott Fife, "Our Education Tomorrow," in *Me Tomorrow: Indigenous Views on the Future*, ed. Drew Hayden Taylor (Madeira Park, BC: Douglas & McIntyre, 2021), 121–37.

71 Interview with Fife, 4:47.

72 Ibid., 5:24.

73 Ibid., 7:41.
74 Ibid., 8:26.
75 Ibid., 8:41.
76 Fife, "Our Education Tomorrow," 125.
77 Ibid., 127.
78 Interview with Fife, 16:02.
79 Ibid., 17:02.
80 Ibid., 17:41.
81 Ibid., 22:13
82 Ibid., 22:13.
83 Ibid., 49:51.
84 "Peterborough Area: Indians Rated Normal Students," *The Globe and Mail* (1936–2017), 16 September 1976.
85 Ibid.
86 Ibid.
87 Georgia Elston, *Giving Ojibwa Stories and Legends from the Children of Curve Lake* (Lakefield, ON: Wapoone Publishing and Promotion, 1985), 7.
88 Ibid., 44.
89 Ibid., 32.

CHAPTER EIGHT

1 Barbara-Ann MacEachern, "In His Own Words: Residential School Survivor Turned Artist Shares His Healing Journey," *Peterborough This Week*, updated 30 September 2022, https://www.thepeterboroughexaminer.com/local-peterborough/news/2019/08/17/in-his-own-words-residential-school-survivor-turned-artist-shares-his-healing-journey.html.
2 RG10 School Files Series, C-8207, Letter from Daniel Whetung to Department of Indian Affairs, 15 February 1909: 2328–30.
3 RG10 School Files Series, C-8207, Letter from Chief Joesph Whetung to the Department of Indian Affairs, 29 October 1910: 1391.
4 RG10 School Files Series, C-8207, Letter from Indian Agent McCamus to the Department of Indian Affairs, 4 January 1918: 1659.
5 RG10 School Files Series, C-8207, Letter from Chief Daniel Whetung to the Department of Indian Affairs, 18 September 1923: 1750–51.

6 RG10, photograph of Wendell McCue, although a Mud Lake band member, lives in Peterborough, Library and Archives Canada/Department of Indian Affairs and Northern Development fonds/e011308214, http://central.bac-lac.gc.ca/.redirect?app=fonandcol&id=5320364&lang=eng.

7 Jorge Barrera, "St. Anne's Survivors Lose What Could Be Final Battle with Ottawa over Documents," CBC News, 7 May 2018, https://www.cbc.ca/news/indigenous/st-annes-residential-school-appeal-decision-documents-1.4652573.

8 Jackson Pind, "Day School Survivors Need Access to United Church Archives," *Broadview Magazine*, 5 August 2022, https://broadview.org/day-schools-united-church-archives.

9 Ibid.

10 "Response to Broadview Article," United Church of Canada Archives, n.d., https://www.unitedchurcharchives.ca/archives/colonizing-institution-records/response-to-broadview/.

11 Ibid.

12 Ibid.

13 Ibid.

14 Ibid.

15 Interview with Val Whetung, April 2024, 49:20.

16 Interview with Shelley Knott Fife, April 2024, 55:04.

17 Interview with Chief Keith Knott, April 2024, 1:17:39.

18 Interview with Stanford Taylor, April 2024, 47:53.

19 Ibid., 48:18.

20 Ibid., 49:18.

21 Ibid., 50:34.

22 Interview with Val Whetung, April 2024, 24:04.

23 Ibid., 29:09.

24 Ibid., 48:40.

25 Interview with Lorenzo Whetung, April 2024, 20:58.

26 Ibid., 24:13.

27 Ibid., 24:44.

28 The Missing and Murdered Indigenous Women and Girls Executive Summary explains, "In many truths shared by witnesses, the normalization of violence could be traced back through family lines to

trauma experienced in residential and day schools, to the Sixties Scoop, and to other forms of colonial violence." *Reclaiming Power and Place: Executive Summary of the Final Report* (Gatineau, QC: National Inquiry into Missing and Murdered Indigenous Women and Girls, 2019), 33.

29 RG10 School Files Series, C-8207, Letter from Indian Agent R.J. McCamus to the Department of Indian Affairs, 4 April 1925: 1793.

30 Leanne R. Simpson, "Anticolonial Strategies for the Recovery and Maintenance of Indigenous Knowledge," *American Indian Quarterly* (2004): 378.

31 Peggy J. Blair, *Lament for a First Nation: The Williams Treaties of Southern Ontario* (Vancouver: University of British Columbia Press, 2008).

32 "Indians Charge Branch Stalls Island Inquiry," *The Globe and Mail*, 7 July 1960. Madeline Whetung also explained how the government systematically removed the land around the waterways of the Trent-Severn Waterway with reference to a dispute over the value of flooded land. Both Daniel Whetung and Alfred McCue represented the community interests in their fight with the federal government. Madeline Whetung, "Nishnaabeg Encounters: Living Indigenous Landscapes," 70–1.

33 Ibid.

34 Ibid.

35 Annie Burns-Pleper, "Bad Water Sickens First Nations. But Government Doesn't Track the Toll," *The Tyee*, 22 February 2021, https://thetyee.ca/News/2021/02/22/Bad-Water-Sickens-First-Nations-Government-Track-Toll/.

36 "A message from Chief Emily Whetung," Curve Lake First Nation Website, 2 February 2021, https://curvelakefirstnation.ca/2021/02/03/a-message-from-chief-emily-whetung-february-2-2021/.

37 Burns-Pleper, "Bad Water Sickens First Nations."

38 "A message from Chief Emily Whetung."

39 Olivia Stefanovich and Richard Raycraft, "First Nations and Ottawa Agree to $8-Billion Setttlement on Drinking Water Advisories," CBC News, 30 July 2021, https://www.cbc.ca/news/politics/drinking-water-class-action-proposed-settlement-1.6123251.

40 Kirk Winter, "Local Man Concerned about Future of Anishinaabemowin Language," *The Lindsay Advocate*, 21 May 2021, https://lindsayadvocate.ca/local-man-concerned-about-future-of-anishinaabemowin-language/.

41 DJ Fife, "A Brief Introduction to Anishinaabemowin," *Ontario Parks Blog*, 6 June 2021, https://www.ontarioparks.com/parksblog/introduction-to-anishinaabemowin/.

42 Ibid.

AFTERWORD

1 Paul Bourgeois, personal communication, 12 February 2023.

2 Union of Ontario Indians, *Anishinaabe Chi-Naaknigewin*.

3 Dan Pine, Sr, *Prophecy Song*.

INDEX

Page numbers in *italics* denote illustrative material.